Sir Alister McIntyre is a disting. ....uonal figure and academic. He studied at the London School of Economics (LSE) and Oxford University and taught at the University of the West Indies (UWI), where he was latterly Vice-Chancellor. He has served in a variety of high-profile roles in UN agencies and in Caribbean regional government. He has been awarded the Order of the Caribbean Community (OCC), conferred by the CARICOM Heads of Government; the Order of Distinction and the Order of Merit conferred by the government of Jamaica; and the Cacique Crown of Honour from the government of Guyana. In 1992 he was knighted by the Queen. He has also received the Chancellor's Medal for Excellence at the UWI, as well as honorary doctorates from the Universities of the West Indies, Toronto in Canada, and Sheffield in the UK.

'In the realm of international development and the economic integration of Latin America and the Caribbean, no practising economist has commanded more respect over the past fifty years from politicians and policy makers than Sir Alister. His story is unmissable.'

Prof. The Hon Bishnodat Persaud, former Director of Economic Affairs, Commonwealth Secretariat

'In this honest and wonderfully engaging account of his incredibly varied career of service to the international community and his beloved Caribbean, Sir Alister shares his origins, motivations, key friendships, triumphs and disappointments. A truly inspiring read.'

Gerry Helleiner, Distinguished Research Fellow, Munk School of Global Affairs, University of Toronto

'*The Caribbean and the Wider World* is arguably the most significant aspect of Sir Alister's legacy to contemporary and future Caribbean society. It documents the lived experience of one of the principal architects of the post-independence Caribbean – its ideology, its institutions and its place in the globalized world. Sir Alister's autobiography abounds with energy and optimism. Readers will be inspired by the continuing relevance of the values and ideas that motivated him as a committed regionalist. The book gives a concrete demonstration of what can be achieved by a Caribbean leader, conceptualizer and a brilliant defender of Caribbean integration who had a commitment to public service, a conviction that regionalism was the only option to save the Caribbean from marginalization in the global environment, and an acceptance of a development agenda based on trade, strategic production and appropriate human resources development. Caribbean leaders, academics, technocrats and students of my generation are deeply indebted to Sir Alister for his profound impact on our individual and collective consciousness, and I recommend this book as an indispensable tool in the realization of Sir Alister's vision in the future.'

Prof. Sir Kenneth Hall, former Governor-General of Jamaica

'*The Caribbean and the Wider World* provides important insights and perspectives on several of the major regional and international issues which demanded attention by the countries in the region, during the last four decades of the twentieth century. The book is an excellent resource for students, educators, and policy makers, as well as persons holding a general interest in the Caribbean and its development. Readers of the book will find an authentic account of the life and career of a virtuoso who was involved in the search for solutions of regional issues, within the framework of the global landscape. The book also reflects Sir Alister's concurrent commitment to assist the peoples and institutions at the national level, so as to resolve pressing problems of a strictly internal focus. The episodes that deal with the author's contribution to university education further reveal the scale and complexity of his seminal influence on the spread of knowledge in the region during a long and distinguished career. The intellectual genius of Alister McIntyre, expertly sharpened on the whetstone of unparalleled experience, has generated this brilliant book that should attract a very wide readership within the Caribbean and the wider world.'

P.J. Patterson, former Prime Minister of Jamaica

'Having worked with him in UNCTAD and later observed his dedication and commitment to development in the Global South, it is heartening to peruse Alister McIntyre's reflections and analyses. Sometimes regions and individuals punch above their weight in world politics. These pages provide privileged access to the private life and public career of an extraordinary Caribbean and exemplary global citizen.'

Professor Thomas G. Weiss, The Graduate Center, The City University of New York

'I am very pleased to endorse this excellent biography of my dear friend Alister McIntyre, which pays testimony to an exceptional career and a life full of commitment and great contributions to knowledge, academic life, the development of Caribbean countries and the construction of a better international community. This book describes an exceptional academic career, mostly in Great Britain, as well as a preponderant role in the construction of an independent Caribbean. Alister's extraordinary faith in the idea of regional integration took shape in his participation in CARIFTA, then in CARICOM and in his multiple cooperation interventions in most of the Caribbean countries, highlighting his role as a leader committed to the destiny of his region. Alister is, without any doubt, among the great men and women that built the Caribbean, strengthening an exemplary democracy, trying to overcome the limitations of its insularity and proving exemplary in the defense of human rights.'

Enrique V. Iglesias, Former Executive Secretary, United Nations Economic Commission for Latin America and the Caribbean (ECLAC); Former Minister of Foreign Relations of the Republic of Uruguay; Former President of the Interamerican Development Bank; First Iberoamerican Secretary General

The Caribbean and the Wider World

Commentaries on my Life and Career

Alister McIntyre

The Radcliffe Press
LONDON • NEW YORK

An imprint of I.B.Tauris

Published in 2016 by The Radcliffe Press
An imprint of I.B.Tauris & Co. Ltd
London • New York
www.ibtauris.com

ISBN: 978 1 78453 634 3
eISBN: 978 1 78672 083 2
ePDF: 978 1 78673 083 1

A full CIP record for this book is available from the British Library
A full CIP record is available from the Library of Congress

Library of Congress Catalog Card Number: available

Typeset by Saxon Graphics Ltd, Derby
Printed and bound by CPI Group (UK) Ltd, Croydon, CR0 4YY

MIX
Paper from
responsible sources
FSC® C013604
FSC
www.fsc.org

This book is dedicated to the late William Demas, a stalwart Caribbean scholar and public servant.

He was my colleague and very good friend.

Contents

CONTENTS

Illustrations

ILLUSTRATIONS

Acknowledgements

Apart from those mentioned in the Preface, I acknowledge the contribution of the following persons in preparing the text.

Drs Dhiru and Laura Tanna, who showed particular interest. Laura persuaded me to start the process by recording conversations with her of my recollections. Although I was unable to access those recordings, nevertheless I wish to recognize the initial encouragement of her husband and herself.

Mrs Gillian Glean Walker, who helped me with the review of several chapters of the text, particularly the first two that dealt with my early life in Grenada.

Dr Angela Ramsay, who reviewed and edited the manuscript, leading to valuable suggestions for improvement.

I wish also to acknowledge the valuable assistance provided by staff in the office of the Secretary-General of CARICOM and on the three campuses of the University of the West Indies in helping me to locate photographs that now appear in the book. They carried out this responsibility with consummate courtesy and promptness.

It goes without saying that I am particularly indebted to Dr Lester Crook, editor at I.B.Tauris, who guided me throughout the preparation of this book and made invaluable suggestions for its improvement. I am also indebted to the other members of the I.B.Tauris publishing staff for their contributions and to those persons at Saxon Graphics, in particular Mr Dave Wright, who were especially helpful.

Preface

My purpose in writing this book is to illustrate how a young person with very modest means could overcome the obstacles in the way of his own personal development, particularly in securing a higher education and developing a professional career. Those two pathways converged to provide me with very many opportunities for personal satisfaction in the career that I chose in pursuit of Caribbean and global development.

The opening chapters of the book contain reflections on my early life growing up in Grenada; the compulsion that I experienced for securing a higher education; the knowledge that I accumulated about the working world that, in the end, made me more humble in dealing with people and situations; and the period during which I secured my higher education and the satisfaction and frustrations which arose out of that. During this period, I began receiving important exposure to the rationale for, and the advantages to be derived from, West Indian economic integration.

On the whole, my period in pursuit of higher education in Britain, and the opportunities for strengthening my academic capacities that became available in the United States, served to make me more focused and confident about the contributions I could endeavour to make, particularly to the English-speaking Caribbean. It also alerted me to avoid prescriptions and assessments that were not sufficiently founded on reliable information, to judge issues on their merits and to guard against relying on unsubstantiated assumptions.

As the countries of the Commonwealth Caribbean moved into independence during the 1960s, they had to contend with a series of public issues that materially affected their opportunities for economic development.

At a more general level, they needed to respond to a network of economic and financial institutions, starting with the World Bank and the International Monetary Fund (IMF). These two institutions had been set up after World War II to implement the decisions taken at the Bretton Woods Conference that established ground rules for the conduct of international payments, and to complement the decision to establish an open system of multilateral trade. The work of these two institutions was reinforced by the General Agreement on Tariffs and Trade (GATT), which provided for the freeing of international trade in goods and services, apart from exceptions that conformed to specified criteria.

The first two independent Caribbean countries, Jamaica and Trinidad and Tobago, set a pattern that in subsequent years was followed by other Caribbean countries. In effect, by membership of these international institutions, the English-speaking Caribbean had established rules and procedures that, with some exceptions, were virtually common to all of them. This was later to make it possible for them to establish special arrangements among themselves for the integration of their trade. In other words, paradoxically as it might appear to many, the decision at independence to join the World Bank and IMF on the terms established turned out to be one of the first building blocks towards the Caribbean Free Trade Area (CARIFTA) and the Caribbean Common Market (CARICOM).

Like other developing countries, the Commonwealth Caribbean experienced the shortcomings and constraints of the global system of trade, aid and finance. This was further underlined by their growing acquaintance, over the years, with the economic work being undertaken by the United Nations and, in certain respects, by leading personalities in the international academic community. Most influential was the work of the Argentine economist, Raoul Prebisch. He made an important mark on the thinking of senior officials in the United Nations about the problems of international trade and development in the newly independent developing countries. As his work gathered increasing international attention and support, it became the foundation for reform of the international arrangements applicable to developing countries for their trade and payments.

Prebisch's work became increasingly the foundation for discussion within the United Nations about how to proceed with the issue of reform. This led to a decision by the United Nations General Assembly to convene a conference on international trade and development which took place in 1964. At that meeting, the decision was taken to establish the United Nations Conference on Trade and Development (UNCTAD) of which Dr Prebisch became the first secretary-general.

Among the insights emanating from the deliberations and work of UNCTAD was enhanced interest in economic integration among developing countries. This contributed towards the resurrection of the notion of integration among the countries that first established the Caribbean Community and Common Market.

As will later be discussed, the growth of interest in the development of international trade and payments along lines favouring economic development lit a spark in the minds of several Caribbean intellectuals who, as the text will indicate, contributed to creating a technical basis for Caribbean integration. My own espousal of the case is contained in two articles and papers that I wrote and published during the mid-1960s: 'Aspects of Development and Trade' (*UN Economic Bulletin for Latin America*) and 'Decolonization and Trade Policy in the West Indies' (First Conference of Caribbean Scholars, 1964). These were intended to join the earlier work of fellow economist and Caribbean integrationist, William Demas, known as 'Willie' to many of his friends and colleagues. The work that we both did on integration and development laid the basis for continuing intellectual collaboration with Willie that I enjoyed for the remainder of his life.

At a wider level, Caribbean economic integration became the leitmotif for the work of both of us in the succeeding years. In fact, Lloyd Best – a close colleague and Research Fellow at the Institute of Social and Economic Research (ISER) – was not far off the mark when, in a public lecture, he described Demas and me as belonging to, and leading, a West Indian political party!

This constituted the philosophical platform from which I tried to contribute to the advancement of the economic integration process and the development of supportive institutions, of which the University of the West Indies (UWI) was and is the most important. It also gave a *raison d'être* for the work that I have done over my life for individual Caribbean countries – the public activities in which I engaged at different times throughout the region, but especially in Jamaica and Trinidad and Tobago where I lived, are described in this book. However, my stance had always been that, coming from the UWI and later from the CARICOM secretariat, I had a fundamental obligation to make myself available to all the countries in the region where I had the relevant skills and experience to contribute to particular issues of problem-solving.

Without going too much ahead of my text, I leave to others to assess the outcome of all of these mostly hurried attempts at problem-solving. In this connection, I would like to use this opportunity to thank those governments and institutions that have honoured me for my work. Despite the frustrations that arose, in the end I was a more rounded individual for having undertaken the assignments and the opportunities they gave me to broaden my perspective and increase my knowledge of the world.

I tell friends that over my career I have been privileged to visit 81 countries – or perhaps I should say airports in 81 countries! But whatever the particular experiences, they certainly served to widen my vision and make me a more perceptive and understanding person.

In ending the account of my life and career, my thoughts inescapably extend to the future. I find this an exciting venture, although at this stage I can only make very preliminary suggestions about some of the principal tasks that might become apparent. However, I hope that they will provide sufficient food for thought for readers who, in the end, will be better placed than I am to take those brief reflections further into concrete discussion of the specific possibilities that lie ahead. In that endeavour, I wish them every good fortune. I look forward to hearing more in the future about the subjects involved.

In putting together these preliminary paragraphs, my thoughts turn naturally to the persons who provided me with valuable support and assistance in completing this manuscript. I single out for special mention Ms Rosalie O'Meally, who has been of outstanding support to me at every stage of the book. I cannot speak too highly about the indispensable support that she has provided and I thank her sincerely for it.

My wife, Marjorie, has been at every stage, an indispensable ally and an invaluable source of friendship, encouragement, and wise counsel. I take this opportunity also to mention my four children – Arnold, Andrew, Helga and Nicholas – who have been sources of encouragement and support at every stage of the work.

Other members of my family, especially my brother, Dunbar, deserve acknowledgement because of the consistent interest they have displayed throughout the preparation of this text.

I underline the role that members of my family have played throughout my career by including a few photographs of them, along with others illustrative of personalities and events which have significance at different times in my career.

SECTION 1

BUILDING CAPACITY

1

Growing up in Grenada

I was born in 1932. At that time, Grenada was a British colony, a part of the British Empire, and accordingly functioned in the manner then being followed by other British colonial territories in the Caribbean and elsewhere. Our family lived in a town called Gouyave, which was principally known for its fishing. My father had grown up there.

Most of the information on my ancestral roots came from my cousin Hope Stewart, née McIntyre, whom I met in Jamaica in 1988. She was very familiar with a number of interesting family details. For example, she sent me a photograph that she had obtained in Scotland of a person named Alister McIntyre. She pointed out that my name was rarely spelt 'Alister'. On that and subsequent occasions, she continued trying to interest me in the McIntyre family history. Eventually I agreed that she should acquaint me with all the information that she had.

As Hope recounted, there were three young Scottish McIntyres who were anxious to seek their fortune abroad. Initially, all of them came to Jamaica to work as engineers in the sugar industry. One of them remained in Jamaica; of the other two, one went on to Latin America, and the other, my paternal great-grandfather, left Jamaica for the Eastern Caribbean. He initially went to Dominica, seemed to have started a family there, but eventually was attracted to Grenada and accordingly became my ancestor.

The McIntyres of Gouyave became a leading family there.

My grandfather, Meredith McIntyre, was one of three brothers and was something of a wanderer. He married, had six boys, of whom my father was the youngest, then left his entire family in Gouyave and went travelling the world. Five of his sons were later to follow him. Originally, he went to Brazil, but it is unclear for how long he stayed there as there are some scraps of information that indicate that he had also gone to other countries such as Argentina. He left the responsibility for my father's education to his two brothers and, from all accounts, never again communicated with his wife. As far as my father was concerned, he was left to grow up with his mother and an aunt who lived with them.

My father's name was actually Meredith Adelbert McIntyre but he disliked the name, so everyone called him 'Merry' McIntyre. He continued the tradition of naming a son Meredith and I disliked it as well and never used it, but kept the tradition.

My father was not well provided for and had to struggle very hard. His uncles put him to work in the family firm, the largest pharmacy in Gouyave, at a very early age. He barely completed the equivalent of what would now be entry-level into secondary school, and decided that the one thing he could do was pharmacy, because the pharmacist in the family firm was willing to teach him. In those days, to qualify as a registered pharmacist you went into the capital, St Georges, to take an exam set by the government. He went and did it when he was 18 and passed very well, which attracted great attention. When his two uncles heard of this they persuaded the Governor to declare that he was ineligible to receive a licence because he was not yet 21 years old.

My father was furious. He had to wait, and considerable animosity developed between his uncles and himself. He turned his attention to planning in detail how he would organize himself after he became 21 and received his licence to practise as a pharmacist. His aunt, who had become his confidante and had some resources of her own, helped him to start his own business.

He decided to go into wholesale pharmacy. This allowed him to develop a cadre of retailers who could provide customers with small quantities of the drugs and pharmaceuticals provided by my father, the wholesale pharmacist, on a credit basis. This business venture was a great success. Apart from the pharmacy, in the 1920s and early 1930s he became a businessman, selling both groceries and dry goods to retail customers. Then he opened a petrol station, and owned a car that he rented out for weddings and similar occasions.

In 1928 he married my mother and built a huge house, right on the sea. Downstairs he had his business. We lived upstairs and my sisters, my brother and I grew up in a very nice atmosphere. Our home had amenities that were not generally available to other families in Gouyave, or perhaps in other parts of Grenada.

In the course of the 1930s my family had a series of negative experiences. The first was the untimely death of my second sister Marcelle, who was eight years old when she was diagnosed with meningitis. In making the diagnosis, the doctors had not held out any hope for her survival, and in fact she died within a week. We were all highly traumatized, and this was compounded by the onset of the Great Depression, which hit Grenada very badly. Grenada's economy was largely dependent on the export of cocoa and nutmegs – minor crops largely grown by the peasant farmers who were the mainstay of my father's business.

In order to attract business away from his uncles, my father had developed his business by giving credit to the smaller shops patronized by the peasant farmers. When they crashed, as a result of the Depression, he also crashed because they could not pay him. Eventually, he had to declare bankruptcy, and the most hurtful thing, from his point of view, was that he had to seek employment.

Our father informed us that he was losing his business and we would have to move to St Georges so that he could find a job. We said: 'But Daddy, why are we going to Town? We're happy here.'

It was really quite a crisis in my family because in Gouyave we were very comfortable by the standards of those days. We had a large house. We had electricity, which very few people had. We had hot water, hot showers and all the rest of it.

It so happened that the owner of the largest pharmacy in St Georges, Mr Mitchell, had just died, so his wife asked my father whether he would come and work with her as the pharmacist. He accepted the offer and accordingly, in 1939, an unhappy family moved to the capital city of St Georges, which then had a population of about 5,000, representing about a quarter of the total population of Grenada.

What a change from our large roomy home! We felt cramped. I had to share a room with my brother for the first time, and then the five children of my maternal aunts also moved in with us about that same time. Three of our cousins – Eugene, Clifford and Tracy Murray – had recently been orphaned, and the other two stayed because they were the children of my aunt, who was a single mother. My mother was extraordinary: her biological children could never detect that she had any preference for them. She was warm, caring, magnanimous and imbued with strong Christian beliefs.

My father stayed at Mitchell's Pharmacy for the early war years, but he was anxious to return to self-employment. The opportunity presented itself because of the critical shortage of imported products during the war. He started up his own business again and experienced a short period of relative prosperity as there was a high level of demand in the mid to late 1940s for locally produced pharmaceuticals that had previously been imported from outside sources, principally from Canada.

However, shortly after the end of the war, the British government decided on a liberalization effort as a way of compensating Canada for its exceptional support during the war. It focused on traditional products from Canada to the West Indies, of which pharmaceutical products were one of the principal items. The immediate implication of this was that the import substitutes that my father had been producing were unable to compete with the flood of products from Canada. Within a comparatively short space of time my father's business once again began to fail because of external forces over which he had no control. Accordingly, from the late 1940s until his untimely death in 1952, my father had to contend with an extremely small business based on producing a greatly reduced range of products.

When I reflect on those things today, the person most affected was my father, who became very withdrawn. He really had very little to do with us. He showed parental interest in the things that mattered, like our schoolwork, but the personal empathy was very limited, except that he took me with him to the cinema every Sunday night, in the days when people dressed to go to the cinema. Occasionally, he also took me to the races with him. I think he was overwhelmed by the number of children and just could not cope with it.

In the relatively cramped accommodations that were available, he kept reassuring the four of us that he was going to find somewhere better for us to live. His first shot at it was not very successful. He moved us to another house that was no better than the house in which we were living at the time. In a certain sense it was worse, because it was on the fringe of what was then a lower-income area. On the fringe, but still we sensed that there was a change in our quality of life, and subsequently my mother went looking and found a very nice house to rent, which we moved into and stayed there for most of my youth until just before my father died.

It was during my Sunday afternoon outings with my father to the Empire Theatre that I became aware of how different the living conditions in the Caribbean were from those that I saw represented in the movies as the standards of living principally in the United States and Europe. I became acutely aware that for the majority of people life in Grenada and, by extension, the Caribbean was sharply different from the standard of living enjoyed by the numerically small upper classes of the region. This sharpened my awareness of the need for economic and social change to bring about significant improvements in the standards of living of the population as a whole.

My mother was a great reader. I think most of my values were shaped by her. Even as a child, I read voraciously to the point where I had read all of the books in the children's library, and there was only one library on the island for children. They had to take a decision whether they would allow me access to the adult library. Of course, it went to the board and they were basically negative and said that adult books should be checked before I had access to them. I had some limited access after the text had been scrutinized. I was often in the library and sought books from the adult section.

When the librarian was not about, I read anything I wanted. So it did not matter anyway.

The information available to my family about my mother's ancestors indicate that they were originally from Martinique, French Antilles. I was told that her great-grandmother's family name was 'Chateau', and that her family had received a grant of land from Napoleon when he visited Grenada with his French Antillean wife, Josephine. My great-grandmother bequeathed most of her land and other assets to members of her family, including my grandmother, and the family lived on the produce of their land, principally nutmegs, cocoa and vegetables.

She married my grandfather, 'Tommy' Robertson, and he lived on her assets all his life. He was regarded as a kind of unofficial mayor of the little village of Birchgrove. My mother used to joke that as the first automobile arrived in the village, her father went out with loudspeakers and said: 'I have just been informed by telephone that an automobile is on its way to Birchgrove. All children indoors. All adults on the side of the road.'

I remember my grandfather very well. He also was a great reader. Whenever he came to see us, he always questioned us on things like the rules of syntax and how to spell various words. He was a gentleman. At 83, he decided to remarry, which my mother and the rest of his family considered to be unusual and teased him accordingly.

On becoming a student of economics

My first school was an Anglican primary school in Gouyave. Mr Miller, the headmaster, had the equivalent of a private class within the class to which all boys of our age belonged. The smaller group was essentially middle-class children like my brother and myself. We were attracted to the larger group where the boys seemed to be having a lot of fun. Accordingly, the other boys and myself in our smaller group spent a lot of time in the larger class because of the sporting and other relationships that we built up.

By the time we moved to St Georges, my brother Dunbar and I were able to settle easily into the primary school run by the

Methodists – the St George's Methodist School. I was eight years old at the time.

The headmaster, Mr Samuel Graham, showed an interest in me straight away. He took me under his wing and began special classes for me in Latin, Mathematics and French. Mr Graham was really responsible for laying my educational foundation because he dealt with me personally. Every Thursday I had to go to his home where he gave me special classes. He said: 'You must now sit the entrance exam to get into the grammar school', which was then the only boys' secondary school on the island. When I was nine, he made me sit this exam. Normally, you sat at eleven and then went on to the grammar school. I sat it and my father became very worried because he heard that I was doing very well and might in fact get into the school immediately. He disagreed initially, saying that I was too young to be in a class with much older boys. Mr Graham responded by saying he would keep me for a year to do more mathematics, which would give me advanced standing when I went to the secondary school, which they did. When I eventually went to the Grenada Boys Secondary School (GBSS), I was placed in the advanced form of 3A as against the entry level form of 1.

As for my relationship with Mr Graham, he stayed in touch with me for several years. In the meantime, however, he himself changed profession; unknown to most people in Grenada, he had been quietly studying law. Eventually he went off to London to 'eat his dinners' at one of the Inns of Court and returned to Grenada as a qualified barrister. Subsequently, he entered the government legal service and began a career progression in law that eventually ended with his becoming the Chief Justice of the Windward Islands and Sir Samuel Graham, knighted by the Queen. Altogether, Sir Samuel had a distinguished career, also serving for a time in a legal capacity in Belize.

Here I was then at the GBSS. The big problem about it, however, was that I was the youngest child in the class and they all thought of me as a little boy, a bit of a nuisance. What was worse, I was coming first in the class, which did not endear me to my colleagues at all. So I found myself in Form 3 with the big boys. They knew all sorts of things and really gave me a warm time. I was ten and they were thirteen. But I started being tall and gangly so I sort of got into this group; my nickname became Bean, because they said my head was shaped like a bean. Actually, it was the best-looking boy who called me that because he was jealous. We were competing for the favours of a girl who said she preferred me, but he persuaded her otherwise.

Sometimes I think that I never really mixed with children of my own age. Once you get into a higher class like that, what you want to do is get into the group and so, as we moved up the school, I just moved with them. I was always the youngest among my contemporaries.

The school leaving examination in those days was the Cambridge Senior School Certificate. In the year I was due to take it I developed malaria and was at home for six months. In spite of initial resistance, however, I sat the examination and passed, not very well, but I passed and moved up to the sixth form. I was thirteen; the other boys were three years older.

I was moved up to a sixth form that in those days offered the equivalent of today's A levels (the Caribbean Advanced Proficiency Examination, or CAPE). They were just then developing the Cambridge Higher School Certificate Programme. Some of the top schools in Trinidad offered it; in Jamaica, there were two schools, I think, that offered it then. In later years, when I told some Jamaican friends in London that I had passed it, they were surprised that Grenada had the Higher Schools Certificate at the time.

I got into the sixth form and was annoyed that they did not make me a prefect. I was forgetting that I was only thirteen in the sixth form. I thought that since I was a fully fledged sixth former and quite responsible, I should be made a prefect. The headmaster squashed my dreams, saying: 'How can we make you a prefect? You're just thirteen. For goodness sake! Who would listen to you?'

I said 'Is that so, sir?' And you know what? I decided that I had had enough of school.

Actually, when I came to the sixth form I had great difficulty in deciding which subjects I should do. I was more inclined towards the arts than the sciences. I liked mathematics and loved history very much, but beyond that I could not decide. Then I went to visit a friend of mine, Yorke Marryshow, the son of Grenada's foremost politician, T. Albert Marryshow. In the 1920s he started the agitation for constitutional change and he also started the newspaper called the *West Indian*, advocating that the West Indies must be West Indian, which became a slogan in support of federation.

My father did not like Marryshow, but he was a very talented man. He had a wonderful baritone voice and used to sing at concerts. He was someone whom you could not ignore, the political leader known as the Father of Federation, the West Indian Federation, advocating it long before many of his contemporaries did.

Anyway, I went to visit my friend Yorke and while I was there I saw that his father had two books written by W. Arthur Lewis (the St Lucian-born economist Sir William Arthur Lewis, who got his doctorate from the LSE in 1940 and won the Nobel Prize in Economics in 1979 for his role in economic development). One was called *Economic Survey 1919–1939*, a set of lectures dealing with the interwar years that were so highly regarded that people insisted they should be published. The other was called *Economic Problems of Today*. I said, 'I would like to read these two books.'

So Yorke said: 'I'll ask my father.'

His father came and said: 'Young man, these books have been given to me by the author, a very distinguished man. He is now with the London School of Economics. He is an economist. Be very careful with them when I lend them to you.'

I read them and was highly enthused. So I went to the school, asked to see the headmaster and said to him: 'Sir, I'd like to do economics in the Higher Schools Certificate.' He said: 'No, you can't. We have one master here who knows a little bit about it. He could probably teach you for one unit.' In those days, you had to do three units. 'But he can't possibly do more. No, you can't.'

I told my father: 'Listen, I'm not going to do any courses that I'm not interested in.' He looked at it again: 'Don't you do English Literature? You used to like literature.'

I said: 'Yes, as a hobby, but I really do not want to get too deep into literature.' Then I said to him: 'I am leaving school.' I did not tell him I had gone to the Civil Service and asked to see his friend,

Mr Emerson Gittens, who held a very senior position in the Administrator's Office.

I had said to Mr Gittens: 'I'd like a job.'

He said: 'Alister, are you crazy?'

'No.'

'How old are you?'

'Thirteen.'

'Good gracious,' he said. 'Thirteen and you want to come into the Civil Service? This is a place for men!'

'I know that, sir, I want to work. I want to earn some money and help my parents. I'm really not interested in school. I'm fed up with school and would like to get to learn something of practical use.'

He said: 'Let me think about it. Call me back this afternoon about four o'clock.'

So I called him at four and he said: 'All right. I'll take you into my office as a Class 3 Clerk, and remember, this is not glamorous work. You have to do a lot of things.'

'I'm very happy. When can I start?'

'Come at the end of the month.'

The Administrator's Office was the colonial equivalent of the Colonial Secretary's Office. I suppose you could say that the closest equivalent to it today is the Prime Minister's Office, but it was headed by a non-elected official. I now had to go to tell my parents that I was going to work at the end of the month. They were both aghast that I was leaving school. My father decided to see the headmaster himself and told him that I was leaving school because I had been offered a job in the Civil Service.

The headmaster rejected the notion and said that he would have a discussion with me to find an alternative. When he did, he questioned me about the reasons for my wanting to leave school, and when I told him, he said that he would not make me a prefect now, but he would make me one next year. In relation to the Higher Schools Certificate Examination, the headmaster told me that the school wanted me to do eight units: three units in history, a unit of mathematics and a unit in English. If I wanted to do three units of economics, he could only offer teaching for one unit. However, he was willing to accept my proposal to do three units if

I could offer satisfactory arrangements for receiving tuition in the other two units. I accepted this proposal and advised him that I had sufficient access to the necessary reading to prepare successfully for the other two units. He agreed, somewhat reluctantly, to my proposal. So I remained in school. I suppose I have been a negotiator from my boyhood!

Anyhow, I went and did that and passed, though I don't know how. And that set me on the road to economics as my profession and lifelong commitment.

2

Early employment and initial political education

Early employment

Having completed my secondary education by the age of 16, I had to confront the question of pursuing further studies in economics at university level. At that time, the teaching of economics at the University of the West Indies had not yet begun, and even when it did, it was at general degree level until 1960.

In effect, then, my only option was to go abroad for university work. In the context of the time, this meant travelling to Britain, and I had already heard about the prohibitive cost of the voyage, not to mention university fees and other expenses. It was also not feasible to think of getting a job and saving sufficient to meet those costs at some period in the future. The only option, although a distant one, was to try and secure a scholarship to attend a British university. My heart was then set on attending the London School of Economics because Professor Arthur Lewis had studied there and was, in fact, to become a member of staff.

The Co-operative Bank

Good jobs were not always available in a small island so I really perked up when I heard that a vacancy existed at the 'Penny Bank'. This was the popular name for the Co-operative Bank, which began by accepting deposits of one penny. It was started in 1932 by some young Grenadians, including W.E. Julien, Arnold Williamson and Sam Brathwaite, who found the banking system in Grenada not sufficiently accommodating for them. Large numbers of people on the island subscribed to it, so it was a very popular institution and remains one of the most respected banks in Grenada.

My application to the bank for a job was successful. I was happy because I began to see myself, however remotely, armed with a university degree some years down the road. I was also happy at work because my boss, the Chief Clerk Adrian Mitchell, an old boy of my school who was years ahead of me, was an excellent on-the-job coach. I stayed there for a year or so, and then Adrian got an opportunity to go to work in Venezuela where some members of his family were already residing. He resigned, so the question was who would take over. He told the Manager, Kenneth Williams: 'Sir, Alister has been running the place for the last six months or so. He does most of the work and I just look it over. I've never had any cause to complain.'

Mr Williams said: 'Is that so?' He brought me into his office and gave me a long interview. When we finished, he said: 'Yes, you know everything. So let us try and get you appointed.' Now that would have been some jump. I was the most junior person in the bank now being considered for the most senior post. When it went to the directors, they said I was too young. I would have to wait. They could not appoint me before I was 21.

I said: 'Really? I'm 17. I have to sit down here for four years? No! This is my resignation. I'm off.'

The situation somehow reminded me of the profound frustration experienced by my father, who had been placed in a stalemate position when he could not function as a pharmacist even though he had passed the examinations.

The nutmeg exporter

Although I was disappointed, I soon became more determined to get a position where I could use my mind to good effect. My next job was at a co-operative that exported nutmegs which were the island's principal crop. The attraction there was that they paid me more. The bank was giving me $40 a month and these people offered me $60 – a 50 per cent increase. What bothered me was that every day I completed my job responsibilities in about an hour. I had nothing to do for most of the day! I asked my immediate superior, who was the senior person next to the General Manager, to give me more work. He said, almost with relief, 'Well, the only thing I can teach you is my job.'

'Whatever you teach me, I'll go and do it,' I replied eagerly.

So he happily passed over many of his responsibilities to me and I felt active and engaged. Not long after that, the General Manager saw me doing my supervisor's work. 'What are you doing there?' he asked sharply.

I told him I was helping my supervisor. He looked at the work and threw it down in disgust. He proceeded to upbraid my supervisor: 'You're exploiting the youngster, you're a disgrace! Do not ever give him any more of your work. He has his own to do!' With his face still thunderous, he called me into his office and ordered me not to do tasks that were not stipulated in my job description. I tried to reason with him: 'Sir, I understand your point, but it would mean that…'

'Boy, don't talk nonsense to me. If you can do your job in such a short time, you must be doing something wrong.'

After that incident, the atmosphere at work became charged. I felt that neither my supervisor nor the manager really wanted me around. I discussed my plight with a former schoolmate. He assured me that I had picked up enough knowledge in the two jobs to do the work of the accountant at his office, a position which would soon become available because the incumbent was leaving to complete his legal studies. With two disappointments under my belt, I was not about to get my hopes up again so quickly. I doubted that any company would consider my qualification to be sufficient, but my friend kept on encouraging me.

Nothing ventured, nothing accomplished, my mother used to say. I learned from the man who was leaving the accounting position that the job involved updating and analysing the cash book, the ledger and the journal. He offered to show me how to do the books but I told him that I had already learned to do them at the bank. Generous in nature, he convinced the boss that I was the right person for the job, because I had correctly answered all the questions he had asked me. The boss said he could take me on probation.

My former salary of $60 per month was doubled now that I was Chief Clerk, but I soon discovered that I had jumped, as the saying goes, 'from the frying pan into the fire'. My boss had a complete disregard for proper accounting procedures and systems. The first time I realized his flouting of procedures was when we ordered American apples for the Christmas season. My boss offered to clear the apples at Customs himself.

I cautioned politely: 'Be careful. If an invoice says that the company got 100 cases of apples, you have to receive exactly that amount. If there is a shortfall, we'll claim insurance.'

He seemed to agree with me, and since I was young and naïve, I was satisfied with his response. When he returned to the office he told us that just after clearing the apples he had coincidentally met some acquaintances and invited them to taste the apples he had just cleared at Customs. The apples were so delicious that these acquaintances wanted to purchase them immediately. The clerk and I checked the shipment that arrived in the office, to discover a heavy shortfall of apples. I instructed the clerk to make a list for the insurance company. The boss, who overheard, said: 'You can't do it like that! The insurance would never pay for it like that, you have to have it certified by Customs.'

My visit to the Customs Office served to enlighten me about the character of my boss. The officer insisted that the full consignment had been delivered to him. So I charged my boss for the shortfall of apples, which angered him immensely. I suppose he thought that since I was his junior I would simply comply with everything he did. Charging him was an ethical procedure that I had learned from the auditors, with whom I had an excellent professional relationship. The auditors were a respected Barbadian company, Bovell and Skeete, with offices in Grenada, headed by the highly competent Mr Lyle Webster. I asked him to undertake a spot audit and became more urgent in my requests because the relationship

17

between me and my boss was deteriorating, and I did not want my boss's actions to affect my own reputation.

Mr Webster said: 'I'm going to pen a nasty Auditor's Report but I have to be cautious because I don't want them to think you're involved in any way. What I will do is to interview the staff before submitting the audit.'

His interview with the six staff members revealed that they had heard me insisting to the boss virtually on a daily basis that he must adhere to proper procedures, and that he could be charged for any shortfall of goods. Mr Webster completed the audit and his report, unsurprisingly, contained a number of queries. He submitted the report to the head of the firm, because he was so concerned about the gravity of the anomalies.

Working with my boss became untenable. Once, he offered fire insurance to a man who had just constructed a mansion. He skipped over the first step in offering insurance, which is to secure an independent valuation of the house. Over the weekend, the client gave my boss his own valuation of the mansion and my boss accepted the premium for that valuation. He advised me on Monday that he had worked out the valuation for the house and said offhandedly, 'Here's the money.'

I protested: 'Who did the valuation? Sir, we can't do it this way at all.'

He erupted. The only thing that finally stopped his shouting was the abrupt ringing of the telephone. It brought the news that the house had burnt down! I could not prove that this was a premeditated act.

'What on earth are we going to tell Bankers and Traders?' I asked angrily. This was the Australian insurance firm that we were representing. 'We can't tell them you insured the house without a valuation, that we insured the house without the issuance of the necessary insurance document before it burned down! If I were them, I wouldn't even look at this case!'

We received no communication from the insurers in Australia. My boss insisted that the client was to be compensated for the burnt house, and I countered that the house had not been legally insured. The argument went on and on. Finally the insurance company settled the case, in the interests of sustaining their reputation, but they terminated business with the agency. By that time, I had already left the job.

The final straw had actually come just before my departure. Around the same time that the house had mysteriously burnt down, I had been trying to persuade a wealthy farmer to purchase life insurance. This was not an easy premium to sell – he was only able to see me on Sundays, and then would insist that I join him in a drink of white rum, which for me in those days was like taking poison. But I took my 'doses of poison' because the antidote to it was the selling of a policy worth $150,000, a massive amount of money in those days. Finally, he decided to buy the policy. I calculated the premium and arranged with him to visit the office so that we could do the required paperwork. Before he was scheduled to arrive, I was called away suddenly on urgent business. When I returned, my boss informed me rather casually that 'This fellow came in about his policy and rather than make him wait, I just filled out the form to issue the policy.' I made the mistake of thanking him very much.

'You don't need to thank me,' he replied. 'This is my policy. You didn't fill out the form so your name is not on the policy.'

Imagine! All those Sundays! All that rum! All that persuasion! All for nothing! This was deliberate provocation! I thought about the matter and told my mother that I was going to leave the job.

My mother was calm and spoke evenly. She said she understood my decision but asked me to think carefully about what alternatives I could pursue. I agreed to do so, and to inform her on the following morning about what decision I was going to take. Feeling exactly the same way at six o'clock in the morning, I took the keys to my boss at his house and ignored his protestations about my decision to resign. My mind was only centred on what I now had to do because of my lack of trust in him. I phoned Mr Webster, who quickly moved in, did an audit on my work, and said it was in order. There would be no ricochet effect on my future career. I then tendered my formal resignation.

My mother was more concerned about my emotional state than my decision to resign. She suggested that I needed a period of relaxation to relieve the anxiety that I was then experiencing. She reminded me of an invitation from friends to go with them to Quarantine Station for a few days and encouraged me to take it up. Quarantine Station was originally an isolation centre for patients thought to have highly contagious diseases. However, as the years passed, it became a place where people could enjoy a vacation by the seaside.

I arrived at the beach in the evening. The very next morning I received a call that I should return to St Georges immediately because my father had had a major stroke and could not speak. It was a most difficult moment in my life. Here I was without a job just at the time that my father had become severely incapacitated. As soon as we visited him in the hospital, we knew that the doctor had made a correct diagnosis – my father died two days later.

My mother did not wallow in self-pity. She loved her husband, but immediately understood that her priority now was the well-being of her children. Showing her usual resilience, she took a supervisory job in a store; the low pay only enabled her to buy the weekly groceries, and did not cover the basic needs of a family of seven.

The trauma of my father's death

Luckily, friends had been telling me all along to join the Civil Service. I applied and heard along the grapevine that I was to be assigned to the Governor's Office. Again, I held my breath. This seemed almost too good to be true. But I was astounded later when a friend told me that the Governor said I was a security risk and should not be employed anywhere in the service. I hoped that this was mere rumour and shared my plight with my father's friend, Mr Emerson Gittens. He said he would check out the information for me.

Around the same time that I made my application to the Civil Service, interesting developments were occurring in Grenada. Poor working conditions prompted a wide-scale strike led by the charismatic leader, Eric Matthew Gairy. While this was going on, a family friend told me that she had a Trinidadian house guest, an intellectual who was thoroughly bored with the conversation of the people he had met. Could I come over to have a drink with him to relieve his boredom?

I agreed, went and judged him to be a very bright man, but I realized straight away that he held strongly to a belief that the Soviet Union was incomparably superior to Western countries, particularly the United States and Britain. He must have thought that my restlessness about local conditions provided fertile ground for encouraging me to join him in his conversion to communist ideas. I chatted with him and left.

About two weeks after that conversation, customs called me to say that I should collect a large package of documents that they had received. I was confused: 'That must be a mistake. Check it.'

'It's for you, sir.'

And they told me the name of the sender. My surprise package contained communist promotional literature. I was aghast at the nerve of this man, sending me a package without telling me anything beforehand. Later, I shared my annoyance with my cousin, Byron Roberson, who lived with us: 'Imagine, this man I hardly know sends me this huge package and asks me to distribute these materials.'

Byron was equally upset and took it upon himself to write an anonymous letter to the newspaper where he worked, to the effect that there were attempts to distribute communist literature in Grenada. To get an anonymous letter published, he had to give his real name to the editor, who was supposed to keep this information confidential. But in virtually no time my cousin received a call from the Commissioner of Police, a retired Englishman who had been a major in the British Army, who had asked the editor to disclose the name of the author of the letter.

Byron answered all of his questions. The Commissioner of Police then said he wanted to meet with me. On that occasion, he acknowledged my uneasiness about the situation, but pointed out that I could do a service to my country by distributing just a few of the pamphlets, to see if any of Gairy's cohorts, or Gairy himself, showed any interest in this literature. I told him I needed time to consider his proposition. Finally, I decided against it: these things have a way of coming to light in a small country, and I had not only my own security to think about, but that of my family, especially my mother. I conveyed my decision politely to the Commissioner, not realizing that he had kept a record of all this information on his files. When the routine check was conducted on my eligibility to join the Civil Service, this information came to light. The Governor apparently said that he didn't need anybody like that in his office. Mr Gittens told him that there was much more to this story and the Governor decided to set up a Committee of Inquiry to investigate the matter further.

I did get the job eventually, but in the meantime I was broke and really concerned about all this bad luck. Eventually I had to give

Figure 1 Mrs Eileen McIntyre, my mother.

my mother the bad news: 'We can't afford to live in this house; we have to move somewhere about a third of the rent.'

My mother looked at me in disbelief. Where would we find somewhere like that? But again, she showed her resilience and found some rooms that were affordable. But this was a further plunge in living standards for her, and meant that there was no respite from the unfortunate occurrences that she had experienced over a comparatively short period of time.

I went on a mission of mercy. I visited the Anglican High School attended by my sister Pansy and our cousin Tracy, who was in our care, and explained the situation to Miss Bertrand, their headmistress.

'Your sister is a very good student,' she said, distressed at the thought of one of her best students leaving the school. She said she would consult the School Board about issuing scholarships to both Pansy and Tracy. I was sufficiently encouraged by this to approach the GBSS, where my cousin Clifford was studying; my brother Dunbar had already left school. The GBSS also made a similar gesture. So, ultimately, the initiative of going to speak to the two schools proved successful.

As far as living quarters were concerned, we were cramped in two and a half rooms: two bedrooms and a small kitchen. My mother and the two girls shared one bedroom, and my brother, two cousins and myself were in the other room. If visitors came they could only be entertained in the kitchen. How my mother maintained her dignity and resolve after such a fall in living standards amazed me. Though it was unfortunate that all this happened, I would not have seen her strength had life remained on an even keel. She gained greater strength from her Christianity, while I gained greater strength from her resolve.

The radio DJ

I learned from my mother to try new things. That was the reason why I became a radio DJ for about three years. The radio programme had been started by the government after the Gairy-inspired uprisings, feeling that it needed a more personal connection with the general population – and what better way to do that than through music and conversation? The government had initially established a Government Information Service because of the wave of false information circulating within the island. The broadcast was aired every three or four hours, and the feedback from listeners was that it was boring and flat.

Pondering on the feedback was Glynn Evans, who had set up the radio programmes for the government. He knew that one of my favourite voices was that dry, velvety voice of Nat King Cole, and he said to me: 'Everybody loves Nat King Cole. Why don't you start a programme with him and see where it goes?' It didn't seem like such a great idea at first. But when I went to the station and played a Nat King Cole song, I think it was 'Autumn Leaves', a hunger started in the listeners for more of his music.

Glynn said: 'Why don't you expand this programme and introduce some serious ideas? If you had a request programme, you could play the songs people ask for. They would listen in for that.'

This was more than I had bargained for and I convinced a school friend, Curtis Strachan, who had a smooth, melodious voice ideal for radio announcing, to join me. Curtis would eventually become the longest-serving clerk in the Grenadian parliament and was knighted by the Queen. Back then, in our youthful days, we called the programme 'The Curt–Al Show' – easy for people to say. I would occasionally say a few words after changing the records but Curtis did most of the speaking. We did the show twice a week after work for three years. We did it gratis, not even thinking of asking for a penny: we were just happy to get some free records now and then. The sole disadvantage, at first, was that my face and voice were identifiable everywhere, so I had to be careful not to get into any trouble.

But didn't we get into trouble with that programme! It was not at all rare for a young lady to ask us to play a song for a gentleman's birthday, which we did – but then his wife or girlfriend would ring, asking for the name of the lady who made the request. I told them that it was not the station's policy to reveal the names of those who requested songs, but I was upbraided by the enquirer. I was also strongly criticized by any number of ladies who thought that other ladies got their requests heard first. What they did not realize was that we did not want an endless stream of requests that would upset the balance of music to conversation.

There were other surprises in this business. I was listening to the radio one day when I heard a long-winded, monotonous fellow talking. I complained to my mother: 'This man is too long-winded. Why doesn't he get to the point?'

'That man is you, son.'

'No, wait a minute. That's the way I sound?'

'Yes.' She hesitated before she added, 'I think you're a bit too wordy.'

Actually, there was more to that criticism. My mother never liked me being in that radio programme because she felt I was making myself vulnerable in a society that had become less secure since the Gairy uprisings. In fact, I did not enjoy the speaking part of it, but I enjoyed selecting the music.

The Civil Service – finally

When I finally did get the position at the Governor's Office, I resigned from the DJ job so that I could concentrate my energies on a demanding job. At the Governor's Office I was given the position of Cypher Clerk, decoding classified telegrams from London, a task that I learned quickly. I now realized why the security check for this job had been so important.

Soon enough, a new governor, Sir Edward Betham Beetham, arrived. Around that time there were interesting developments in the colonies. These started in Buganda, a kingdom within Uganda that contained the largest ethnic group in the country. The Kabaka or King of Buganda was dethroned when he married an English girl, having thoroughly upset his relatives and the people of Buganda, who felt that there were enough young ladies readily available in Buganda. Interests in Britain were also against the marriage but understood that their position could have a negative impact on all the other colonies. There was a barrage of secret telegrams between England and the colonies to discern their reaction to Britain's position.

One day, the Governor told me he was expecting a top secret telegram from London and instructed me to decode it while he attended another engagement. He showed me how to retrieve the codes from the safe and unintentionally locked the safe without closing the door. I went home, had supper, came back, got the codes from the safe and decoded the telegram. I then asked the policemen on duty to ask the Governor to come to the office. An inebriated Governor stumbled in, read the telegram and said: 'All right, put the codes back in the safe.' So said, so done and he stumbled out again. When it was time to close the safe, it just wouldn't close. I asked the policeman to send for the Governor again. Did he ever curse me for interrupting his enjoyment at the club! With the smell of alcohol pervading the room, he could not stop cursing me. I did not respond but later, relating the incident to my mother, I told her: 'I have to leave. I can't tolerate this abuse.'

Next morning, with the words of my resignation written boldly in my mind, before I could let him know my displeasure, he opened the conversation by saying: 'Alister, I apologize unreservedly for my conduct. I had a little too much to drink, I'm afraid I said some rather terrible things to you which were uncalled for, and I do wish to apologize. Come into my office and let's talk for a bit.'

This was to be a defining moment in my life. He enquired about my career plans and I told him of my high hopes of getting a scholarship to study economics in London, but things were going at a snail's pace. He casually picked up the phone to Britain, in a day when phoning the mother country was considered a big thing to do. He spoke with the Colonial Office, while I held my breath. When he put down the phone at last, he said with the quiet casualness that only the British do well: 'I assume you will get your scholarship.'

Here was a man to whom an apology was not just words but action. He said: 'University starts in October and you will be away from your mother for three years. I am going to give you some leave now so that you can spend some time with her and the rest of your family. And, Alister, I know that your family circumstances have not been the easiest. I am authorizing an interest-free loan of £500 so that you'll have some cash to take to university.'

I realized that the Governor was a decent person. Most people just apologize and leave it at that. I have always thought that there is a particularly fine decency in the best of the British, and it was this degree of decency that created a sharp turn in my life.

While I was preparing to go to the United Kingdom, I married Alice Williamson. Because of the current regulation, I went to London alone. She joined me in my final year, but returned to Grenada for the birth of our son, Arnold.

When Governor Beetham later went to Trinidad, he was the only British officer in that country to get along with Dr Eric Williams. Even after Dr Williams became Prime Minister, he asked Sir Edward to remain as Governor-General for a while, as a gesture to a great man. Later on, the government of Trinidad and Tobago endorsed this gesture by naming one of their first highways the Beetham Highway.

I believe that Sir Edward had a good understanding of the process of independence as a natural chain of events and was able to get along well with a strong nationalist like Dr Williams. While in Grenada, he had already displayed a capacity to accommodate at least some of Gairy's idiosyncrasies, before he found that he could no longer accept any kind of relationship with him.

My early political education: introduction to the idea of federation

My political consciousness was enlivened by listening to the speeches of T.A. Marryshow, the leading political figure in Grenada. The speeches, normally given every Thursday, drew large audiences. Marryshow was the editor of the *West Indian* newspaper, which had as a subheading 'The West Indies must always be West Indian', referring, of course, to the importance of federation.

Marryshow, I think, also understood that independence would not only boost our confidence, but create an abundance of opportunities for building a new nation, especially for young middle-income professionals. He understood the power of speaking to people not as a group but as if he were singling out individuals, to inspire them on what independence would do for each of them. During his speeches, he would point his finger at a number of us, saying something like 'After Independence, do you realize that *you* could become the governor? Do you realize that in an independent Grenada, every job would be open to you?' This was a deliberate strategy on his part to generate personal enthusiasm for independence.

To understand why we were so excited at the prospect of having every job open to us, one needs to appreciate some of Grenada's unique features. Grenada was not a classical sugar plantation society characterized by a large underclass, in the conventional Marxist perception. Because of Grenada's topography, sugar, which thrives on flat land, was never the dominant industry. Crops had been developed that were suited to its hilly terrain. The chief tree crops grown were cocoa and nutmegs – lucrative export crops that could be grown on small holdings. The development of the peasant population received an impetus during the Napoleonic era, as it is reported that Napoleon visited the Antilles and made grants of land in honour of his first wife, Josephine, a creole from Martinique.

Almost from the outset there were two systems of agriculture – plantation and peasant. Thus Grenada, and to some extent the other French colonies of St Lucia and Dominica, emerged with a different system of land holding. Instead of a pure plantation system, their economies were characterized by a strong peasant population – a free coloured class with their own land, who followed the practice of cultivating non-traditional export crops. By the 1940s and 1950s Grenada's strong peasant population was developing small and not so small businesses, and therefore their sons, and to some extent their daughters, could see the possibilities of mobility. Accordingly, this influenced the structure of politics that existed in the closing years prior to federation and, later, independence.

As a result of parallel but somewhat different developments in other islands in the region, smallness became a dominant theme, not only in discussions about the feasibility of political independence, but also in relation to possibilities for economic integration, centred around the constraints of small size and economic under-development.

Continuity in the thinking about federation of young people at the time was captured in the GBSS school song, a visionary set of verses created by two former GBSS graduates, both Island Scholars, L.M. Commissiong and L. Morgan, who were then studying medicine at Edinburgh University. It was and is a rallying song; as fellow GBSS graduate Dr Winston Phillips states in his blog ('The Grenada Boys Secondary School Hostel – Reminiscing on a boarding school life in Grenada'), it is 'a song one can boldly sing anytime, anywhere… but not anyhow!!' The final stanza of the song is as follows:

> And when boyhood days are over,
> Our motto must still remain;
> For only by earnest endeavour
> The highest we shall attain.
> A truly great West Indies
> Be this our constant aim;
> Surmounting insular boundaries
> A people in more than name.

The GBSS school song remained the guiding sentiment in my own efforts at personal development and public service. These words drove me and other boys to really reach the highest we could attain in our personal and professional development, without thinking of boundaries and obstacles. We felt a brotherhood with our Caribbean region.

3

Education in the UK

At the London School of Economics (LSE), 1954–57

By good fortune I had secured a place at the highly prestigious London School of Economics. Then, as now, the reputation of the school was legendary. It came to my attention because of my admiration for the career of Professor Arthur Lewis, who had been a student and, subsequently, a lecturer there. I determined that I should try, as far as possible, to pattern my academic work along lines similar to his own. I was disappointed to learn on my arrival at LSE that he had left to take a chair at the University of Manchester.

On my arrival at the LSE, I was deeply impressed by the very high quality of the faculty in the different disciplines being taught and the academic accomplishments of the staff in their various fields, and I realized what great efforts would be required to succeed in this highly competitive environment. I rapidly adapted to the new situation and became thoroughly immersed in everything going on around me.

In my first few days there, I became acquainted with other West Indian students at the LSE, most of whom were at the same stage as I was. We spent our first days at the school relaying information to each other about the different departments and the formidable challenges that awaited us. It was truly a most enlivening experience

Figure 2 School friends from the LSE – Roy Jones and Pat Cacho.

and I kept patting myself on the back that I had been privileged to secure such a marvellous opportunity. Our impressions were reinforced by the extremely high quality of the lectures that we attended in the different disciplines. The scholarship of the lecturers and their capacity to communicate made a strong impression on all of us. We came to realize that the heights to which we aspired would require considerable work and application. We all burned with the desire to attain the highest levels, and this competitive spirit stayed with me throughout my time at the LSE and beyond.

There were seven other West Indians at LSE in the mid 1950s. Two of them were Lloyd Barnett, who would become an ambassador in the Jamaican Foreign Service, and Jack Clarke, who would attain the position of President of the Jamaica Development Bank. Perhaps one of the few Jamaican colleagues from those days who only recently passed away is Roy Jones, a former director of research at the Bank of Jamaica. Because of our comparatively small number, we all became close friends and remained in touch throughout our professional careers.

31

Among my English friends at the LSE was Sarah Graham, who became a close family friend and later godmother to one of my children. Sarah was in the Department of Sociology at Mona for a time before emigrating to Australia.

The West Indian Students' Union (WISU)

Almost immediately after I arrived in London, my close friend Cosmo Phillips, once a fellow sixth former in Grenada, invited me to attend a meeting of the West Indian Students' Union. Cosmo was the secretary. He had been in London at one of the four Inns of Court to read for the Bar. When we met again in London, he persuaded me to join the WISU, an active student body which, at that time, devoted many of its activities to promoting federation.

The position of secretary was demanding and few students were at the stage in their studies where they could devote a great deal of time to extracurricular activities. I was then completing my first year and did not have to sit exams until the end of my second year, so I could squeeze in some free time in the weeks and months preceding the exams. In order to devote himself exclusively to preparing for his exams, which were close at hand, Cosmo persuaded me to help him out by offering my services as secretary. Accordingly, when he resigned, I accepted the nomination and was appointed.

A major occasion during my time as secretary was the conference on federation organized by the British government and attended by the major political personalities from the Caribbean region. The WISU was not permitted to attend the conference, but a special session was organized for us to meet the representatives from all the islands. Formal presentations were made by Hon. Norman Manley of Jamaica, Hon. Albert Gomes of Trinidad and Tobago, Hon. Grantley Adams of Barbados, and Hon. T.A. Marryshow.

Mr Manley gave a stirring presentation of the case for federation in the context of political independence and its significance for the future of the West Indies. Mr Gomes did not appear to be overly interested in discussing strategy on how to move federation

32

forward, but was more inclined to address his own role after federation, and used a phrase that remained with me: 'I am de facto Governor of Trinidad.' He then proceeded to list a number of responsibilities that the Governor had delegated to him. The Hon. Grantley Adams was surprisingly silent: the students from Barbados who were in the audience explained that he was a man of few words. Nonetheless, I found it difficult to reconcile his silence with the important role being assigned to him in the formation of the Federation. Hon. T.A. Marryshow was at his rhetorical best. He moved away from details to paint a picture of what this independent West Indies would mean for the young people of the region. It was as if I had stepped back into the St George's Market Square in Grenada, in the midst of passionate political oratory.

There was not enough opportunity for an exchange of views with the delegates, but Hon. Norman Manley indicated that he was paying a visit to London later in the year and would welcome a substantive meeting with the WISU to discuss the Federation. We were all greatly excited by this opportunity to contribute to the dialogue on the subject. Different people were given responsibility for preparing substantive proposals for the area assigned to them. I was charged with the responsibility of presenting a statement on the Federal Customs Union. Basically, my reference point was my colleagues at the LSE. However, I had to do most of the legwork and make it available for their comments.

In the course of 1955, Mr Manley visited the WISU. Our preparation for his visit was as thorough as possible. I was quite convinced that the Federal Government had moved towards the Customs Union without sufficient examination of the possible advantages and pitfalls. I presented the results of my efforts to Mr Manley and was gratified by his high commendations. I felt the need to get as firm a grip as possible on the subject as a matter of urgency. Indeed, my own presentation showed that in proceeding towards a Customs Union, the principal concern was how to provide revenue for the participating governments. Virtually no attention was being paid to the economic effects. It was left to William Demas and myself to point out in later contributions that the Customs Union could be used as a principal instrument for the economic development of the contributing countries. We evoked a response from governments on that subject only after the Federation had collapsed and they were moving towards the freeing of intra-regional trade on economic grounds.

The most impressive presentation made to Mr Manley was delivered by Stuart Hall, who represented Oxford on the WISU executive. Stuart was a Jamaican Rhodes Scholar who had attained First Class Honours at Oxford. He was moving towards graduate studies in English Literature, although he had become a major political figure in the Labour Group at Oxford. He was an incredibly bright and articulate person, with a very strong commitment to Federation and West Indian unity.

In his presentation to Mr Manley, Stuart located the Federation in the context of political theory and practice. It was outstanding, so much so that Mr Manley asked him straight away for a copy which he said he would circulate to colleagues in the Jamaican government. We were all enamoured with this outcome, in my own case because it articulated for me, for the first time, how the notion of federation was grounded in political thought and practice, although the possible role that federation could have played in the economic development of the region was understated.

On the whole, my experience in the WISU solidified my commitment to federation and to the economic integration of the participating countries. It goes without saying that the collapse of the Federation was a major blow to my own perception of what the region needed to do to advance its development. My colleagues and I were at a loss to understand how the high measure of accord displayed by the leadership on the visit of 1955 had deteriorated to such a level of discord that it permitted the forces against Federation to succeed as a result of the referendum in 1961.

An incident worthy of repetition was told to me by the Hon. G. Arthur Brown many years afterwards. At the height of the political discord between Jamaica and the Eastern Caribbean, Hon. Norman Manley called to his home G. Arthur Brown and Edgerton Richardson, his two principal advisers. He asked them to prepare a list of the issues that divided the two sides and to suggest compromise solutions in each case. After they completed the report, Mr Manley communicated the compromises to Hon. Grantley Adams, who had been appointed Prime Minister of the Federation, in a sealed letter which was left for Arthur Brown, who was scheduled to visit Trinidad, to deliver personally to the Prime Minister. When he arrived in Trinidad Arthur Brown sought to discharge his responsibility by going to the Prime Minister's residence. When he arrived there he was greeted by Lady Adams, the wife of the Prime Minister, to whom he delivered the letter, because she informed him that Sir Grantley was away on an unscheduled visit to Barbados. There was a stony silence which neither Mr Manley or his advisers could explain. Subsequently, after Sir Grantley's death, Mr Brown received a call from Lady Adams to say that she had found an unopened letter from Mr Manley in Sir Grantley's papers. It was evident that the latter had not opened the letter. One is left to speculate that if those compromises had been received and acted upon, the course of history in the Caribbean might have been radically different.

I conclude these comments with the observation that the West Indies Students' Union was an important learning experience for me, not only because of my substantive engagement with the issues of federation, but because I developed a circle of friends who have remained close to me in the succeeding years.

My personal tutor could also have been considered a friend, not only because we had drinks together, but also because he supported me so wholeheartedly. At the LSE there was a system of personal tutors, that is, there was a member of staff to whom a student could go for personal guidance – even outside of one's own discipline. My personal tutor, who remained with me to the end, was Ralph Miliband. His sons became prominent politicians: David was Foreign Minister in the Tony Blair administration, while Ed has been the Leader of the Opposition in Parliament, but at the time when I visited him, some years after, they were little children. Ralph Miliband and I became very friendly. Towards the end of term, he invited students to his home to have a beer, and he and his wife, a sociologist, went out of their way to be extremely kind to us.

Miliband was a Belgian of Jewish origin, who had fled the Nazi occupation and grown up in England, but he never discussed his personal experience. He also never discussed his political ideas, until nearing the end of my stay at the LSE. I went to the library and borrowed his book *Parliamentary Socialism*, which made me realize his strong advocacy of parliamentary socialism in the UK. What struck me the most was that I had never known that he was a socialist. He never showed us his books. He would simply give us whatever advice we requested. When I became a university teacher, I followed his example of not imparting my political views to students. I made every effort not to influence students with my personal views. The correct procedure was to introduce students to the subject and allow them to develop their own ideas.

Towards the end of my third year, we arrived at the question of my future after the London School of Economics. I told my professor, J.E. Meade, that I was committed to return to the Grenadian Civil Service. He said that while he did not wish to counter the expectations of the Grenadian Civil Service and the Colonial Development and Welfare authorities in London, he nevertheless felt that I had the potential to become a strong graduate student and suggested I should try for a Fulbright Scholarship.

Professor Meade, later to be awarded the Nobel Prize in Economics, was a person whom I strongly admired because of his robust intellectual mind and his exemplary character. I recognized how fortunate I was to be in close contact with an individual of such vast knowledge in economics. I wrote to the Fulbright authorities in London with a supporting letter from Professor Meade, enquiring whether I could be considered for a two-year Fulbright Fellowship, tenable at the Woodrow Wilson School at Princeton University. The Fulbright authorities asked me to submit a research proposal. I already had a proposal because of an article that I had read by William Demas, whom I had not yet met. It imbued me with the ambition to contribute to the discussion on the West Indies Customs Union.

Professor Meade recommended that I consult a Trinidadian who was a Reader in economics at the LSE. I wrote a proposal and sent it to him for his comments. At a later meeting with him, he advised me that he was also working on the subject, so he could not encourage me to work on it as well. Consequently, on reporting this to Professor Meade, he suggested that I try another subject. I tried to do this, but the Fulbright Office responded that it was too late to be considered for that year's awards. I was deeply disappointed. (I could not have known then that I would eventually go to the Woodrow Wilson School, not as a student, but as a Visiting Faculty Member.)

Professor Meade and I examined other options. I could attend Cambridge or Oxford. Actually, he was about to assume the Marshall Chair at Cambridge, the most prestigious chair in economics in the country. I thought better of following him to Cambridge, since he would be settling into a new position. I said that I was thinking about going to Oxford but did not know anyone there. He responded that Sir Donald McDougall, who was at Nuffield College, had the distinction of serving as economic advisor to three British prime ministers – some years later adding a fourth. He went on to say that Sir Donald was interested in the Caribbean, having attended an economics conference on the Mona campus only several months before.

The uncertainty then prevailing about my future work was mitigated by receiving First Class Honours in my final degree.

Life at Oxford, 1957–60

I was accepted at Nuffield College after an interview with the warden and several fellows of the college. Perhaps a sense of humour helps: when one of the fellows asked me, 'Mr McIntyre, what do you know about wine?', my answer was: 'Nothing at all, but I know a great deal about rum!' This pleased the fellows, who decided that I had a very good sense of humour, which was always helpful in a small, defined community.

Graduate work in Economics at Oxford was not at that time as well developed as I had hoped. There was a solidly organized B.Phil. degree at graduate level, intended for students who had not read economics at undergraduate level or who were coming from other institutions, particularly from the United States. For those students who planned to pursue a higher research degree, the arrangement was to get involved immediately in research, under the supervision of either a fellow from their own college, or from another college in Oxford. I was grateful indeed to be assigned to Sir Donald MacDougall, and benefitted from his extraordinary experience working as an economic advisor in the field.

Sir Donald supported my choice of a Caribbean research topic and suggested that I apply for a Beit Travelling Fellowship which would cover my expenses in Jamaica and Trinidad and Tobago. I held meetings with economists in the fields of trade and development, for example William Demas and G. Arthur Brown, who were then heads of economic planning units in their respective countries. Both men wholeheartedly supported my proposal for conducting research on West Indian trade with Canada. At the time the West Indian Federation was still in its infancy, and Canada wished to develop an arrangement that contained ideas and proposals beyond the previous West Indies Trade Agreement with Canada, which was negotiated in 1925 and would in any event need to be brought up to date.

I followed G. Arthur Brown's advice to write a 'think piece' for Premier Norman Manley, and I received encouraging responses from everyone, including Premier Manley and G. Arthur Brown himself. I went back to Oxford with this special proposal, which Sir Donald was pleased to accept and submit to the Board of Studies for their agreement. Once this was received, I could now work toward the full preparation of a thesis for the Doctor of Philosophy (D.Phil.) degree.

One of the subjects on which I needed more information for my thesis was Britain's import policy towards Canada. The British had liberalized imports from Canada right after the war, at a time when Britain suffered from severe foreign exchange constraints. In this way I discovered how the liberalization of Canadian imports had destroyed my father's business (see Chapter 1). I remember my father saying: 'It's all over. The Canadians have come back with their perfumes and other goods. Nobody wants my products anymore.'

I asked my father: 'How could the Canadians have come back so quickly? It's just after the war. Were the Americans there?'

He said: 'Not the Americans. You can't get anything from the Americans without an import licence.'

'That's odd,' I thought.

When I was starting the data collection process for the thesis, I asked Sir Donald if he would help me to retrieve information on Britain's import policy. He was uncertain if he could gain access to the relevant documents at the Board of Trade, but spoke to the senior officials at the board, who agreed to arrange for me to see the relevant documentation because Sir Donald attested to my reliability and integrity.

But while in Whitehall, I examined the files and discovered that the issue of West Indian imports from Canada had been discussed in cabinet immediately after the war. Britain felt a special responsibility to help with the revival of Canadian trade with its traditional partner in the West Indies, because of the strong and continuing support that Canada had provided to Britain during the war. In submissions to the British cabinet, it was pointed out that the West Indies had been a small market with which Canada had had long and mutually beneficial ties.

It is instructive that Canada and the English-speaking Caribbean shared a similar journey for most of the nineteenth century. In the post-emancipation period, after slavery was abolished, the West Indian planters had run into certain problems, and they had asked England whether they could form a union with Canada. I found this fascinating. I discovered that there were several items on the list of imports that Britain had liberalized that were not essential imports and were very similar to the products being produced by my father. Because of my personal interest in the matter, I spent a great deal of time analyzing the movements in trade affecting the items that appeared competitive with my father's products.

Sir Donald, who felt that my first draft chapter was excellent, sent a copy to the Board of Trade as a courtesy in order to assure them that no breach of confidence had been committed. Their response was also very complimentary.

A few months later, Sir Donald said to me: 'Alister, you might be annoyed with me, because I have been requested by the British government to go to Australia to deal with a matter there and the

Australian National University has sweetened the deal by inviting me to be a visiting professor while I am there.'

'How long will you be away?'

'A year.'

'My goodness. This is not good news for me.'

'Don't worry, they'll find a good supervisor for you.'

Despite the genuine efforts made, the new supervisor was not a good choice. At that time, the college was in the early stages of developing faculty resources in the fields that interested me. My new supervisor, a South African, was never able to work closely with me. He displayed very little interest in the topic on which I was working, so there was little common ground between us.

I can recall asking my new supervisor to read the chapters I had written. Three weeks later, I asked him what he thought of them. His annoyed response was: 'Oh, I haven't had time to read them. Who do you think you are? You can't jump the queue.'

What a difference to the way my previous supervisors would have responded! The poor quality of an academic supervisor has created untold distress to many students. He called me one day and asked me to review a book on Puerto Rico. I agreed reluctantly. I was later informed by one of his assistants that he had used my review without any acknowledgement of my contribution. I later indicated to him my disappointment at the way he had handled the matter. If I had expected even a mild degree of contrition, I had a surprise coming! He only replied tersely that I was rude and that he could use his discretion to decide how to deal with the text I had submitted to him.

After some exchanges that were less than pleasant, I decided that I would work independently without a supervisor. No one in the college was aware of the situation: reporting a supervisor is often not in one's best interest. It was a most uncomfortable state of affairs, because I often wondered if I was on the right track with the research. Eventually my supervisor told the Warden of the college that I had been flouting the rules by working independently. The Warden subsequently called me to his office to remind me of the rules before asking me to explain my lack of contact with my supervisor. I related briefly what had taken place. I suspected by his facial expression that he had some sympathy with my predicament, but nevertheless he said I should have discussed the problem with him so that possible alternatives could have been found that did not conflict with university rules. I said that I had not wanted to place him in a difficult position. He also said that if I would not work with my present supervisor, I would need to make a satisfactory arrangement with another supervisor.

I tried other faculty members to no avail. There was an economist named Arthur Hazelwood, and I was very much hoping that he might be available. But he said that he was overloaded with supervisory work. At this point, I decided to return to working independently without raising the matter again with the Warden. On reflection, this was a mistake. Nonetheless, I managed to work on my own for about a year. It was during that time that I learned of a vacancy in the Economics Department of the University College of the West Indies at Mona in Jamaica. I applied for this post and was accepted.

Of course, I advised Professor Meade of this development concerning my employment. Although he congratulated me, he said that I should have tried for an assistant lectureship at the LSE. If that had gone well, I might be able to get a lectureship after three years, and with that experience I would be qualified for a more senior position at UCWI. By this time, however, having already visited Jamaica and enjoyed my stay there so much, I decided that I would accept the appointment.

A considerable advantage to accepting the position at Mona was that it discharged my commitment to return to the Grenadian Civil Service. At that time, the best position that the Grenadian government was able to offer me was that of First Class Clerk. Before I left Grenada to go to the LSE I had been in the clerical group, and thought that this position would not provide sufficient latitude to contribute at the professional level.

My education in Grenada and my experience at the WISU led me to become a strong federationist when I returned to the Caribbean in 1960. The only reason why I was not involved in work on the referendum in Jamaica was because I had been diagnosed with diabetes and hospitalized. I had to direct all my attention to the management of my condition. I still thought we had a good chance of becoming a federation. I was on a medically requested leave of absence when I learned the results of the referendum. That news threw me into a depression and I wondered what my future role would be in the region. I still looked for opportunities, and as later chapters will show, those of the greatest importance to me were building regional economic integration and associated activities. I contributed significantly at the regional level and also accepted assignments from individual countries in the broad area of external trade and development.

SECTION 2

MY ACADEMIC CAREER

4

University College of the West Indies, Mona campus, 1960–64

Establishing honours teaching in economics

I arrived in Jamaica in August 1960 to take up an appointment as a lecturer in the Department of Economics at the University College of the West Indies (UCWI), Mona campus. My thesis at Oxford University was unfinished because of the difficulties I had with my supervisor there. Actually, I had decided to give it up, but on his return to Britain, my substantive supervisor, Sir Donald McDougall, encouraged me to continue with it, although he was not in a position to resume as my supervisor.

On his way back from Australia, Sir Donald had been urged by the British government to return to the Treasury as Economic Advisor to the then Prime Minister for the third time in his career. So he told me that when I finished my draft thesis, I should send it to him so that he could have a thorough look at it. However, as subsequent events will show, I had little time to attend to this during the next twelve months.

When I first came to the UCWI (which at the time was a college of the University of London), there was only a Department of Economics in the Faculty of Arts teaching the subject for the BA General degree. When Professor Arthur Lewis arrived as Principal, he proposed that a Faculty of Social Sciences should be set up, offering, *inter alia*, specialist teaching in economics.

After consultation with the University of London, Professor Lewis invited his former professor at the LSE, Sir Arnold Plant, to come to Jamaica and advise on the implementation of a programme in economics.

On coming to Mona, Sir Arnold discovered me and was pleased to hear that I knew the London system very well. He brought me in to assist him in the design of the programme. This proceeded very satisfactorily and was accepted by all the relevant university bodies.

However, it was not well received by the members of the Department of Economics and I heard 'on the corridor' that there were complaints that Professor Plant chose as his collaborator the youngest and therefore the most inexperienced member of the department. No consideration was given to the fact that I was the only member of staff who had studied at London University under the system that was being proposed for Mona. Indeed, as I recall it, all of the then members of the department were several years away from studying economics and certainly had not taught the subject at university level but had been focused on general degree teaching or research assignments at the Institute of Social and Economic Research (ISER).

The ISER was established first to do research in the social sciences, as a precursor to beginning teaching. It housed people who could, in principle, be transferred immediately to teaching as departments were established. So the Smiths, M.G. and Raymond, and Lloyd Braithwaite went to Sociology and Anthropology and two economists, George Cumper and David Edwards, were transferred to the Department of Economics. But Professor Lewis decided to retain the ISER, not solely as a supplier of teaching staff but as a research institute alongside the teaching departments, as a way of encouraging people to do research.

Paradoxically, although I was the most junior member of the department, I was, apart from the Professor, the most experienced in teaching economics at undergraduate level. While I was at Oxford, my supervisor, Sir Donald McDougall, encouraged me to take up a part-time tutorship at St Peter's Hall, an undergraduate college at the University. I was required to teach a class of 12 students. When they presented themselves at the preliminary examinations, all 12 of them were successful and 11 of them passed with distinction. It was the first time that the Hall had received such good results and I was warmly congratulated by the Master of the Hall who, to show his appreciation, invited me to dinner with my class and expressed very generous sentiments about this achievement. The students also kept in touch with me, often to get advice on the remainder of their studies.

In addition, I acted as unpaid tutor to West Indian students at other colleges when they were experiencing difficulties with the subject. I am glad to say that all of them were successful at the different levels at which they presented themselves.

Notwithstanding my comparative experience, I was somewhat alarmed at the teaching loads assigned to me in the first academic year at Mona, 1960–61. At a departmental meeting held to make these assignments, I found myself with a teaching load of 22½ hours per week. The next person was given 5 hours and others less than that. I simply could not reconcile this situation with my junior status in the department. I accepted it and moved on, but I was very dissatisfied. I had my thesis to complete, which was a not an unusual situation for junior members of a department.

When Professor Keirstead arrived from the University of Toronto some months later to assess the situation in the department, I told him frankly what it was and he agreed that my situation was most unfortunate. I believe that he also communicated a similar judgement to the Principal, Professor Lewis.

The Principal called me to a meeting with him and as, I think, a joke, told me that I was very lucky to get so much teaching because when he was at the LSE as Assistant Lecturer, he had to fight to get a course or a part thereof! I did not see the humour in the comment, but he later went on to demonstrate his sincerity in helping me to get opportunities for personal development.

Closer scrutiny would have revealed the mismatch between the qualifications of the staff and the teaching requirements. Cumper and Edwards had credible records in research: Cumper had done a number of useful papers on the Jamaican economy and Edwards had done an authoritative study of small-scale farming in Jamaica. But neither of those were equivalent to the study and work experience in the area of economics necessary for the B.Sc. (Econ.) degree. This demonstrated a lack of planning in establishing this degree. When Professor Charles Kennedy arrived from a fellowship held at The Queen's College, Oxford, to take up the post of Professor and Head of the Department of Economics, it was expected that his own qualifications and knowledge of the subject would enable him to correct the faculty/teaching mismatch. That did not turn out to be the case. Indeed, it was only the recruitment of another staff member, Michael Faber, that brought us within sight of teaching skills that were in harmony with the degree requirements.

In its first year, the department was not well staffed because the majority of the staff, although very well prepared in their areas of expertise, were not ready to deliver most of the major courses that the degree required. Those members of the department who had been responsible for teaching economics in the BA programme had left the UWI for positions elsewhere and those who remained were only peripherally involved in teaching economics as such. Inevitably, tensions that the Head of the Department could not resolve developed between myself and those of my colleagues who were experiencing problems with delivering the teaching programme. Because of my junior status, there was a limit to the help I could give in resolving this problem.

It was at this time that I was diagnosed with diabetes and hospitalized for three weeks. I went into the University Hospital as an emergency and received immediate treatment from Dr Don Christian, who at the time was a young lecturer and a specialist in diabetes. He prescribed several medications for me and the following day brought a group of his students to examine me and discuss what approach they would have taken to my medication. I was somewhat concerned about the degree of attention I was receiving, which signalled that my condition was serious. When I approached Dr Christian on the subject, he told me that he had put me on a crash programme of medication and if it worked, my sugar should resume acceptable levels in three weeks. At that exact date, Dr Christian was able to discharge me because I was capable of managing the disease at home.

Returning to my teaching responsibilities, I hoped to introduce course material that gave students an introduction to Caribbean economics and then lead into the more standard courses on economics. Some members of the department felt that this background material was not well enough established and they would not accept my innovations. This led to conflicts that might have appeared to be based on personalities, but were actually grounded in more substantive differences over trying to create a relevant Caribbean information base that students could build on and develop.

Others in the department were always interested in discussing what I call minute points in economic theory; for example, whether the Edgeworth Bowley Box diagram should be like this and whether the curve curved this way or that way, and they would sit down and talk about it endlessly. I would say: 'Let us bring it back now. Ground it. What on earth does this have to do with optimization? Everybody has to optimize. Every country has to optimize. But tell me, this optimization theory that you are talking about, how will it help?' I myself had played around with this early in my undergraduate studies. There was no mystery about it. I would ask my colleagues how do these matters apply to the Jamaican situation. They would reply that they were not discussing Jamaica.

Every Thursday night, the department had a meeting at Professor Kennedy's house. He used to encourage people to engage in small theoretical points. I was just fed up. I only went there because I felt I had to. But I was thoroughly fed up. I said: 'This is not economics. Let us deal with the realities out there. What do we have to say to the community that is paying us about what the situation is and what do we think?' My colleagues simply refused to answer my questions.

Eventually, I gave a public lecture one Sunday morning at the Arts Lecture Theatre. I cannot remember who asked me to do it. The topic of the lecture at the time was 'On going into the European Common Market'. When I got there, my reaction was: 'My goodness, what is this?' Someone said, teasing me: 'You are a screen star!' The lecture was exceptionally well attended by both students and the public. But none of my colleagues was there. The lecture went down very well. Then people from the department came to me the next day to ask who had invited me to deliver the lecture and what were the principal matters discussed. I declined to be dragged into a discussion and reminded them that we had met recently for the precise purpose of discussing our teaching and its contents.

I finally said I would agree to continue the discussion at Professor Kennedy's weekly meeting. Accordingly, at the next meeting, I started. But it was different in a seminar situation, because those at the meeting could interrupt while I was speaking. So I was only able to repeat about half of my lecture before Kennedy said: 'We've got to stop now, at least by ten o'clock.'

I said, 'Yes, that's fine.'

Somebody suggested: 'Alister, we'll continue next week? Can you?'

'No!' Kennedy countered, 'We can't devote all of this time to this subject, we've got other things to discuss.'

One or two people, including Lloyd Best, pressed him and asked: 'Please tell us what it is that you have in mind for the next one?'

Kennedy was ready to go back to the same themes. This confrontation went on and I commented sarcastically that I would be encouraging intellectual evenings this year.

A welcome addition had taken place in the department in the form of Michael Faber, whose name was known locally because he belonged to the family of Faber and Faber, the well-known publishers. Prior to coming to Jamaica he had worked in East Africa, so he was very sensitive to the need for relevance in our teaching. We became very close friends. Faber suggested 'Yes, let's give it a try.' Kennedy responded: 'Come on, Mike, you've just arrived. Give yourself a chance.'

Kennedy had done some work on neutral technical progress which was an element in the theoretical literature on economic growth with particular reference to developed countries. With some adaptation, the ideas developed there could be made relevant to developing countries, but his own thinking was not yet focused on that. There was, therefore, a gap between, on the one hand, Professor Kennedy and the members of staff who supported his thinking, and on the other, the other economists for whom I was the principal spokesman.

I was more interested in policy and preparing students for work in Jamaica and the rest of the Caribbean. I was frustrated because in my view we should acquaint our students with the realities of the region from the outset, so that they could develop their own responses to issues that would come up when they went into the world of work. When I met people outside the university, they would say: 'We want to hear more from people at the university. What do you people at the university think of so and so?'

When I came to Jamaica in August 1960 to start at the UCWI, even before I had settled in and reviewed my courses I began getting calls: 'Would I serve on this committee or that committee?' These often emanated from the Civil Service and the private sector.

As far as the teaching itself was concerned, I recruited a number of tutors from the community, as temporary staff, who were graduates in economics from other universities, and were working in the Jamaican Cvil Service and at local technical schools. I encouraged them to accept part-time appointments that could be accommodated within the funds provided for teaching. I met them as a group twice a week to go over the material I was presenting in the lectures and to share ideas about using it in tutorials. The group was very enthusiastic; we were very careful about how they presented the lecture content and I was very pleased by their enthusiasm. Indeed, the London External Examiners who second marked the students' scripts commended us highly on how well prepared the students were. At this stage, Professor Kennedy and my colleagues became interested in knowing more about my approaches. Personal relations did not necessarily improve, but I felt satisfaction in knowing that my ideas were beginning to gain ground.

Altogether, my sojourn at Mona gave me the opportunity to sort out my ideas on the teaching of economics in the Caribbean; this would serve me in greater stead when I assumed more substantial responsibilities for the teaching programme, especially at the St Augustine campus.

5

Teaching in the United States

Woodrow Wilson School, Princeton University

Sir Arthur Lewis was Principal of the UWI and I did not know at the time that the Woodrow Wilson School was then negotiating with him to go there as professor. Marver Berstein, Dean of the Woodrow Wilson School, came on a visit to Jamaica to engage in a form of gentle persuasion.

Professor Bernstein told Sir Arthur that he wanted to get someone to teach a graduate course on development with reference to the Caribbean because there were a lot of people at Princeton who were interested in the Caribbean. It was 1962, right after the Cuban revolution, and independence was approaching. He told Sir Arthur that this course had been scheduled for the spring semester, on the assumption he would be there to deliver it. According to Professor Bernstein, Sir Arthur replied diplomatically that in view of his unavailability, he would try to arrange for me to do it.

I was sitting in my office when I received a call from the Principal's office asking me to receive Professor Bernstein, although I did not know what his specific interest was in seeing me. Upon arrival at my office, he indicated the subject of his concern to me and disclosed that Sir Arthur had promised to arrange for my release if I were interested in taking up the offer. In view of the difficulties that I was experiencing in my department, I was more than eager to take it up.

So there I was at Princeton for the spring and summer semesters. I was impressed with the high quality of the facilities made available to me, both at the office and at the apartment which was assigned to me.

I was also very pleased to discover that two junior members of faculty on the campus, but not in the Woodrow Wilson School, were former student colleagues from Nuffield at Oxford. Right away they got in touch with me and arranged my reception in the community.

The other interesting thing was that the Woodrow Wilson School had never before had a non-white faculty member and only one non-white student in the history of the school. They did their best to prepare for my arrival and were very concerned to respond to any problems associated with my presence on the campus.

I enjoyed teaching this group of students because they demonstrated both an anxiety to learn and a capacity for relating knowledge to actual problems and experiences in the world.

Teaching economic development at Mona, I had always wanted to integrate academic thinking with ongoing policy issues and I was very anxious to take these approaches forward in the classroom. Professor Bernstein would come periodically to see what was taking place there. On one occasion I told him about the approach that I wished to use in teaching students about development problems in the Caribbean. His response was positive and immediate. He indicated that if I wished to arrange a field experience for the class, I should go ahead and make all the necessary arrangements. I was very encouraged by this response.

I took 30 students with me to Jamaica in order for each of them to acquire local knowledge and experience and take forward the preparation of their theses on local problems. The school was very flexible in granting permission for students to address various areas of problem solving. For instance, several students did theses on Jamaica, but one student was particularly interested in Trinidad and Tobago and I arranged for him to do a report on development problems in housing there. Another group of students secured my support for doing a film on developments in Grenada. It turned out rather well and the school arranged a special showing of the film that autumn to which they invited outsiders such as the parents of the team and people from USAID as well as from other agencies interested in development.

Altogether, the experience at Woodrow Wilson taught me what could be achieved with good students, excellent teaching, proper facilities and high motivation to achieve on the part of the students. I so much wished that we could get those ingredients together at Mona, although the subject matter and the level were not the same since Mona was an undergraduate programme.

This is why I devoted so much of my time and attention to building up local capacities in teaching. I succeeded to some extent when replacements had to be found for me.

Conference in Brazil funded by the Ford Foundation

I had hardly returned from Princeton when I got an offer to attend a high-level international conference on Inflation and Economic Growth, which was being convened in Rio de Janeiro in January 1963. When the Ford Foundation representative came to see me with the proposal, I declined it because, as I told him, I never thought that after such a long absence I would get approval to go abroad again. He said nothing, but apparently went to the Principal and told him that I had turned the offer down. Sir Arthur told him to pay no attention to the refusal. The conference was a very important occasion in economics and teachers of the subject should get thoroughly familiar with the issues and the principal contributors to them. He asked the Ford representative to send me the details about the conference and the airline ticket, and he would do the rest.

Sir Arthur called Professor Kennedy and advised him that he wanted me to attend the conference and would he please make the necessary arrangements. Kennedy was furious and wondered what manoeuvring I had engaged in to get on the conference list.

As expected, the conference was a great success. I met all the contemporary personalities who had been contributing to the dialogue on inflation and growth, which was then extremely important for all developing countries, including those in the Caribbean. I picked up a lot from the conference, both in terms of substance and professional contacts. They served me in succeeding years in sustaining intellectual contacts with Latin America and parts of the developed world.

Columbia University 1963: Fulbright-Hays Fellowship

Among the people that I met at the Rio Conference was Albert Hirschman, the renowned development economist. At breakfast one morning, he said to me: 'I had an idea last night. It was to invite you to Columbia, for which I can provide a Fulbright Fellowship.' I said: 'No, I'm afraid this would not be possible, because I have just returned from another overseas engagement.' He then replied: 'Let me talk it over with Arthur.' Apparently, when he mentioned it to Sir Arthur, he also told him of my

Figure 3 Speaking with Professor Lambros Comitas, friend and colleague at the Research Institute for the Study of Man, New York.

response, to which he replied: 'Don't take it too seriously, he needs the outside experience because the department is sadly lacking in that. I shall arrange accordingly.' When Sir Arthur brought the matter to Professor Kennedy there was a virtual explosion among staff members, accusing Sir Arthur of favouritism, since I was the only West Indian holding an established post in the department. But the department decided to accept the decision of the Principal that I should go.

I found Columbia a very exciting place. One of my responsibilities as a Fulbright Scholar was to engage in activities to help institutional development in the teaching of economics. Accordingly, after making enquiries I set up a programme of visits to African-American colleges in the United States. These were highly interesting. I was able to review their teaching programmes and make suggestions in terms of both content and staffing requirements. More often than not, I gave a public lecture on some aspect of development in the Caribbean. I think that my visits were much appreciated. In more than one case, the principal of the college was a West Indian and I felt obliged to go the extra mile in making suggestions about staff development.

With several of them I also raised the possibility of joint efforts at fundraising. However, I made no mileage with that idea at Mona and it had to await my later tenure as Vice-Chancellor to take it forward.

Another outcome of my visit to Columbia was that I was pressured into offering a paper for the first conference of Caribbean scholars held at Mona in Easter 1964. I was asked, at very short notice, to prepare a paper because there were no other offerings in economics. I sat down one evening, worked through the night, and had a paper written by breakfast time the following morning. It was entitled 'Decolonization and Trade Policy in the West Indies' and was sent off immediately to Kingston. The organizers of the programme were in such a hurry that I was allowed no opportunity to read over the paper and make changes. Accordingly, there were one or two mistakes that lived on with the paper. But in general the paper was very well received and is still, today, a reference in the literature on Caribbean Economic Integration.

Policy work with the UN in Mexico

While I was at Columbia, I received a call from the Executive Secretary for the Economic Commission for Latin America (ECLAC). With the admission of several Caribbean countries to the United Nations, and therefore to ECLAC, the Executive Secretary wished to have a paper done on some aspects of development in the Caribbean to demonstrate that ECLAC was interested in the countries of the region. His estimate was that the paper would take about five months and he enquired whether I could come to Mexico City, where the Caribbean work had been established. I explained to him that it was virtually impossible for me to get any further leave; apparently however, when he approached Sir Philip Sherlock, who was then Vice-Chancellor of the UWI, Sir Philip agreed to release me.

When that news reached the department, 'all hell broke loose'. Professor Kennedy said he would insist that I be transferred to another department, because I was of no value to the Economics Department. When that news reached me in New York, I concurred with Professor Kennedy and said in the event that I was

Figure 4 Visiting Sir Philip Sherlock, former Vice-Chancellor, UWI.

removed from his department, I would resign and take up one of the offers of appointments that had been made to me by other institutions.

At the time, I had offers of appointment as an Assistant Professor at Dalhousie University in Halifax and McGill University in Montreal. Furthermore, the Economic Growth Centre at Yale University had offered me an assignment with the Central Bank of Liberia to work on their trade and development problems. That offer was extremely well compensated and was made more attractive by the fact that a former friend of mine at the LSE, Jim Weeks, was the governor of the bank. He warmly welcomed the offer made to me and I was seriously contemplating going there when the ECLAC offer arrived.

I should also mention that Professor Hirschman asked whether I would be willing to stay at Columbia for another year. One advantage would be that I could submit my work for a Doctorate at Columbia. He had read my D.Phil. thesis and thought that with a few minor changes it would be acceptable to them. Within the year, I could write a comprehensive examination for which I needed only minimal preparation, clean up the thesis and submit it to them. This was also an extremely attractive proposition, but I felt committed to undertake this inaugural paper on the region for ECLAC because it could have an important bearing on the Caribbean's standing in both Latin America and the United Nations and could serve as a discussion point for new initiatives in the Caribbean towards freer trade and integration. This forecast was fulfilled.

Exceptionally, ECLAC published the paper – 'Aspects of development and trade in the Commonwealth Caribbean' – in both English and Spanish, and for many years it was a standard reference on Caribbean development. It also served as a base document for the preparatory work on the formation of the Caribbean Free Trade Association (CARIFTA).

As far as my future at the UWI was concerned, Sir Philip Sherlock came to New York on a working visit and told me that he would not accept my resignation. If I was reluctant to return to the department at Mona, there was a good possibility of an appointment at St Augustine in Trinidad. They were working towards the full BA General programme with the hope that they could proceed towards a B.Sc. (Econ.) programme in a few years' time. They were looking for a leader and would happily accept me if I was ready to come. I agreed to go to St Augustine and I left ECLAC in November 1964, went on a winding up visit to New York and then on to St Augustine in December of that year.

6

UWI, St Augustine, 1964–67

Developing academic programmes

I was very encouraged by the fact that in Trinidad I would be able to work closely with my best friend, Willie Demas, then Head of the Planning Unit in the Office of the Prime Minister, Dr Eric Williams. When we first met in London in 1956, we bonded almost instantaneously because of our close intellectual interests and passion for Caribbean integration and development.

At Cambridge, Willie had worked as assistant to A.R. Prest, who had been officially commissioned to undertake a fiscal survey of the Caribbean. Dr Prest relied heavily on Willie to assemble the empirical data and to interact with officials in the field. It was particularly fortunate for Willie that when they were undertaking the Jamaican leg of the project, he was able to interact regularly with academics at the Institute of Social and Economic Research, which exposed him to many of the nuances surrounding public policy in Jamaica and elsewhere in the Caribbean. In that spirit, he wrote, independently of the survey, an article on Customs Union which was published in the *Social and Economic Studies* journal and which, as indicated earlier, provided one of the foundation documents for my later attempt to present a proposal for undertaking a research dissertation on that topic.

After that assignment, Willie moved to Oxford because he was recruited to work on a review of economic development problems in the region by Ursula Hicks, who with her husband had earlier done a report on *Finance and Taxation in Jamaica*. However, the work was not completed because of his call back to Trinidad to head the Planning Unit.

Like myself, Willie had been advised by some people to remain in the UK, because of the limited opportunities available for economists in the Caribbean. We were not persuaded by this line of thinking and accordingly pursued our enthusiasm for finding appropriate opportunities in the region. In the case of Willie this bore fruit in the decision of the government of Trinidad and Tobago to establish a Planning Unit in the Office of the Prime Minister.

At the time that Willie and I met, he had an important assignment at the West Indian Trade Commissioner's office in London, headed by Sir Garnet Gordon from St Lucia. I had not yet graduated, so it was really a common interest in the Caribbean that brought us together. When we met at the Trade Commissioner's office, we started chatting and had a marathon session that lasted over six hours. That session went beyond trade problems to encompass a virtual review and assessment of the development problems in the region as a whole. He told me that although the Trade Commissioner had not yet been informed, he had been offered and accepted the lead post of Economic Planning Advisor to the government of Trinidad and Tobago.

Because of my relationship with Willie, I became involved in the government's policy work. Dr Williams was always looking for additional talent. He was thought to be a very complex person and I cannot honestly say that I had easy conversations with him. I recall that people in the Prime Minister's Office and elsewhere in the government would say that the Doctor seemed to like me. I would respond by saying that I had no concrete evidence of that. In my own assessment his relationship with me was essentially linked to my close friendship with Willie. Dr Williams considered that Willie felt I was really giving him intellectual support, that we were on the same wavelength and that Willie had a lot of confidence in my prescriptions. I think he just took it up from there. I was asked to sit on the Industrial Development Corporation Board, the Board of the Public Utilities Commission and the Board of the Cypriani Labour College. It would appear that the government wanted me to be involved in a variety of matters.

The Institute of International Relations, St Augustine

From the very beginning, in both formal and informal discussions it was recognized in the region that training in foreign affairs would be an indispensable requirement to deal with the new international issues that would arise as a result of independence.

Dr Williams had been one of the early champions of the need for training officials to support the work of governments in the international field. This became an important part of the 1961 Chaguaramas Agreement with the United States, in settlement of the controversy surrounding the existence of US naval bases in that area of Trinidad and Tobago. Since that agreement was never fully implemented, its provisions for the training of diplomats did not come into force.

Accordingly, in the preparations for West Indian political independence, the Federal Government took action to pepare for the training of diplomats for the region. With the collapse of the Federation, the government of Trinidad and Tobago realized that it had to make its own arrangements for the training of its staff. To that end, informal conversations began between Mr J. O'Neil Lewis, a senior official of Trinidad and Tobago, and Professor Jacques Freymond, Director of the Graduate Institute of International Relations in Geneva, to find out whether the Swiss would be interested in helping the government with training in that area upon independence. Mr Lewis, whose nickname was Scottie, was also a graduate student at Oxford working towards a degree. He was there just before me and because he was planning his return to Trinidad he more or less handed over a few things to me when I was going up to Oxford. At the same time, wishing to acquaint himself with the modalities of the GATT, because it would be necessary to join that organization after independence, he requested and received a six months' posting to Geneva. While there, he took the initiative to open discussions on a strictly informal and off the record basis with the Institute of International Relations in Geneva to provide training opportunities for diplomats.

Those discussions bore fruit after independence when a formal agreement was reached with the Swiss government to establish an Institute of International Relations in Trinidad and Tobago, to be developed with the support of the Graduate Institute of International Relations in Geneva, led by Professor Jacques Freymond.

At that time, UWI Mona was, quite independently, making arrangements to teach International Relations at graduate level, and had invited Professor Uwe Kitzinger to serve as a visiting professor to help them to establish a graduate teaching programme. Kitzinger, whom I knew quite well, was a Fellow of Nuffield College, Oxford. When I was at Oxford, Uwe was a research fellow at Nuffield because he had produced the first book in English on the Common Market, entitled *The Challenge of the European Common Market*, which became a bestseller. So I knew him from those days.

When it was announced that Trinidad and Tobago was taking steps to establish a Graduate Institute of International Relations, all of the relevant officials at the UWI were taken by surprise. They were not clear how a graduate programme at St Augustine would be developed since, at the time, there was not a full undergraduate programme in social sciences at the St Augustine campus. Accordingly, after very intense discussions which were held initially in the Bahamas, an understanding was reached that Mona would undertake graduate degree programmes in international relations, while St Augustine would do the graduate diploma programme, targeted towards the development of career diplomats.

This understanding was only partially implemented, because the progress envisaged in establishing a graduate programme at Mona took much longer to implement than was initially foreseen. As a consequence, it was only a matter of time before the Institute at St Augustine started graduate degree programmes with the admission of students from all over the region, including students from Mona.

The implementation of the agreement with the Swiss was left to the government of Trinidad and Tobago and the St Augustine campus. As the newly appointed Chairman of the Division of Social Sciences at St Augustine, I was drawn into representing the UWI in coming to an agreement with the government of Trinidad and Tobago and the Geneva Institute on the detailed provisions for implementing the plan.

Agreement between the three parties concerned was reached separately. The St Augustine campus was asked to take responsibility for the university's implementation. The institute would be an affiliated institution of the UWI. It would be run by the Swiss and UWI and would be on the St Augustine campus, but not strictly speaking part of the UWI. The latter would work with the Swiss in setting it up, would contribute to the teaching if asked, and the students would work for UWI diplomas. In furtherance of this arrangement, I was asked to represent the UWI in negotiating a separate affiliation agreement with Trinidad and Tobago, the institute and the UWI.

I represented the UWI in the tripartite discussions on the affiliation agreement. We were able to settle the details of that agreement very quickly. The teaching staff, the books and other academic material were to be provided by the Swiss. Trinidad and Tobago was to put up a building immediately.

In my own case, I was asked by Professor Freymond to teach the course on International Economic Relations. I thanked him for the honour, but said that I had to decline because I already had my plate full. I had a major teaching load in the Division of Social Sciences and, along with that, the government of Trinidad and Tobago had persuaded me to accept several official appointments to serve on boards in a number of capacities. Nevertheless, I agreed, after persuasion from Professor Freymond, to help the institute to get going by agreeing to teach the course for the first term on the basis that a replacement could be found to take over from me for the rest of the academic year. However, despite genuine efforts by the institute to recruit a replacement, the first term turned out to be the first year. The first year turned out to be the second year. Indeed, I taught the course in the third year as well. So for the following three years, while I was in Trinidad, I continued teaching the course.

In fulfilling its own obligations for implementing the tripartite agreement, the Trinidad and Tobago government constructed a building and met the recurrent costs, and the institute is still in operation, largely on the basis of Trinidad and Tobago meeting its full costs. However, because of the attendance of other Caribbean students, they or their governments make a small contribution to the current budget.

Ulrich Haeflin, the first director, was eventually replaced by an excellent colleague, Roy Preiswerk. Altogether the institute has produced some very successful graduates and has really justified its existence over the long term. It has trained most of Trinidad and Tobago's diplomats and a large number of other Caribbean diplomats. A number of well-known Caribbean scholars were associated with the institute for varying periods, including the late Professor Norman Girvan, who was a distinguished member of the staff for several years. It can therefore be characterized as a home for Caribbean scholarship in the field of international relations and development.

I think that both the Swiss and the government of Trinidad and Tobago can reasonably claim that they made a good investment.

At the Mona campus, the development of a graduate programme in international relations has been more modest but the small staff there have made valiant efforts to implement the responsibilities foreseen for them in the agreement made in Nassau.

Department of Economics

When I arrived at St Augustine in December 1964 there was a small Department of Economics with two members of staff. With such a small department it would have been difficult to build up a programme for an honours degree. Willie had been telling me that there was a large demand for economists in the government, which only emerged when they began to prepare the government for the

65

responsibility of independence. Many of the people concerned could not leave Trinidad and Tobago for overseas studies because of heavy personal commitments. Accordingly, the government of Trinidad and Tobago began, at an early stage after my arrival, to indicate their need for a local programme in economics at honours degree level. For its part, the university felt obliged to respond to this need. In fulfilment of that commitment, I had to build up a staff virtually from the ground up. The then existing staff of three people was not in a position to teach the new programme because they required further work in the subject. I managed to find support to finance graduate work in the United States for two members of the staff. The third staff member was expected to go abroad as well at a later stage. In the meantime, I had to make contingency arrangements to get the programme started.

In considering what should be my priorities, the first order of business was to set up the B.Sc. (Econ.) programme and to secure temporary staff for it. The budget made provision for three additional lecturers, who with the three of us already on the ground would make a total of six members of staff. This permitted me to proceed with the recruitment of two staff members in the fields of Money and Banking and Quantitative Economics. With that core staff of six we were able to set up an initial B.Sc. Economics programme and to graduate our first class of students with honours degrees.

The new staff members were a stroke of luck: Eric St Cyr had done a doctorate at Manchester University in Quantitative Economics; Carlton Bruce had graduated from Mona with a first class degree in Economics and had gone on to do a doctorate in that field at Rochester with a fellowship that I had secured from the Ford Foundation; and Roy Thomas, one of the foundation members of the department, had also arranged to go to the US and complete a doctorate in Industrial Relations. These members of staff, together with those already on the ground, constituted a critical mass for teaching at honours degree level. Our first group of students did exceptionally well and convinced the sceptics at Mona that we were capable of delivering honours students of exceptional calibre.

Department of Management Studies

In considering what particular courses we could organize as specializations, I was drawn to the area of Management Studies, partly because of the encouragement given by the local business community. Some leading members of that community were showing great interest in encouraging the university to build up a management studies programme.

Among the personalities whom I met shortly after my arrival at St Augustine were Sydney Knox, Chairman of Neal and Massy, and Tommy Gatcliffe of Angostura Holdings. They criticized the university for being alienated from the business community. I, in turn, asked them what they had ever done to become more knowledgeable about the university.

The upshot was that I devised a week-long business studies conference on the campus with the help of a friend, Bill Carmichael, who was the Dean of the Cornell University Business School. I had met Bill at Princeton where we were both working as Assistant Professors. I sent the plan for the conference to Sydney and Tommy and said that if they wanted to fund it I would organize it, which they agreed to do.

Willie advised me to make the participants stay on campus for all five days so that they could really get a feel for what the university was like. I persuaded the university to assign 30 rooms in Canada Hall. Right after Christmas, before the students returned, the businessmen all left their homes, came and lived in the dormitories and ate in the cafeteria. I gave the overall lectures on Caribbean economies and policies and Cornell University sent down professors to give business studies lectures. I ate lunch on campus with the 35 participants every day.

The programme was a great success, and led not only to the business community providing other funds, but I brought in my final-year students to meet and speak with the business leaders and many of the students made contacts then that helped them get employment after graduation.

In organizing the business studies seminars for the private sector, Dean Carmichael very graciously agreed to help me with the development of Management Studies at St Augustine. Cornell provided the core staffing for the weekend business programme and were a source of advice in designing undergraduate programmes to suit the circumstances and needs of Trinidad and Tobago and the rest of the Caribbean.

After discussions on campus and with the business community, we considered that we could offer two specializations in management studies under the B.Sc. (Econ.) programme. One was in Industrial Management, designed to introduce students to subjects which would be relevant in preparing themselves for careers in the non-agricultural private sector. The other was in Agricultural Management and was aimed at student intake for employment in the agricultural sector, where, like elsewhere in the economy, graduates with a background in management were badly needed.

The eventual outcome in the Division of Social Sciences and the Institute of International Relations at St Augustine was that finally I was able to build the kind of course work that provided a solid foundation for understanding the Caribbean's problems and needs.

The contentiousness I had experienced at Mona developed precisely because I wanted to introduce course material that gave students an introduction to Caribbean economies and societies before leading into the more standard UK/US courses on economics. Some others in the department felt this was not well enough established and they would not accept my innovations. Now, in Trinidad, I was able to develop the Economics Department and Programme of Management Studies along the lines that I felt were most relevant to that country and the Caribbean as a whole.

Initially, there was unease at Mona about the speed with which these programmes were being put in place at St Augustine. Rumours developed about the expense involved with the Cornell programme. The unease reached a point where the Vice-Chancellor asked the University Bursar to visit St Augustine and enquire into the management of the programme, especially the financial situation. The Bursar did visit the campus and was surprised to find that the budget for Management Studies was showing a surplus because of the relatively large inflow of private sector and foundation support.

The Cornell connection was critical in a number of respects. First, they provided their top MBA students to teach the courses being offered at St Augustine and were therefore the core initial staff in Management Studies. In the meantime, we selected three of our B.Sc. (Econ.) graduates to go to Cornell to get their MBAs on the basis that they would return and constitute a core in Management Studies for the undergraduate teaching. They were complemented by visiting senior staff from Cornell to help with the more specialized courses and to provide continuing advice on delivery of the standard courses for the degree. We were therefore able to be the first campus in the UWI to be delivering a comprehensive programme in Management Studies.

Equally critical to the success of the programme was the assistance provided by the Ford Foundation, which basically financed a substantial part of the programme through the Cornell connection, including staff development and a variety of supports as the programme gained momentum. This was essentially the base from which the programmes at the Arthur Lok Jack Business School were eventually elaborated and developed.

Return to ECLAC in Mexico, 1967

In early 1967 I received a telephone call from the chief of the Mexico office of the Economic Commission for Latin America, with whom I had worked when undertaking the earlier study on 'Aspects of development and trade in the Commonwealth Caribbean'. He asked me to return to the office for a period of approximately three months to do a preliminary study on the possibilities for economic co-operation between Belize and Central America.

They knew I was knowledgeable about Belize as a result of the friendship with Raphael Fonseca (later Financial Secretary in Belize) that I developed while I was at university in London; and my very close association with Patrick Cacho, which originated when we were both undertaking our undergraduate studies at the

LSE. On his return to Belize, Cacho was asked to head up the Planning Office. I was therefore in a close relationship with the two most important civil servants in Belize.

I had only three months to undertake the study and accordingly had to work exceptionally long hours, including weekends, in order to complete it on schedule. When I was finished, the then Executive Secretary said to me, 'This is an excellent paper but we cannot publish it because it could have political implications.' He may have felt that the Guatemalans would be critical and this could lead to difficulties at the inter-governmental level in ECLAC and other fora.

Having spent three months of my life working intensively only to find that it led to a negative outcome because of being politically difficult was a grave disappointment to me. They would not allow me to publish it even as an individual. However, later in my career, after I had served in the United Nations for a period of ten years, I appreciated much more than I did at the time the extent to which the Executive Director was constrained by United Nations rules and procedures. Truly, he had no alternative but to prevent the publication of my work.

Among the things that created concern with the findings of my report was that it identified good possibilities for co-operation between Belize and the countries of Central America. As had been anticipated, news of my study began to circulate even before it was finished and the spirited response of Guatemala to this news confirmed the anxieties that developed among the management of ECLAC. Guatemala did not recognize Belize as an independent entity. They considered that the British government had illegally annexed a part of their territory and called it British Honduras (later Belize). They therefore felt impelled to disassociate themselves from recognition of any action taken by Belize that had become the subject of discussion in any forum in the United Nations. It was felt by the ECLAC management that my report corroborated the recognition of Belize and was, accordingly, unacceptable to Guatemala and other member states of ECLAC that held the same point of view.

Guatemala has had to recognize Belize now because the English-speaking Caribbean pushed for Belize to be admitted to the UN.

Guatemala voted against it. Once Belize was admitted to the UN it became part of the Economic Commission for Latin America, like the rest of the Caribbean.

To this day Guatemala retains its basic stance on this matter. However, it has both formally and informally accepted projects and schemes of co-operation involving both sides. But, as I indicate later on in this book, there are still prospects that an arrangement for co-operation will eventually be worked out between the two states.

Returning to my time at the St Augustine campus, I can say that they were three years well spent in laying foundations for the development of social sciences and management studies at St Augustine. I consider that my academic work, alongside my activities as advisor to the government and, in some instances, the region as a whole, constituted a very worthwhile phase in my career.

As far as academic work was concerned, I should mention the book that I wrote jointly with Kari Levitt in 1966 on *The Political Economy of Canadian–West Indian Relations.* This was in response to an invitation from the Canadian Trade Committee of the Private Planning Association of Canada. This committee, a leading private sector organization in that country, invited us to prepare a book on the subject for use by their organization in taking part in the Canada–West Indies Conference convened by the governments to consider the revision and upgrading of the Canada–West Indies Trade Agreement of 1925. That book was well received by all of the parties and it appears that they drew from it in undertaking the revision.

I returned to the Mona campus with reluctance because I felt that the innovations that I had introduced at St Augustine had not reached a sufficiently mature stage for me to give up the leadership of them. However, I was conscious that the university administration had made persistent efforts to identify a director for the Institute of Social and Economic Research following the departure of Dr Huggins to take up the post of Principal at St Augustine. I was also aware that some regional governments had been expressing disquiet at the vacancy at the ISER at a time when they were looking to the institute to undertake innovative work on their decision to establish a process of regional integration; I shall be taking this up in future chapters. Moreover, the Ford Foundation, which had identified the ISER as a critical institution for their support, was gently reminding the university authorities of the urgency of settling the leadership question.

These considerations influenced me in yielding to the urgings of the Vice-Chancellor and his senior advisers.

7

UWI, Mona, 1967–74

Director, Institute of Social and Economic Research (ISER)

When I arrived in 1967 to become Director of the Institute of Social and Economic Research, I thought I would have opportunities to make the institute a more vital force in the development of teaching and research oriented towards addressing some of the major development problems of the region.

As a first step, I invited staff both in the institute and the teaching departments to take responsibility for developing specialist knowledge on the individual countries in the region. I perceived that in so doing we could become the first stop for researchers and policy analysts wishing to investigate specific development problems and possibilities. The institute would therefore be seen progressively as a primary source on the development problems of the area. Accordingly, I invited individual staff members to adopt a country and/or a particular development issue.

The first opportunity I got to test this approach was in responding positively to a request from the government of St Vincent and the Grenadines to assist them in the preparation of a Ten-Year Development Plan. The staff in the departments and the institute showed commendable enthusiasm for undertaking this project. Unfortunately, their lack of experience in dealing with the public and governmental establishment led eventually to a suspension of the project because of the deep differences in their assessments of the extent of critical poverty in the islands. Predictably, the ISER team identified it as a more critical problem than the local commentators would accept. Since the two sides could not find common ground, we ultimately had to abandon the project. However, this was good experience for us in handling local interests when engaging in policy research. A subsequent attempt in Grenada to undertake a background study, out of which material for a development plan would emerge, was more successful.

My idea was to assemble these analyses in the form of country surveys that could be used to create a pool of information relevant to the principal problems of the area and suitable for use in teaching and further research. I intended to address the more glaring information gaps, typically in the smaller islands since more work had been done on Jamaica and Trinidad and Tobago.

My own perception included the development of strong working contacts with the other research institutes located in former British colonies in Africa, which had been set up around the same time as ISER. I felt that, working together, we could constitute a knowledge resource available to our governments to assist with problem solving, particularly in relation to issues arising in the international community.

Accordingly, I made my first approach to the Director of the ISER at the University of Nigeria at Ibadan, Professor Adebola Onitiri, who had been at the LSE with me and had been in touch for some time sharing views on development, especially as they pertained to the external relations of our respective countries.

We agreed to start the process by exchanges of staff so that at each institution there would be staff who were familiar with the co-operating institution, its programmes and its staff. A few people, including a staff member from the University of Guyana, went to Nigeria to commence the process. However, we were hindered later in advancing this process because of a shortage of funds. Nonetheless, the initial contacts still provided us with a small window on Africa. Less formal contacts were also initiated in institutions in Mauritius and the Pacific. In the Caribbean, we also started developing links with universities in the French and Dutch Antilles, Puerto Rico and Haiti.

Because of my perception that the institute should become a centre for research and policy information in the Caribbean, I discussed with senior colleagues, particularly with Lloyd Braithwaite who had been acting director of the institute before my appointment, the need for a detailed exchange of views among colleagues on the three UWI campuses about the research priorities for the area, for which the institute could provide support.

It was agreed that we should hold a conference on research. I arranged to convene it at Cave Hill and it was very well received by the faculty and by the institutions and agencies interested in the institute and supportive of its work.

The conference convened for one week and produced a comprehensive document outlining the different areas that represented the research interests of individual staff on the three campuses. It also provided the institute with material that could go into an application to the Ford Foundation for a grant to support a programme. The grant was designed not only to develop individual projects but to provide for the publication of the documents representing the outcome of particular investigations.

I persuaded the foundation that they should also support the publication of dissertations and other studies as an encouragement to the staff and to make those documents more accessible to the general public. Accordingly, the institute was able to publish six books by staff members that were quickly taken up in teaching and by relevant people outside the university. It also served as a marker for outside institutions who were interested in building working relationships with the UWI.

My friend Bill Carmichael, who had now taken up the vice-presidency of the Ford Foundation, was instrumental in helping me access research funds for faculty and students to travel and do research on various topics. While I was head of ISER, the Ford Foundation gave well over US$1 million dollars, which allowed us to carry out and publish as much research as we did.

In particular instances, field researchers generated controversy about the fieldwork they were undertaking. When the late Dr Roy

Marshall became Vice-Chancellor (1969–74) he was very upset when he was told that the institute, without prior consultation, had a team in the field studying at first hand the development of the Black Power Movement in Trinidad. I heard he was ready to fire me. Actually, I made an error in approving the project and handing over its supervision to a member of the teaching staff. I was then unaware that the staff member had not done any field research before and basically left it up to the team to take the relevant decisions on their modus operandi.

On the other hand, I was unhappy that the Principal decided to take the matter to the central university committees to seek a disciplinary decision against me. I felt that he should have consulted me before taking the action that he had set in train. In the midst of this, I was told that he had received a very commendatory letter from the Prime Minister of Trinidad and Tobago, highly congratulating me on the outcome of another project in the field of foreign investment where I was the lead researcher. I gather that because of this the Principal felt it was not now appropriate for him to propose disciplinary action against me. But I had learnt my lesson: to be more cautious in the future when colleagues proposed projects of policy research.

Returning to academic subjects, some of my colleagues envisaged a more activist role for the institute in policy development – not restricted to work with governments in the region. I understood the good intentions that lay behind this approach, but argued that we had to keep a close eye on the balance that we should maintain between government and non-governmental groups. My colleagues did not exactly disagree, but felt that I tended to place more weight on our role with governments as against non-governmental institutions and groups. This was to occasion a controversy that would later assume much greater proportions than I wished.

I had always wanted us to be thought of as a major source of expertise available to provide a measure of support to different policy interests, but I felt that we needed to be careful in so doing since we were basically funded by regional governments. Unfortunately, that became a significant area of misunderstanding between myself and academic colleagues, largely in the teaching departments. It was one of the factors that led eventually to my decision to leave the university and accept the post of Secretary-General of CARICOM. In any event, I was being propelled by my deep commitment to doing whatever I could to advance the process of regional integration.

Association of Caribbean Universities and Research Institutes (UNICA)

Sir Philip Sherlock, Caribbean scholar par excellence, arrived at a critical juncture in my university career and our friendship remained close after his retirement as Vice-Chancellor. He was the principal force in establishing the Association of Caribbean Universities and Research Institutes, after I had returned to ISER at Mona in 1967. A principal goal of this organization was to strengthen relationships between Caribbean universities, and from our standpoint, between the UWI and those institutions.

Sir Philip insisted that I should be the UWI's representative on the UNICA board, based on my previous Latin American and international experience.

UNICA was a dynamic association which grew exponentially under the additional influence of Victor Urquidi, the outstanding Mexican scholar and head of El Colegio de Mexico. An equivalent source of dynamism came from Henry King Stanford of the University of Miami, then president of his institution. He agreed to take up the presidency of UNICA, thereby opening opportunities for contact and collaboration with a large number of academic institutions, particularly in the United States and Latin America.

The Ford Foundation was impressed with the goals of the organization and provided the first grant in support of its work. There were also indications that once the institution was up and running, other sources of support would present themselves.

In 1969 UNICA established offices in Kingston and Sir Philip became its first secretary-general after he retired as Vice-Chancellor of the UWI. During the hiatus after his departure, Sherlock advised whoever was going to act for him as Vice-Chancellor, prior to the arrival of Dr Roy Marshall, that he wanted me to remain as the UWI representative on UNICA because I had worked with him on its formation, arguing that I had many contacts with academics in Latin America.

Politics at Mona were difficult to navigate, as I found out in my own case. William Demas called me on one occasion to say that he wanted me to travel as an advisor to some CARICOM trade delegation that was going to Europe, but later on indicated that the government of Jamaica had objected to my presence on the delegation. It would appear that their objections were based on unfounded rumours that I was a deeply committed socialist. It turned out later that the supplier of these rumours lost his position with the government and I agreed to help him to get a position with the UNCTAD/GATT Trade Centre in Geneva. Later on the minister recognized that the rumours about me were without foundation and withdrew his reservation about my being an advisor to future delegations.

Contacts with Michael Manley

I met Michael Manley on a social occasion in 1967, when we had no substantive discussions on any matters. Later on, however, he telephoned to invite me to meet with him about a book he was writing, which eventually became *The Politics of Change*. I agreed to look at his manuscript because in the period subsequent to our initial meeting, I had come across his influential article in the *Foreign Affairs* journal, entitled 'Overcoming insularity in Jamaica'. Following upon the results of the referendum I was pleased to see that there were political personalities in Jamaica still strongly engaged with support of regionalism.

In preparation for our meeting, I read carefully the draft manuscript that he had sent me. In so doing, I developed mixed views about it because there were some propositions with which I had difficulty. However, overall, I had positive views about several sections in the manuscript. I telephoned him to indicate my reactions to the text and to remind him that I did not wish to influence his draft unduly, because I had different views from himself on several political issues.

'Look, I'd very much appreciate getting your criticisms of it and for you to feel free to say anything you want. Could we meet over drinks or dinner, whatever?' He added: 'I live in a very humble situation.'

I accepted the invitation. On that occasion, I expressed myself very frankly on the subject of his book. He made a lot of notes, and then said he would like another meeting because, if I would forgive him, his economics was not what it should be. He repeated his request, said that he would review my comments and asked whether I would agree to have a further consultation about them. I did not hear from him again for a little while and then he asked whether we could have another meeting.

On that occasion, we had a discussion about linkages and their importance to economic development and their relevance to Jamaica. We spent the entire evening on that subject. I did not see Michael again until he called me about bauxite, years later.

The role of ISER in policy choices

When I look back at my period at the ISER, I felt that under my direction the institute had made progress on a number of fronts, but I must say that in the latter part of my period there I felt very uncomfortable with the negative views that were then being expressed about the role of the institute under my charge. It was being represented that I was too willing to accept personal requests for help with policy problems from the political establishment in several Caribbean countries. It was then argued that the ISER should give priority to intellectual/academic issues rather than policy issues. I myself had an entirely different view because, given the history of the ISER, the expectation was that it would address local problems of relevance to the communities to which it related and from which it drew basic support. In this context, the ISER had to maintain its relevance in order to ensure continuity. Of course, this did not mean taking political sides, which in the end was what the critics were often doing themselves.

It mattered little that these criticisms were without foundation and I was later to hear from some of my critics that they had misjudged the reports which were in circulation about my orientation on development issues and the importance I attached to serving the regional governments as against private groups.

Matters reached a head in the early months of 1974, when I came to the conclusion that I could not work fruitfully with people who made unjustified assumptions about my political and social predispositions. I need hardly say that these were totally unwarranted representations of me and later events served to propel some of the principal people involved to apologize directly to me.

SECTION 3

WORKING AT REGIONAL AND GLOBAL LEVELS

8

Working for the region

Preparatory work on the Caribbean Free Trade Association (CARIFTA)

When I arrived in Trinidad and Tobago in December 1964, Willie Demas involved me in a number of activities. As I have already indicated, while in Mexico I had produced the paper 'Aspects of trade and development', published it in both English and Spanish. This had a very good reception from both ECLAC and a number of personalities in the region. In that paper, I tried to set out a rationale for integration in the Caribbean.

When I got to Trinidad, Willie told me that he had shown the paper to Dr Eric Williams, who liked it and said that it should be distributed throughout the region. He asked Willie to send it to all the governments and particularly to those ministers responsible for economic planning, the Bank of Jamaica, and so on, which he did. Dr Williams also suggested that, having sent it out, a working meeting of experts should be convened to discuss it.

Exploratory working meeting at Mona

Willie called to tell me what they were doing and asked me whether the university could sponsor the proposed meeting of experts. I suggested that he contact the then acting director of ISER, Lloyd Braithwaite, who readily agreed. Braithwaite also indicated that he would ask Lloyd Best and myself to act as rapporteurs for the proceedings.

Accordingly, we held the meeting at Mona. It was not well attended, except in the case of Jamaica and Trinidad and Tobago. There was also a representative from St Lucia. Notwithstanding the paucity of numbers, we had the two principal officials in the Caribbean, so it was agreed that we should proceed with the discussion. That part of it went very well, and the recommendation was made that a report of the meeting should go to all governments, proposing that official work should begin immediately to set up a free trade area and then to consider the more comprehensive arrangements for integration.

As part of the package, I persuaded them to recommend that governments should also finance a programme of research on integration, because there were a number of areas which could not be dealt with in one paper. The governments agreed, contributed, and out of that came a number of studies; the most prominent, and perhaps the best known, among them was by Havelock Brewster and C.Y. Thomas, 'The dynamics of West Indian integration'. George Beckford contributed a paper, Norman Girvan as well, and there were several other contributions on particular topics.

The private sector contribution to proposals for freeing trade

This programme of work started and was going on, but alongside it Carlton Alexander and Aaron Matalon, prominent Jamaican entrepreneurs, went on a region-wide tour, proposing the phased freeing of trade. Eventually, the whole of the private sector was more or less committed to the idea of Caribbean Free Trade as a first step.

Alexander and Matalon were also enthusiastic when they heard about what was going on at the ISER. They fully endorsed that programme, so there was a fairly wide consensus that the time was opportune to take steps to free intra-regional trade.

Initial decision to establish a Caribbean Free Trade Association

Prime Ministers Forbes Burnham of Guyana, V.C. Bird of Antigua and Barbuda and Errol Barrow of Barbados did not know how to proceed after the collapse of the Federation in May 1962. Although Guyana was not a part of the Federation, Burnham was a federationist with supportive members in his cabinet, notably Shridath 'Sonny' Ramphal, who was Attorney General and went on to become Foreign Minister as well. After preliminary contacts between the three prime ministers, a meeting was proposed for Dickenson Bay in Antigua to examine possible provisions for a free trade area, taking as their model the European Free Trade Association (EFTA) that preceded the European Common Market, and to discuss how the three countries might proceed with the idea.

They met in Dickenson Bay and discussed a draft essentially prepared by Guyana (Sonny Ramphal and a group in Georgetown) and largely modelled on the EFTA agreement, with some modifications. They drew up an agreement that, along with Trinidad and Tobago, was signed on 15 December 1965, establishing the Caribbean Free Trade Association. The three prime ministers accepted it as a basis for further discussion and sent it out to the other governments.

Caribbean Heads of Government meeting, Barbados, 1967

Accordingly, in the second quarter of 1967 the governments had three documents before them: the Dickenson Bay agreement, the report on the Mona meeting on Caribbean Integration and my study, 'Aspects of development and trade in the Commonwealth Caribbean'. These constituted the documentation for the Heads of Government meeting in Barbados in October 1967. As the author of one of the documents, I was invited to the meeting.

I had never been to a Heads of Government meeting before. It seemed hard to get the preliminary discussion going, so I was asked by the chairman of the meeting, Prime Minister Barrow, to make some introductory remarks. Following my presentation, it appeared that the discussion by the Heads of Government was not automatically proceeding, so, on the suggestion of the chairman, they decided to adjourn and take a coffee break.

I went out of the room and encountered the officials from the Jamaican delegation. We had a jovial exchange of views and I teased them that having broken up the Federation, it was their responsibility to start off the discussion about a proposal to restore some regional arrangements. The officials confided to me that there was a division of opinion among the ministers in their delegation and they were trying to get the head of delegation, minister Hugh Shearer, to take a stand and indicate support for the proposal. After the adjournment, I was surprised to hear Mr Shearer propose that I should be asked, as one of the authors of the papers, to make a brief presentation of its principal findings. The chairman offered the floor to me and in my response I indicated that this was an important opportunity for governments to take the matter forward beyond discussion to a firm decision to proceed and work towards the establishment of a free trade area. The chairman then nudged me into suggesting that the government of Jamaica should break the ice and proceed as I had proposed, since informal contacts suggested that the other governments would support this. This did not sit well with the Jamaican delegation and one minister left the room. Thereafter the atmosphere became more relaxed and it quickly became apparent that the other delegations were strongly in favour of taking a decision to establish a free trade area. At that stage, the head of the Jamaican delegation associated himself with the proposal.

An adjournment was then taken and during that time, ministers agreed informally among themselves that Guyana should be asked to host the secretariat of the Free Trade Area. On the return to plenary, this proposal was greeted enthusiastically. A drafting group of officials was set up to make the arrangements for establishing the secretariat. When we came back from lunch, we dealt with the Caribbean Development Bank, and agreement was quickly reached to establish it in Barbados.

Having secured these two outcomes, the meeting closed in an atmosphere of very high accord.

The establishment of the CARICOM secretariat

After an initial period of teething problems, when the proposed secretariat was under the interim leadership of Fred Cozier, a permanent secretary from Barbados, the establishment of the secretariat was regularized with William Demas as Secretary-General. He proceeded with great energy to fill several vacant posts and to embark on a programme to familiarize member states and their populations with the case for integration and the initial steps that had been taken or were in prospect.

Willie Demas had an extraordinary capacity for leadership and for keeping otherwise disparate officials on a single course of working to create a strong base for the programme of integration that was then envisaged.

Secretary-General of CARICOM, Georgetown, Guyana, 1974–77

In early 1974, I was carrying out a short-term assignment with the Inter-American Development Bank in Washington when I received a telephone call from the Jamaican Mission to tell me that the then Permanent Secretary to the Prime Minister, Mr Vin McFarlane, was in Washington and wished to see me urgently. Later that evening I met him at the Embassy. He told me that his Prime Minister had asked him to brief me on some informal consultations he was having with his colleagues in the other islands about filling three important regional posts that were then becoming available. The first was the imminent departure of Sir Arthur Lewis as President of the Caribbean Development Bank; the second was the consequent replacement of William Demas as Secretary-General of CARICOM, should he be appointed to the Caribbean Development Bank; and the third was the vacant post of Vice-Chancellor at Mona, following the resignation of Sir Roy Marshall. The heads of government wanted to hear from me which of those vacant posts I would be interested in filling.

I told McFarlane that I knew that Demas was reluctant to leave CARICOM, but would do so if I was agreeable to offering my candidature as his replacement. I told him also that, in my view, Aston Preston was the best candidate for the vice-chancellorship, and I would not wish to be a contestant for that post. Accordingly, he suggested to me that I should accept the post at CARICOM if it was offered to me. Following the discussion with McFarlane, I received, in short order, an offer of the post of Secretary-General.

Accordingly, my family, which then consisted of my wife Marjorie, my son Andrew and my baby daughter Helga, and I arrived in Georgetown in September 1974. My son Nicholas was born later while we were in Guyana.

In succeeding Willie Demas as Secretary-General, I felt confident that I could build on the solid foundations that he had already laid. In so doing, I decided that my initial focus should be on strengthening the structure of the secretariat as it moved to support new areas of work, while responding to immediate requirements for advancing the technical work in two areas: one was the proposed Caribbean Food Plan, which was seen essentially as a response to the economic and financial crisis then taking place in the region, and the other was the proposed negotiations for entry into an association agreement with the then European Common Market. Accordingly, much of my initial energy was devoted to these tasks, and I proceeded immediately to take up the substantive work that Demas had left behind.

The first task was to prepare a Heads of Government meeting in St Kitts and Nevis that was scheduled to be held before the end of the year. The second was to pick up on the flow of technical work that was already taking place on an association agreement between the African, Caribbean and Pacific States (ACP) and the then European Common Market. Already, the two most senior members of the secretariat staff, Deputy Secretary-General Joseph Tyndall and Director of the Trade and Integration Division Edwin Carrington, were in Brussels dealing with particular matters. I had to pick up the cudgels to deal with the remainder of the items coming up for negotiation. The work on this matter is discussed further in the next chapter. Thirdly, my predecessor had begun technical work on major aspects of the proposed Caribbean Food Plan, which was then proceeding satisfactorily.

Needless to say, these three areas of work, taken together with the other work of the secretariat and the need to prepare comprehensive documentation for the forthcoming HOG meeting, resulted in a very heavy workload for me. To start with, governments were anxious that I should bring the work in Brussels under my direct leadership; they felt that I was already fully prepared for this and I received several messages encouraging me to do it and asking when I could take up the responsibility in Brussels.

Secondly, no arrangements had been made to start the preparation for the Heads of Government meeting. When I examined the proposed agenda, I found that some 14 technical documents had to be prepared. My colleagues had assumed that I would deal with this after I arrived; so I had, without much previous knowledge of the technical capabilities of the staff, to assign individual staff responsibility for them. I then found out that I had myself to take responsibility for the 14 documents. Accordingly, I arranged with my personal office to clear my desk of appointments so that I could stay at home and draft the papers without distractions. On doing so, my office telephoned me to say that a new senior staff member had arrived and they wondered whether I would wish to meet him, since he might be able to help me with some of the documents. This person turned out to be Dr Kenneth Hall, who I already knew when he was a student at the Institute of International Relations in St Augustine. He came to see me at home and without any equivocation took responsibility for drafting five documents. This was highly appreciated because it significantly reduced the burden of drafting for me. Dr Hall undertook his assignments with enthusiasm, did good drafts and, between the two of us, all of the documentation was ready on time for the meeting. The St Kitts Heads of Government meeting proceeded very smoothly and I was congratulated by them for having taken up the responsibilities of the post very promptly.

However, on my return to Georgetown I was convinced that a systematic structure should be designed so that the work could be organized in more efficient and effective ways. I decided to ask the United Nations Development Programme (UNDP) to provide me with a small group of advisors to design a staff structure for the secretariat which, until then, had relied upon ad hoc initiatives. The group of advisors did excellent work and their recommendations

Figure 5 My first CARICOM Heads of Government Conference as Secretary General, with the late Hon. Robert Bardshaw, Prime Minister of St Kitts and Nevis, Chairman of the Conference.

Figure 6 The late Prime Minister of Dominica Dame Eugenia Charles, Sir Shridath Ramphal and me.

were fully accepted to provide the structure for the secretariat. Among other things, a permanent staff group was established to deal with Heads of Government conferences and other major meetings. The management of the secretariat staff was supposed to be a function of the Deputy Secretary-General, but he indicated that his plate was already full and declined to take on further responsibilities. I therefore decided to assign the responsibilities to other senior staff members, substantially to Dr Hall, who was willing and able to do the additional work involved.

The Caribbean Food Plan

Apart from organizational matters, I took a direct interest in the substantive work programme, principally the technical work on the Caribbean Food Plan and the Brussels negotiations. As far as the Food Plan was concerned, the initiative was taken by the Prime Minister of Trinidad and Tobago, who proposed that as a response to the oil crisis at the time, existing food deficiencies, and development needs for higher income and employment in all of the member states, a regional development plan should be set in motion. He consulted with Prime Ministers Burnham, Barrow, Manley and others. Prime Minister Manley agreed and drew attention to Jamaica's urgent need for the construction of an aluminium plant, which was not feasible in Jamaica because of the unavailability of the energy needed to achieve sufficiently low power costs. He suggested that Trinidad could erect a plant to convert the alumina to primary aluminium and return it to Jamaica for use in fabrication industries.

In agriculture, the two principal needs identified were for corn and soya as inputs into the production of animal feed. These two products, in turn, constituted the basis for an expanded livestock industry to meet growing demands for meat and meat products. In relation to fisheries, it was considered that catches in the Leeward and Windward Islands could satisfy a substantial part of the regional demand for those products.

As Secretary-General of CARICOM, Willie Demas was called in by Dr Williams to assume responsibility for developing the Food

Plan, since this was essentially a regional matter. Willie conceptualized it into a Caribbean Food Plan, to be jointly formulated and implemented by the member states of CARICOM, which would be aimed at substantially reducing major food deficits in the region. He assembled a very good group of technocrats for the purpose of identifying the priority projects that should be developed, specifying locations for them with estimates of the professional and technical staff needed for their implementation. This entailed the preparation of pre-feasibility studies and the drafting of statutes for a Caribbean Food Corporation, which would be the implementing agency for the Food Plan.

Because of the urgency of the situation, the Food Plan proceeded by attempting to implement major projects before the entire programme had been worked out, costed and the financing of it arranged. Accordingly, the secretariat was urged into action to work out high priority projects for meat and fish production. My predecessor had assembled a very knowledgeable group of technocrats to prepare projects for beef production in Guyana and black belly sheep in Barbados, both of which would supplement local production in supplying the region's need for meat; and for corn and soya production in Guyana and Jamaica as inputs into animal feed. Projects were also being designed for increasing the supplies of fish in the Leeward and Windward Islands. The secretariat had organized small technical groups with representation from member states to follow up these projects. At the same time, other possibilities were being discussed for projects in the remaining member states.

Despite the valuable work that was going on, I was very anxious to place the existing programme, together with additional project ideas, under the discipline of a formal programme containing a draft financial section in which the financing could be fully discussed. Once that draft was ready, I would propose convening a Heads of Government conference to secure formal endorsement of it. I had already discussed the matter with Willie who, as President of the Caribbean Development Bank, would have assumed the lead role for financing. Both Willie and I had already had preliminary conversations with sources of development assistance including the World Bank, the Inter-American Development Bank and major bilateral sources. We had positive responses, although no commitments could have been made at that stage.

All of these preliminary actions were disrupted by the major disagreement that occurred between the prime ministers of Trinidad and Tobago, Jamaica and Guyana over the decision made by the last two to seek associate status with COMECON – the grouping led by the Soviet Union and including virtually all of socialist Eastern Europe. As it turned out, this became a major disruption of the CARICOM work programme and slowed down significantly progress towards putting a number of major integration initiatives in place. Advances of project finance were terminated by Trinidad and Tobago and this brought to a halt, among other things, the corn soya project in Guyana and the budget for the Caribbean Food Corporation, which was intended to be the administrative agency for implementing the Food Plan; this brought the entire initiative to an unfortunate suspension.

Looking back over this period, I have to say that with the collapse of the preparations for the Food Plan no major initiative emanated from the secretariat in subsequent years. However, Secretary-General Roderick Rainford made admirable attempts to interest member states in undertaking other initiatives to achieve substantive progress during his period in office. Otherwise, the years were characterized by interim arrangements and short periods of office, except for the extended period of time spent by Secretary-General Carrington. His successor has since been trying to build on Dr Carrington's efforts and restore active programmes in the secretariat.

The Independent West Indies Commission: report to the Heads of Government, 1992

The West Indies Commission was originally conceived by A.N.R. Robinson, who was then Prime Minister of Trinidad and Tobago (1985–91). Robinson was an ardent Federationist concerned about two things: one, that the movement (CARICOM integration) appeared to be losing its dynamism; and two, that Trinidad and Tobago had not participated in a Heads of Government (HOG) conference for seven years after Dr Eric Williams had suspended his government's participation. However, during that time Trinidad and Tobago had continued paying their full subscription to the secretariat.

Prime Minister Robinson felt strongly that he should do something to resuscitate CARICOM, because of his own personal convictions. So he called Sonny Ramphal, who was the person they contacted whenever they wanted to do something like that and asked: 'What can we do?'

Sonny suggested: 'Well, let us take it to the next HOG conference and get them to agree on setting up a commission to review the whole CARICOM process and come up with some proposals for strengthening it.'

Accordingly, at the Heads of Government meeting in Grand Anse, Grenada in July 1989, which as Vice Chancellor of the UWI, I attended, it was decided to take some initiatives to revitalize CARICOM. Prime Minister A.N.R. Robinson, as Chairman of the Conference, requested that a draft declaration should be prepared containing all of the agreements that the conference might wish to approve. He asked Sonny to take responsibility for a draft. In turn, Sonny consulted Willie Demas and the two of them eventually, turned to me to put any appropriate finishing touches. I took the initiative to include a paragraph to the effect that the University of the West Indies would remain a regional institution indefinitely. As far as the university was concerned, the relevant paragraph in the declaration represented a re-statement of the regional commitment at a time when some reservations were beginning to be expressed about its continuance as a regional institution. To the present day, most university people do not know exactly how it happened. And I never told them. This is the origin of the retention by the university of its regional status.

The document was unanimously approved by the conference and became known as the Grand Anse Declaration. It served to revitalize interest in the regional movement and to provide CARICOM with a more active mandate.

Coming back to the conference, as part of the Grand Anse Declaration the Heads decided to set up the West Indies Commission to undertake the necessary investigations and discussions and to propose those steps forward that would strengthen regional integration. Sir Shridath Ramphal was appointed as chairman. First of all, he consulted the governments regarding the most convenient place to establish the secretariat and it was agreed that Barbados should be asked to become the location since it has the most convenient airline connections. Then the University of the West Indies offered to accommodate the secretariat at the Cave Hill campus. DeLisle Worrell, who is now Governor of the Central Bank of Barbados, was appointed as the staff economist. Sir Shridath, as Commonwealth Secretary-General and being in London, had to have somebody there liaising with the West Indies Commission, which took up a lot of time.

We met, discussed, defined our tasks as outlined in the terms of reference contained in the Grand Anse Declaration, and then agreed on a series of consultations to be carried out in each of the CARICOM member states. Four of us, Sonny, Frank Rampersad, who was then Director of Economics at the Commonwealth secretariat, Willie Demas, then President of the Caribbean Development Bank, and myself constituted an informal drafting committee. We had our meetings in Barbados, London, indeed in several countries, depending on where we were at any particular time. And we had countless meetings on the telephone – long telephone conversations. I told Willie once that the Trinidad telephone company should give him some kind of special honour because of the contributions that he had made to their budget. (Subsequently, on his retirement as Governor of the Central Bank of Trinidad and Tobago, the telephone company gave him free phonecalls for life!) We were on the phone for hours exchanging views, Rampersad and Ramphal in London, myself in Jamaica and Willie in Trinidad. Of the other members of the Commission, Professor Rex Nettleford from the outset said: 'Look gentlemen, I won't waste your time. I have handled the cultural side so let me carry out the consultations on the cultural side.'

We actually had meetings in every single country in CARICOM. The central budget of CARICOM paid for the transport. The central budget came from all the countries, but then each country paid the costs of our meeting in that country. We flew in, they picked us up and provided a hotel and local transport. We interpreted our Terms of Reference as requiring us to report on measures to improve the functioning of CARICOM, how to revitalize the whole process. For instance, I was among those who contended that the Regional Food Plan did not succeed because there was no explicit provision for participation by the private sector. I thought that if it had been so, it would not have just been interrupted by Trinidad's decision to withdraw financing. The projects that we had lined up were projects that made a lot of sense to the man in the street or other interested parties. From a technical point of view, they were well-grounded ideas. My own view was that we should have returned to the programme but with explicit participation from the outset by representatives from the private sector, and in appropriate cases, where inputs were required, from the investment community abroad.

The West Indies Commission had meetings with an open agenda in every country, where anything could be discussed. The public were invited, they came, asked questions, and they expressed views as they considered appropriate.

I remember we went to St Vincent and held a meeting on the Leeward coast. At the public gathering, where we could sit down to talk, Sonny said: 'If you had a choice and the means to do so, what is the country in the world you really feel you would like to visit?'

There was almost a single cry: 'Barbados!' We were surprised! Everyone expected New York, London, and so forth. Until someone came up and I said: 'Tell me, why Barbados?'

'Because Barbados is the only television station we can get here.'

They had never seen anywhere else. That was the rural point of view and a good rural, agricultural point of view it was. We were all taken aback. Our chairman said that we should explore what could be done in Trinidad, Jamaica, Guyana and elsewhere in the Caribbean community to expand their television coverage.

We sensed that St Vincent was not unique and that in several member states television coverage of other member states was rather weak. Indeed, we saw a case for a CARICOM media policy to ensure that all parts of the community were in contact with each other.

Ramphal really did a phenomenal amount of work on the West Indian Commission and its report. He has to be given the credit for it. He was carrying out this heavy assignment in conjunction with his substantive duties as the Commonwealth Secretary-General and it was highly commendable that his colleagues on the Commission felt that he was giving almost undivided attention to our assignment.

Our central idea was that the problem with CARICOM really was one of implementation. It largely had, and still has, to do with the fact that at the national level, when a proposal or decision from any of the CARICOM main committees gets to the capitals, there was no established procedure for taking steps to implement it. In most instances, they get bogged down because the people who are the first recipients do not know what to do to move it forward. Should we get a policy decision here? Should we send it on to the Attorney General to get a draft? Is legislation required? Not required?

I would not put the onus only on the civil service, because of course the ministers were responsible. The Prime Minister, after all, attended a big meeting and now it was report time for action. So what is the action? What are they doing? I would say that the immediate difficulty arose because the civil servants did not fully grasp what the intentions of their governments were on the issues in question. I put part of the blame on us, because when we wentto the various countries, it never occurred to us to have separate sessions with the civil servants. We had a public session, at which they were of course invited to ask questions. And anybody who got in touch with us would find us open to discussion, but we did not invite the civil servants specifically.

We entitled the report 'Time for Action' in order to draw attention to the central issues of implementation, which has already been mentioned. But the biggest problem in our report was our proposal for a commission. The European Union has an elaborate, much more powerful body than we proposed in our report. Our proposal was rather modest: a commission of three – a chairman and two commissioners – confined to implementing decisions taken by the principal organs of CARICOM. So when CARICOM takes a decision, the next step should be the commission contacting each of the capitals to see through the implementation. We would not have a large commission. One commissioner would deal with external economic relations and everything that followed from that, which everyone agreed was being done well on a group basis – nobody had a problem with that.

Another commissioner would handle the social sector, which was education, health and so forth. Nobody had a problem with the Caribbean Examinations Council or the University of the West Indies or what I was trying to set up at the time, the Association of Caribbean Tertiary Institutions (ACTI).

A third commissioner would work on the common market itself, which was intra-regional trade and all the problems that were occurring in that area which every so often required honest brokerage. So when a decision is taken by CARICOM, it would be left to the commission to interact with member states in order to ensure timely implementation of those decisions. In any case, this was just a proposal to set up a commission of three.

It would appear that when the report was submitted, governments focused only on the appointment of the chairman of the commission, which gave rise to a number of unfounded rumours. There was underlying anxiety about it, largely to do with rumours about who would be the prospective candidate to be considered for selection to the post. In the weeks and months that followed the submission of the report to Heads of Government, it appeared from informal conversations that governments were widely divided on the choice of a chairman. Informal efforts to bring governments more closely together were not successful.

No progress was therefore made with the establishment of the commission. In fact, one could say, the report sank like a stone!

The members of the West Indies Commission were obviously very disappointed at the lack of an outcome to their report. We ourselves felt truly committed to the strengthening of the regional process. We also held the view that unanimity among governments was desirable but not a necessary condition for starting the process.

It would be feasible if in some areas a critical minimum of governments were ready to move forward, leaving the door open for others to participate as and when they indicated a desire to do so. As an example, there was then some talk of Barbados joining the Organization of Eastern Caribbean States (OECS). But there did not appear to be consensus within Barbados on the matter, so it was not pursued.

Notwithstanding the lack of a successful positive outcome, the report could have been of value as a starting point for any future consideration of strengthening regionalism.

Caribbean Regional Negotiating Machinery: Chief Technical Advisor, October 1998 to May 2000

As I mentioned, the CARICOM Heads of Government came to the view that they needed to set up a permanent negotiating office to provide continuity in undertaking the necessary preparatory technical work.

The Regional Negotiating Machinery (RNM) was established in 1997 when negotiations with the Free Trade Area of the Americas (FTAA), WTO and post-Lomé were coming up simultaneously. We really needed to have a hard core of permanent people supporting the process by undertaking/organizing the technical work that was required for each negotiation. Sonny Ramphal agreed to become Chief Negotiator on condition that he maintained his office in London and a working office was set up in Barbados.

My son Arnold, who had completed his Ph.D. and come back from the University of Toronto, had started teaching at Cave Hill. Sir Shridath offered him a staff position at the RNM's Barbados office. He became in effect, the senior person at that office.

I joined the RNM as Chief Technical Advisor, reporting to the Chief Negotiator. An arrangement was made with the Jamaican government to provide me with an office. Since office space was at a premium, the Prime Minister helped by providing an office at Jamaica House until a more permanent location could be identified. I had excellent working relationships with the Prime Minister and his staff at Jamaica House.

As Chief Technical Advisor, I had responsibility for preparing all the technical briefs that went to the Chief Negotiator for clearance and providing him with advice on technical issues arising during the negotiations and on the strategy for harmonizing these positions with the other delegations involved on our side of the negotiations.

I remained with the RNM for approximately two years, but eventually separated from it because I wanted to turn my attention to issues in other fields.

Figure 7 Commemorative stamp issued by the government of Jamaica on my receipt of the OCC.

9

External economic relations of CARIFTA/CARICOM

Advisor to the CARICOM delegation: preparing for Lomé I negotiations, 1972

The Lomé Convention was the first agreement between the European Common Market and the countries that became known as the African, Caribbean, and Pacific (ACP) countries, former colonies of different European nations. The trade and aid agreement was finally signed in February 1975 in Lomé, Togo, hence the name. But the history of the negotiations leading up to it is quite a story.

The European Economic Community (EEC) had an agreement starting in 1957 covering French African countries, because of France's economic and trade ties with them. So when Britain was about to join the European Common Market in 1973, the question arose whether they would also accept into a relationship the British ex-colonial countries that had special trade arrangements with Britain.

The progress towards an eventual agreement was very interesting. The Commonwealth secretariat was then looking for someone to study the question of the association of the former British colonies with the European Union. I was Director of the Institute of Social and Economic Research (ISER) at the Mona campus, and someone suggested me to the Commonwealth Secretary-General, Mr Arnold Smith.

I was retained as a consultant to do the study for a meeting of Commonwealth Trade Ministers in London. I completed the study, which was entitled 'Some economic issues arising from the options offered by the enlarged European Economic Community to developing countries in Africa, the Indian Ocean, the Pacific Ocean and the Caribbean', in 1972.

My study was not well received by the government of the United Kingdom because it was very critical of the Yaoundé Convention and suggested major changes to it. This convention had been signed in Yaoundé, Cameroon, on 20 July 1963 between the then European Common Market and 18 African countries, former colonies. It was deficient in several respects and had to be revisited and upgraded.

As I said earlier, the British criticized the study. The Canadians were mildly critical, but the Commonwealth secretariat with the Secretary-General and his Director of Economics were strongly in favour. Eventually, the Trade Ministers meeting supported the broad thrust of my proposals, although they may have differed on details. The British were then more or less committed to getting some revisions of the Yaoundé Convention so that the English-speaking Commonwealth could be fitted into the European Union, especially as the existing Yaoundé Convention was due to expire in 1974. The meeting went very well from the point of view of the developing Commonwealth countries because they were able to exert pressure on Britain to propose to the EEC certain arrangements for a new convention in which Commonwealth countries in Africa, the Caribbean and the Pacific could participate. This went beyond the current thinking of the existing Common Market members and Britain.

Sir Shridath (Sonny) Ramphal, Foreign Minister of Guyana, took the opportunity during a meeting of the Non-Aligned Group of Foreign Ministers in Georgetown in August 1972 to arrange a meeting with the African ministers taking part, as a follow-up to the discussions at the London meeting of trade ministers. He invited Willie Demas, Secretary-General of CARICOM, and myself as the author of the London study, to attend.

I went to the meeting and present were President Burnham and the Heads of Delegation from a number of Commonwealth

African countries, including Nigeria, Ghana and Sierra Leone. President Burnham said that he had called the meeting because of our involvement in preliminary contacts with member states regarding the possibility of an association with Europe. He considered that we could all benefit from a preliminary exchange of views to see whether there was sufficient basis for developing a common position on the matter.

The African ministers attending were enthusiastic but explained that they knew very little about the technicalities that would have to be negotiated. The Foreign Minister of Nigeria went on to propose that CARICOM should send a team of officials to the different African capitals to brief them on the issues. We were surprised to discover that those African ministers present who were signatories to the Yaoundé Convention were not particularly conversant with the issues – or did not wish, at that stage, to share their information with the Commonwealth African states and other countries like the CARICOM, which had a potential interest in the matter.

We met separately with the so-called Associable Countries, that is, those Commonwealth African countries which were now being invited to join Europe, and they were very frank and told us that they had not yet had a chance to acquaint themselves sufficiently with the issues. Since the CARICOM countries seemed to be very well briefed, they proposed that if we were to develop a common position, they needed to be better informed on our positions with respect to the issues.

Following the meeting, the CARICOM Heads of Government decided to follow up the suggestion made by Nigeria to send a team of Caribbean officials to Africa. It was agreed that the team should be headed by one of the permanent secretaries from the Caribbean who were themselves not briefed. So Sonny Ramphal, President Burnham and Willie Demas called me at the end of the meeting and said that in their view it was essential that I should be part of the team. I was hesitant because I did not think that the other members drawn from the civil service would be comfortable with that. On their side, they assured me that they could set those anxieties to rest.

It was agreed that the CARICOM countries would send a delegation to some of the countries in East and West Africa in September 1972 to explain the implications of association with Europe. It was one of the most satisfying things that I have done. Although I was not a government official (I was then at the university), whenever it was time to speak, throughout our visit to Africa I was the spokesperson for the group. Frank Francis was there from Jamaica, John Donaldson from Trinidad, Laurence (Bunny) Mann from Guyana, Jean Holder from Barbados and two from the OECS – altogether a team of seven including myself.

Those European countries in the EEC without strong links to Africa were not too keen on France bringing in their whole contingent of African states, and now that Britain was entering, she was bringing hers as well. They thought that this was changing the entire character of the Community, which it was, and they were not too sure that they wanted this. It was rumoured that Germany was of this view, as were Italy and the Netherlands. They were not too pleased, but they went along. So the whole character of the Europe of the six – Belgium, France, Germany, Italy, Luxembourg and the Netherlands – was being changed by the enlargement.

I think it gave Europe greater influence than they originally had in the international community, such as at the UN. They now had two seats among the permanent members of the Security Council. The Russians were totally against all these colonial links. They were not part of it, but they did not want the European Common Market to become embellished by all these African links. It changed the global arrangements. The Americans were sceptical and unenthusiastic. Canada was part of the Commonwealth so they offered no objection to the arrangement.

When the so-called Commonwealth Associables (meaning the countries of Africa, the Caribbean and the Pacific who were being considered for inclusion) came in, we brought to the table a number of development issues that the French had managed to contain within the context of the Yaoundé arrangements. They did not like our approach very much because it was based upon unity among the participating developing countries. We did not want to go in there and have different groups, English-speaking African, French-speaking African, the Caribbean and the Pacific. We should be united. If it is to make any sense at all as a development arrangement, it must be based on unity among the recipients. It was quite easy to maintain that unity amongst our own group because on the technical issues there were no major divergences among the Caribbean countries. This was what we explained at the private meeting we had during the Non-Aligned Conference in Guyana and we continued this theme throughout our visits to Africa. Frank Francis, considered to be the leader of the delegation, would initiate the discussion by pointing to the unity among CARICOM countries and then introduce me as the technical advisor, indicating that I would speak for the group as a whole. So, as already explained, I became the technical spokesperson for the group.

Some of the African governments had good economic sections dealing with the matter. This was the position in Kenya, and was also true in Ghana, Nigeria and Sierra Leone. Cameroon was then not too well informed but when we went there and spoke with them, they were responsive.

We did not know how the Yaoundé countries, particularly the major ones – Senegal and the Ivory Coast – would react. They were negative! I think they did not want this large number of English-speaking countries to join their arrangement, which they believed they were running quite well. They were the leaders in the francophone group, so they did not want their position to be threatened by a large number of new members. After a while, the Senegalese were more co-operative. Their spokesperson was very learned, a classical scholar and well regarded by President Senghor. He was exceptionally well versed in literature and kept quoting to us from a number of French authors. He was also an *enfant chérie* of the Europeans, though he was not at all interested in any marriage between the French- and English-speaking countries – certainly not between the francophones and the Caribbean – on cultural grounds. The Ivory Coast was not particularly co-operative initially either, as they had special understandings with the French that they wished to preserve.

Our team flew first to Kenya, then Tanzania, and were in transit in Uganda when we were advised to pay a protocol visit to President Idi Amin, who was then the current President of the Organization of African Unity (OAU). We arrived there at 5:30 in the morning. Since we were in transit and did not have a hotel, we went into the VIP lounge in Entebbe, had a shower, a cup of coffee and went off to the presidential palace. It was a very brief meeting, simply designed to recognize him as the then serving President of the OAU.

Our delegation had asked me if I would speak for them at the meeting. We did not expect the President to be conversant with the issues, so we kept the conversation at a general level. I thanked President Amin on behalf of the group, told him we recognized his greatness and his great contribution to African unity. We hoped that on this occasion he would give his fullest possible backing to the mission and help us in any way he could. He agreed and we ended on a pleasant note. We toasted each other and he left the room.

At the conclusion of the meeting with President Amin, the Protocol Officer took us back to the VIP lounge at the airport. We did not want to check into a hotel since we were leaving at 4:30 or five o'clock that afternoon to go by Ethiopian Airlines to Ghana. We were comfortable, except for our uneasiness about the situation with the Asians who were trying to leave the country and had been waiting for several days to achieve this.

When the time was drawing near for the aircraft to arrive, I went to the check-in desk on my own initiative to confirm that there were seven of us in the lounge with first class reservations on the flight to Ghana. We simply wished to know that we could be boarded at the appropriate time.

The airline representative said that there was absolutely no room on the flight and we were not the only people with confirmed reservations who were waiting to board, some for more than a day. Although we had tickets, there were no reservations.

I returned to the lounge and reported to my colleagues on the outcome of my conversation with the airlines ticket counter. As we were discussing the matter, the Protocol Officer arrived and we told him about the situation. He immediately repudiated what the airlines representative had said. He told us not to worry and that he was ready to take us now to the aircraft. We went and he led us right through, no boarding passes or immigrations procedures, up the stairs and into the first class cabin. There were seven vacant seats. We sat down, got ready and the flight took off. But we noticed great hostility on the part of the cabin staff. I said to the steward: 'Excuse me, you haven't even offered us a drink, a glass of water, asked us if we're comfortable.'

He said: 'We are furious, sir!'

'Why?'

'Because the Ugandan government, without any consultation, removed from the flight eight passengers from Mobil Oil, who were on their way to Ghana on business, in order to make sure that you had seats. They were coming from Ethiopia and they're stranded now in Uganda. The government officials there told them: "Get off the flight. This has been booked for some very distinguished diplomats and representatives. The government of Uganda would be highly embarrassed if they were not on the flight." So the businessmen had to get off.'

On receiving this information, we were highly embarrassed and felt very badly, but could not do anything about it.

In every place that we visited, after the formalities were over, we discussed the proposed agreement with Europe and what the implications were for each country, as far as we knew. At all our visits, we presented the country concerned with an aide memoire summarizing our understandings and agreements.

We met with the head of state in every country as a courtesy, although there was not much of an exchange of views at that level, except in Ghana where we met with President Rawlings. While we were in Accra he invited us to his home for drinks in the evening. President Rawlings was very interested in the Lomé Convention, asked us a lot of questions and obviously wanted to be involved. We found him to be one of the more responsive people. He said Ghana would be 100 per cent behind the Caribbean on this matter. We also had that assurance from the Ugandans, though from one of his permanent secretaries, not from the President himself.

Every day I had the responsibility of organizing the technical presentation wherever we went, and then I had to prepare the mission notes that eventually would have to go back to the governments. I remember that in Nigeria I was so tired that I missed the official function given for us. I told them: 'I can't go any further. I'm going to bed.'

Most Nigerian officials had a very good grasp of the substantive issues so it was an exchange of views there more than our presentation. In sum, we had a highly successful visit. Everywhere we had to do the same thing, go through all the issues in considerable detail and get their responses.

Participation in Lomé I negotiations in Brussels, 1973

The CARICOM Council of Ministers had a meeting in Georgetown to agree on the official position that we had been articulating. It was agreed that the ministers together with the officials, some of whom had been participating in the preparatory work, should constitute the delegation to the negotiating conference in Brussels. I got to Georgetown only to pack my bags again and head off, this

Figure 8 In conversation with Hon. Prime Minister Michael Manley on the occasion of receiving the Order of Merit with another recipient and recipients of other honours.

time with Sonny Ramphal, who was then the Minister of Foreign Affairs in Guyana. We went on the same flight to Brussels.

When we got there, we discovered that the English-speaking countries joining the group had been able to persuade the francophone countries to let Nigeria be the spokesman, because Nigeria was the largest country. Numerically, the English-speaking countries were now greater than the francophone. The latter countries could therefore not object to that arrangement. Trying to make contacts with the officials we had met in Africa, since most of them were there, I got in touch with the Nigerian delegate, whom I knew quite well because we were at the LSE together. I called him and said: 'What's the position. We'd like to know. You're speaking first, Africa, then the Caribbean and then the Pacific. We'd like to get an idea of what you want to say, so that we could finesse our speech accordingly, since the conference opens tomorrow.'

'Alister, I have news for you.'

'What?'

'We have no speech. We've been struggling to try to put together a speech and we haven't managed to do so.'

I said: 'Good heavens! OK, I'm going to get Ramphal and we'll come over to have a drink with the minister and yourself.' The name of his minister was Colonel Briggs.

Sonny had been appointed the spokesperson for the English-speaking CARICOM countries. So I went to him and said: 'The Africans do not yet have a speech, so why not offer our speech to them as coming from the group as a whole?' He was surprised, but eventually saw merit in the idea as a sign of ACP solidarity.

We spoke with Minister Briggs, who said: 'We're still drafting, you know. We're not ready to talk.'

So Sonny said (nonchalantly): 'Look, we have a bit of a draft. We've kind of put together something and rather than put you to the trouble of having to spend your whole evening drafting, would you consider accepting our draft as the draft for everyone? To tell you the truth, we feel strongly there should be a single spokesperson from the ACP group to demonstrate to the Europeans our unity and towards that end, we offer our speech as a contribution, but we'd be very happy if Nigeria made the speech on behalf of all of us.'

Minister Briggs was delighted. We left the speech with him, and he told us later that he had read it from cover to cover.

The next day, he delivered the speech and it clearly had the intended result of surprise. The Europeans were troubled. When it was announced that the minister from Nigeria would speak on behalf of the African group of Associable Countries, Colonel Briggs got up and said: 'Yes, Mr Chairman, but I speak not on behalf of the African group, but on behalf of the African, Caribbean, and Pacific group of Associables.'

You could have heard a pin drop in the room! They were completely taken aback, not least, of course, by the content of the speech, which was not what they were hoping the Africans would present. So that changed the tone of the meeting immediately! There was evidently great support among the English-speaking delegations from the ACP countries for the Nigerian statement. However, the French-speaking Africans had difficulties, largely because it diverged from the content and tone of the speech that they had presented for their group.

Senegal and the Ivory Coast were furious, and said that the English-speaking Africans had allowed themselves to be duped by the Caribbean. They were not going to spend their time here just discussing sugar, bananas and rum. They had other issues. They already had a good arrangement with Europe and did not want too much interference with that arrangement, so their attitude was extremely negative. But Nigeria said: 'Look, we want a meeting of all of the African states with the Caribbean and the Pacific.'

Ghana came out in support of Nigeria and thus the de facto ACP group emerged, African, Caribbean and Pacific. At the meeting we said: 'As far as we are concerned, we are willing to go along with the English-speaking African countries and we suggest that we have one spokesperson. We suggest that everywhere, on every subject that we have to speak, there's a single spokesperson from this group.'

But that was a shock for the Europeans. I remember afterwards that the European ministers castigated their commission for not knowing that this was going to happen. Some of the commission staff later told us: 'You got us into trouble that evening. All our ministers wanted to know why we were not aware that this "unity" was taking place.' Yes, you could have heard a pin drop in the room.

In relation to trade, Sonny Ramphal and P.J. Patterson led the Caribbean presentations. The Africans were assigned responsibility for all the discussions on financial aid. I was there along with Frank Rampersad, a Trinidadian colleague who was a senior member in the Commonwealth secretariat, to provide support as required.

The CARICOM ministerial team consisted of Sonny Ramphal from Guyana, P.J. Patterson from Jamaica, Errol Mahabir from Trinidad and Tobago, Branford Taitt from Barbados and Derek Knight from the OECS. They assumed that I was their chief advisor. Initially, this led to some discussion among the ambassadors and senior civil servants from the CARICOM countries as to what their role was, in relation to mine. Jamaica and Trinidad and Tobago were particularly concerned. The matter was clarified by the ministers, led by P.J. Patterson, that I was the Chief Technical Advisor for CARICOM, without prejudice to the ambassadors from member states of CARICOM. I had done a study for UNCTAD, which had been published, on trade preferences between France and the francophone countries and the English-speaking Caribbean. I had also done the study for the Commonwealth secretariat on the question of Britain's entry into the EEC and its implications for the developing Commonwealth countries.

However, some of the civil servants felt that their status was somehow being diminished by my coming on the scene. They were representing their countries in Brussels and it was their job to do it. They felt that the ministers just took me from the university to be the spokesperson. So they decided to blank me out in the sense that none of the documents from the EEC came to me. The documents all went to the various missions, and they in turn prepared briefs for their ministers. I was sitting in the hotel doing nothing.

I did not know at first that this was happening. But I decided to find out what was going on and I asked Laurence Mann, the ambassador from Guyana, what the position was. He told me. He did not agree but this is what they were going to do.

I said; 'OK.' So I went, invited to a meeting of the Caribbean delegation when the ministers were there. Either Sonny or PJ was chairing the meeting and the diplomats said: 'Well, where do we go from here?'

PJ said: 'Alister, would you take us through this?'

'Take you through what?' I said. 'I haven't seen a single paper. Ask your ambassadors. They have taken the view, which I suppose has merit, that they are here to be your diplomatic representatives and advisors and I am intruding in the whole thing. I would be happy to be helpful in any way I can, but as a matter of fact, if you are well staffed with ambassadors, what am I doing here? I have a lot of work to do in Jamaica. I have no intention of wasting the university's money sitting around to listen to a dialogue between yourself and your ambassadors. I think it only fair that I return to Jamaica.'

Well, the ministers responded angrily. They said: 'How dare you fellows sit down and sabotage the arrangement we have made? This is the man who took you all through Africa and had to explain everything to the African countries and now you want to carry on in this way? We will not have it and we are telling you now that he is the Chief Technical Advisor for CARICOM and any technical advice that we want we are going to get from him. So if you don't want to work with him, maybe it is time you go.'

This was reinforced by an understanding reached between the ministers and the Vice-Chancellor of the UWI. He had expressed his desire to be as supportive as possible in settling any details of the assignment that required my presence in Brussels. That was how the matter was settled. So it was a very awkward situation, I must say.

These meetings lasted about six weeks, after I had spent a similar period on the mission to Africa, and my health still had not recovered fully, though I had stopped smoking. I tried to absent myself from all social functions and only went to the meetings where my presence was thought to be essential, because I was worried about my health. When I arrived in Brussels, I spoke to the hotel concierge, who identified an English-speaking cardiologist who would be at my disposal should I need a doctor. Fortunately, I never did.

Lomé I negotiations in Brussels through the latter part of 1974

Following upon my initial visit to Brussels for these negotiations, I assumed the post as Secretary-General of CARICOM in Guyana in September 1974. Throughout the time I was at CARICOM I worked on the Lomé Convention because it really developed momentum in 1975–76. We definitely made a breakthrough with the first Lomé Convention.

After it had become clear that the negotiations with Europe would be prolonged and substantial because we were negotiating a completely new treaty, the CARICOM Heads of Government decided to formalize all the arrangements that had been put in place. They set up a ministerial group and a technical working party of officials, which I chaired as Secretary-General of CARICOM.

The technical group consisted of one member each from Barbados, Guyana, Jamaica, Trinidad and Tobago, the Windward Islands, the Leeward Islands and the Caribbean Development Bank, so seven or eight people – a small enough group that you could call them at short notice. They knew each other, so those who could not come would call me and say: 'Look, we're discussing so and so. I can't come but this is the position of the government. If anyone objects, let me know.' The rapport was extremely good.

Special commendation must be accorded to P.J. Patterson and Sonny Ramphal who were the principal leaders in the negotiations. Unfortunately, many of the others who were involved have since died.

Our technical team used to meet in Georgetown to examine strategy and get clearance from the group of ministers handling EU matters in the region and the negotiations, which were prolonged but eventually we thought were very successful.

I would sometimes initiate the process by travelling to Brussels and gathering together the officials who were involved. Whenever we were ready, we called the ministers to discuss particular subjects coming up for negotiation. We were briefed on every single aspect of that draft convention so that any of us at meetings in Brussels could speak on anything because we all had the dossiers and were very well prepared.

The Europeans had created an elaborate machinery for the negotiations, including a large number of negotiating committees. When the ACP group was identifying negotiators, they had drawn on a wide cohort of ministers from different countries. In the case of the subjects assigned to CARICOM, the Community fell short of the number of ministers required.

The Europeans had said: 'We want a discussion and a negotiation on the monetary arrangements and we want it now.' The negotiations were at a very advanced stage and the CARICOM ministers were fully engaged with their respective assignments.

In the circumstances, they hit on the idea of designating me as a principal negotiator, but I pointed out to them immediately that I did not have the ministerial status required. In response, some of them indicated that they would, nonetheless, designate me as such and get confirmation from their capitals. So for a little while I was a minister and designated as the negotiator on monetary arrangements. My European counterpart was the Prime Minister of Luxembourg. However, some of the officials in CARICOM were very concerned about this apparent breach of protocol. They said that we should have tried to get a minister and should not mislead the Community. In fact, after it was finished, the CARICOM ministers said that they would get the Heads of Government to agree that the CARICOM Secretary-General should have ministerial status. They did not!

As far as those negotiations were concerned, we have seen that the French had their own arrangements with the Africans while the English-speaking Africans had no kind of monetary union. Things became complicated when my counterpart negotiator, who seemed to be impressed with my grasp of the subject being negotiated, invited me to prepare the draft of the outcome of our negotiations.

'Could I have a secretary?'

And I went into an adjoining room, dictated something, cleaned it up, brought it back, he initialled it, I initialled it, and we had an agreement.

The country with which I worked best was Ghana, worked best at the official level that is, and the ministerial level too. I also worked well with Nigeria, but Nigerians are a little bit sensitive on protocol issues, who is a minister and who is not a minister and all that sort of thing. But I got on well with them because on the technical issues they relied on me to provide the necessary advice. My relations with some of the delegates were formed while we were undergraduates at the LSE. Some of them rose to very high ranks in their respective governments, including one who became a head of state.

Notwithstanding the complexity of the group in terms of differences in economic situation and negotiation priorities, we managed over the period of the negotiations to reconcile different interests and come up with a group position on all of them.

It began as a very hard negotiation. The Europeans punished the Caribbean by settling all the other issues except ours. They must have found out what we had done on the question of ACP unity.

But the fact of the matter was that we were approaching the end of the negotiations, and everything else was settled except sugar, rum and bananas, which were the Caribbean products. The European side had problems. According to one account they could not make contact with the French President whom they wanted to approve the changes being proposed to settle the outstanding matters in the agreement, all of major interest to the Caribbean. We were getting worried because the Africans had all their issues settled and were finished.

The European countries insisted on calling the final plenary but they could not get the ACP group to agree to do this. Eventually, they succeeded in pressuring us to accept their proposal to convene the plenary, and we then informed the chief Nigerian negotiator that it was unlikely that we would join the agreement because none of our issues on bananas and rum had been accommodated. In turn, Colonel Briggs discussed the matter with the other ACP heads of delegation, and they agreed not to accept the draft agreement without settling the issues on bananas and rum. This decision caused considerable consternation among the European delegations. A final effort was made by the French to contact their president in Paris because it was they who had the major reservations about those commodities. That effort succeeded and the EU was ultimately able to provide an acceptable settlement.

The Lomé Convention was one of those events in my life that I would consider a great success. I was very proud of the achievement of CARIFTA/CARICOM in negotiating its first international trade and economic agreement in a situation where our delegations were highly respected on both sides. I was proud of Lomé I, but it was a long, ongoing affair that was not implemented until April 1976. After that, it meant that three years later we had to negotiate the successor agreement, Lomé II, January 1981–85. Altogether I enjoyed the Lomé negotiations very much and learnt a great deal from them.

Lomé II and Lomé III

When the second Lomé negotiations came around in 1979, I was at UNCTAD in Geneva. I told CARICOM that I could not be involved in the negotiations, but I would arrange for technical assistance. There was a Dominican working at the UNCTAD secretariat under a temporary UNDP contract, and I asked him whether he would be interested in going to Brussels under an extension of his contract to give ongoing advice to the ACP group for the period during which Lomé II was being negotiated.

He agreed and did a thoroughly good job. The ACP delegations in Brussels were very pleased with his work.

Lomé III was agreed in March 1985 for trade and in May 1986 for aid. I did not participate in these negotiations nor in those of Lomé IV, which were perhaps the most substantial of all.

Lomé IV 1989–99

I regard the negotiation of Lomé IV as Sonny Ramphal's finest moment. From a textual point of view, based on the brief that was provided for him by the CARICOM secretariat, we got everything that we had asked for in Lomé IV.

The Europeans wanted to have terminal arrangements with sugar and bananas. We got good terminal arrangements, good in the sense that they looked good at the time with the amount of money that was supposed to be paid to sugar farmers and to get farmers resettled into other crops.

During Lomé I we broke the ice. As I said, the French had been having these Yaoundé Conventions with the francophone African countries and were very fixed in their views as to what should be done, and they were then the most influential member state in the Europe of the Six. The British had come on board but it was thought that they were viewed with some suspicion by the other five. In certain circles, they were not thought to be Europeans and so they could only help at the margins. Politically, the other Europeans were not thought to be well disposed towards the developing countries. France was in tune with their line of political thinking, but on development issues were prepared to go some distance because of their colonial links with Africa. The views of the Germans coincided only to a very limited extent. The Dutch were sympathetic but not very influential. So there was quite a struggle among the Six.

As previously explained, forming the ACP group came about because the non-francophone African countries joined the agreement, particularly Nigeria and Ghana, who came with a completely different view of development co-operation; Nigeria especially was very influential. The ACP group came to the negotiations with a menu that was quite different to what the Europeans expected and they blamed us in the Caribbean for having done it.

The outcome of Lomé IV was that the Europeans negotiated a separate agreement – an Economic Partnership Agreement (EPA) – with CARICOM to implement its provisions, separate and apart from the agreements that were proposed for the other two regional groupings.

That Economic Partnership Agreement negotiated in 1994 with the Europeans was unsatisfactory to some Caribbean countries. That happened because there were too many changes in the arrangements. There were also many changes in personnel. There were a lot of outside pressures and I think the CARICOM representatives agreed to matters that they should not have accepted. However, there are mixed views in the region about these questions.

In some circles, it was questioned whether the Europeans were attempting to follow a strategy of divide and conquer. When I was consulted on the matter, I urged caution on the part of CARICOM. I reminded them of the importance of unity among the ACP countries from the time of the first agreement. However, insufficient attention was paid to these warnings, partly because of the anxiety among some of the technical advisors and the ministerial leadership to conclude the agreement as quickly as possible. CARICOM ended up negotiating alone for the first time. As a result, CARICOM agreed on a number of important provisions that were premature. Taking a long view of the matter, one wonders whether the Europeans considered the concessions then offered to CARICOM as a price worth paying to secure the end of the ACP as a unified group.

As far as I am aware, we are the only sub-region that has signed with the Europeans. The Africans indicated that they were not ready to conclude a new agreement. From the available information, it appears that East Africa, West Africa and the Pacific have not signed, and in the meantime, the Europeans have given them further concessions.

Actually, what happened in Lomé IV so far as the Caribbean was concerned was that in the implementation phase of the agreement the EU insisted that they wanted to treat the Caribbean as a whole. Accordingly, they wanted to negotiate with CARIFORUM, which was CARICOM plus the non-English-speaking countries, Haiti and the Dominican Republic.

On the other hand, CARICOM wanted all members of the agreement to be part of CARICOM. Haiti has since become a member of CARICOM but the Dominican Republic has not; they are still hanging on to the CARIFORUM arrangement, which in effect allows the EU to give the Dominican Republic a special status. The Dominican Republic left no one with any doubt that they felt that as the largest country they should be leading the group. I understood where they were coming from, because they got on very well with the Europeans, with the Spanish, in particular, pushing very hard for them.

Spain was assigned the post of Commissioner-General for Development, so they were then in charge of formulating development policies in the EU Commission, including the allocation of aid. Of course the Dominican Republic was first on the track to be recipients of aid to the region.

To some extent, it was CARICOM's fault that this occurred. The secretariat mismanaged it at a certain point, and the Dominican Republic was able to argue successfully that their development assistance from the Europeans was not being well managed by the CARICOM secretariat. Because CARICOM insisted on a regional allocation and regional administration, the actual management of the development assistance was then shifted to Santo Domingo. So we lost out on that.

Only time will tell whether it would be possible to find other arrangements with the African and Pacific countries where the convention would offer a promising opening for solidifying economic relationships between the Caribbean and the other ACP countries.

In retrospect, I would say that the Lomé relationship was a very significant part of my career, since I devoted a lot of time, thought and effort to it.

Service with the Commonwealth

While I was Secretary-General of CARICOM I was asked to undertake, as part of my regional responsibilities, a very important assignment as Chairman of the Commonwealth Group of Eminent Persons on the New International Economic Order (NIEO).

The NIEO came to international attention during the Sixth Special Session of the UN General Assembly in New York, 9 April–2 May 1974. There was considerable political ferment among delegates from the developing countries, who were pressing for discussions about negotiations for an NIEO. They had long put forward the view that the existing order had been developed without sufficient consideration of their situation in the world. Bretton Woods had largely been negotiated between Europe and North America. The whole division of leadership was settled by a comparatively small number of countries. It was then agreed that the World Bank would be headed by an American, the IMF by a

European and the United Nations by one of the smaller developed countries.

The GATT had been an outgrowth of that, as in fact had been the whole postwar architecture for the management of the world economy. The developing countries maintained that they were not sufficiently involved because, at that time, most of them were colonies. They insisted that it was now their time to be involved because of the shift that was occurring in the world as a result of the oil price increases that had altered the comparative resource position of the two groups of countries in their favour.

They argued this position with great force and in the face of strong opposition from the more conservative among the developed countries, principally the United States, Britain and Western Europe. Northern Europe was somewhat more flexible because they tended to be sympathetic towards the developing countries and the claims that were being advanced by them.

Commonwealth Prime Ministers' meeting, April 1975

Prime Minister Michael Manley, along with his other Caribbean colleagues, thought that the opportunity of the Commonwealth Prime Ministers' meeting being held in Jamaica should be used to advance the idea of negotiating the NIEO. In prior consultation with his Caribbean colleagues, principally Prime Ministers Burnham and Barrow, they decided to push for the NIEO agenda, knowing that they had a friend in Pierre Trudeau, Prime Minister of Canada. There was some uncertainty about Prime Minister Malcolm Fraser of Australia, but he ended up with the progressive leaders.

Some of the Commonwealth Heads of Government from the developing countries said that this was the time to press for negotiations because of the ambience in which the present meeting was taking place. It was thought that countries such as Britain and Australia could be persuaded to support any proposals brought forward about commencing work on the NIEO negotiations. It was considered that Prime Minister Harold Wilson was intellectually with the developing countries and had in fact come to the conference with a proposal on buffer stocks for commodities.

The way the Commonwealth Heads of Government Conference is organised, the first day of the conference is devoted to what is called 'the economic debate'. At the time of the 1975 meeting I was Secretary-General of CARICOM. I got a call from Sonny Ramphal, Guyana's Foreign Minister, who told me that, in informal conversation, the Caribbean Heads had decided to ask William Demas and myself to come to the conference to assist Prime Minister Burnham with the text of his speech, in his capacity as the region's spokesman in the economic debate. To facilitate our arrival, they sent an aircraft to Trinidad to take us to Jamaica.

On our arrival, I spoke again with Ramphal and we agreed that we should meet, draft the speech and deliver it to Prime Minister Burnham's hotel room. We worked for the better part of the night and slipped the text under the door of his hotel room at about 3:30 am.

The next morning when we attended the conference, we found that Prime Minister Burnham made no use of our draft and we were somewhat perplexed about the situation.

The speech he did deliver seemed to appeal to some of the leaders, but Willie and I thought it contained too much rhetoric and too little substance. Accordingly, the quality of the economic debate suffered because it lacked sufficient direction.

Willie and I were concerned and went to see Sonny Ramphal to discuss what could be done to rectify the situation. However, Sonny said: 'Let us move on because I have been called to some private consultations. The Canadians seem to be developing a proposal. I spoke with Ivan Head [who was then Prime Minister Trudeau's chief of staff] and he has asked me to come to a meeting. I want you fellows to come too.'

The Canadians indicated some concern about the big divide between North and South that had been apparent during the Sixth Session of the United Nations General Assembly. They considered that the occasion of the Heads of Government Conference could be used as an opportunity to agree on an initiative that would be directed towards reducing the tension that had arisen. The Commonwealth was a group that contained representatives of both sides. An attempt should therefore be made to find a middle way between the two positions. The idea emerged of a group of eminent persons on the New International Economic Order which would try to identify possible common ground between North and South.

A member of the British delegation whom I knew – I think we were at Oxford together – met me in the conference hotel and said that his prime minister was insistent on putting up a proposal for an international buffer stock of commodities. He indicated that they needed an input from the Caribbean, and from myself in particular.

As requested, I prepared for the meeting, but heard nothing from the delegation. I decided to check with my friend and he indicated that he and his colleagues were perplexed because, without any explanation, the Prime Minister had indicated that he did not wish to spend any further time on this matter and they should submit the draft in its present form.

As directed, the members of the delegation put the unfinished proposal before the conference. But it did not attract any attention. What we did not know was that Prime Minister Wilson had gone back to London for unforeseen medical attention. Later on, we heard that he had resigned and been succeeded by James Callaghan.

The concept that Prime Minister Wilson had hoped to promote came very close to the position being taken by developing countries in the UN/UNCTAD for a system of international buffer stocks. Prime Minister Wilson's proposal was of long standing, since he had developed the idea when he was an academic at Oxford.

As indicated elsewhere, there was at the time an existing buffer stock in cocoa, and as a prelude to the discussions described in the next chapter, at the time of the Commonwealth Heads of Government Conference discussions were already in train about creating stocks of other commodities. At UNCTAD IV, the relevant producing and consuming countries reached agreement to set up a buffer stock for natural rubber. In the end, it became the only buffer stock that was successfully negotiated because of the strong support provided by the US to the scheme, presumably because of their desire to be particularly supportive of the South East Asian producing countries.

The British proposal at the Commonwealth meeting failed because the Canadian proposal was more inclusive and more in keeping with the proposal made by developing countries at UNCTAD IV.

At the Commonwealth HOG meeting, the particular issue of buffer stocking was referred to the Group of Eminent Persons for consideration as part of the consolidated list of measures that were being proposed for further work by the group.

Chairman, Commonwealth Group of Eminent Persons to examine proposals for an NIEO

During the Heads of Government Conference I heard that I was going to be proposed right then at the conference as Chairman of the Group of Eminent Persons to examine proposals for the NIEO. The CARICOM Heads of Government indicated their interest in my accepting the assignment. I hesitated initially because of the implications for management of the secretariat in Georgetown, but the Heads felt that it was simply a matter of my assigning interim responsibility to my deputy. The chairmanship of the Group of Eminent Persons represented a great opportunity for the Caribbean to involve itself at the UN in the leadership of the developing countries.

On reflection, I accepted the appointment as chairman of the group because it was apparent that the Caribbean HOG considered it to be an important part of my responsibilities as Secretary-General of CARICOM. The big item at the conference was the appointment of Sonny Ramphal as Secretary-General of the Commonwealth, and I felt assured that he would give us his leadership in the work of the Eminent Persons Group. He did not disappoint us.

In short order, Ramphal took up his position in London and indicated that one of the first things he wanted to do was to launch the Group of Eminent Persons as a matter of top priority. Accordingly, he was urging me to go to London because he was finalizing the list of persons. He had got nominations from different countries and wanted my advice so that the final membership of the group could be settled.

Based on consultations with the Commonwealth Heads, it was decided that the Secretary-General should name a group of ten people. On my first visit to London, we agreed on the membership of the group. I did not myself know most of them, but was glad to see that the Nigerian representative was a good friend from LSE days, Adebola Onitiri, the Director of the Nigerian Institute of Social and Economic Research, with whom, as I have already mentioned, I had remained in contact. He himself had visited the UWI, but I had not yet managed to schedule a visit to Ibadan.

As far as the rest of the group was concerned, I knew some of them by reputation, but had not yet met them personally.

We had an organizational meeting in London and the first substantive meeting in Ottawa. We ran into all sorts of difficulties – one of these was with the secretary of the group, who had been seconded from the UK Treasury. It appeared that his perception was that, following upon our discussions, he would write the report and just present it for our signatures. So during our meeting he kept saying that his time was limited and that we were talking too much. I responded by telling him that in these initial contacts we had to give every member of the group sufficient opportunity to express themselves on the issues. It was my job to see where the differences among the members lay and to develop proposals for reconciling them. Indeed, we had extremely enlightening exchanges; the areas of consensus became evident as well as the openings there were to resolve differences. I felt strongly that we had to give the members every chance to settle issues among themselves.

A good opportunity presented itself for the members to exchange off the record views about areas where a consensus on the substantive issues seemed to be imminent. The High Commissioner for Malaysia in Ottawa visited me and said that he would like to invite the group to his residence. I seized the opportunity as providing some space for informal exchanges to achieve a meeting of minds. I also concluded that this would give me some space to prepare a working draft for discussion after the group had reconvened.

Accordingly, I remained in the hotel and wrote the draft report. My secretary, Sheila Chang, worked very hard to prepare the draft so that when the group returned they were able to find it slipped under the doors of their hotel room. On the following morning, when we reconvened, members of the group were, by and large, satisfied with the draft. Their job therefore really became one of fine tuning by agreeing on any further amendments required.

But the secretary was highly offended, and felt that the group, led by me, had essentially done his job. He submitted his resignation, which I accepted after consultation with the Commonwealth Secretary-General, who found as a replacement a very accomplished economist on secondment to London from Trinidad and Tobago. This substantially simplified the completion of the draft and thereafter the very smooth functioning of the group itself.

During the Ottawa meeting I received valuable assistance from the Prime Minister's Office. Prime Minister Trudeau was very interested in the work of the Group of Eminent Persons and made available Ivan Head, special assistant in his office, to help us in sorting out any difficulties that occurred.

One of the problems that had to be resolved was what recommendation the group would make concerning a target for official development assistance. The target then was 0.7 per cent of GDP, but we wished to propose an increase to 1 per cent of GDP. We were aware that proposals along those lines were being strongly resisted in the UN and other forums, but we felt that an increase at that time was justified, given the difficult situation facing a large number of developing countries because of the negative changes in world oil markets and in the international economic situation as a whole.

The Canadian representative on the group was generally a flexible person, but he indicated firmly that he could not associate himself with the proposal on aid. On our side, we felt that we should exercise strong powers of persuasion to encourage Canada to support the proposal. As a result of our contacts through Ivan Head in the Prime Minister's Office, we were able to get an instruction to the Canadian representative to support the increase. Accordingly, we achieved a consensus on the figure of 1 per cent, but the Canadian officials, other than Head, were most reluctant to break rank with the official OECD position.

In recognition of the difficulties that the Canadian representative was experiencing, the Prime Minister's Office advised their Foreign Office to relieve him of attendance at the group when it was settling the issue of development assistance. Apart from this, he was an extremely helpful and constructive member of the group.

Apart from the organizational meeting in London and the substantive meeting in Ottawa, the Group of Eminent Persons also had a second meeting in London and a further substantive meeting in Ibadan, arising from a specific invitation made by the Nigerian representative Adebola Onitiri. Unfortunately, our visit to Ibadan coincided with a very unfavourable spell of weather caused by the Harmattan wind, which curtailed the length of the discussions.

Accordingly, we decided to complete our work in one day so that we could return to our respective capitals. This was an unwelcome occurrence since so much effort had been made to arrange for our meeting and related hospitality. I was particularly regretful because I had hoped to use the opportunity to spend time at the University of Ibadan campus, with which we at the UWI had very important relations.

After the meeting in Nigeria, I decided that we had enough material for our report and further meetings were not warranted in the light of the timetable before us. We were to present our findings in time for the Commonwealth Heads of Government meeting that was, at that time, scheduled to be held in London. The Commonwealth Heads meet every two years – they met in 1975 in Kingston and in 1977 in London. Secretary-General Sonny Ramphal was pressing to have the final report ready for the London meeting. We did succeed in doing this, and by that time the atmosphere of controversy had somewhat abated, which seemed to coincide with the chairman's own predilections. The report was warmly accepted without reservation.

As far as discussions about the NIEO were concerned, it was agreed among the major OECD and OPEC countries that they should meet in Paris under the auspices of the OECD to exchange views on the subject as a means of advancing consideration of the matter in the United Nations. Accordingly, the Conference for International Economic Cooperation (CIEC) was subsequently held in Paris. It was said to be the idea of Dr Henry Kissinger to take the discussion of the NIEO out of the UN and to have a select group of northern countries meet with OPEC to discuss possible avenues for an understanding of how they would proceed. The OPEC countries were under pressure to have some non-OPEC countries invited to the meeting. They put pressure upon the OECD and the latter invited some non-aligned countries, of which Jamaica was one. These countries believed, in hindsight naively, that the OPEC countries would take a strong stand and insist on acceptance of all of the concessions being sought by the developing countries. It did not happen because the balance of interests was much more delicate than the developing countries realized. Accordingly, OPEC as a group were not in a position to give enthusiastic support to the developing countries. Some of the non-aligned countries were very disappointed at the results of the meeting and, as a consequence, they tried to switch the discussion back to the General Assembly.

It was at UNCTAD IV in Nairobi in May 1976 that Dr Kissinger made a concession. He announced that the US would agree to negotiate an integrated programme of commodities as part of a package of proposals in the field of development support, and this would include a common fund that would provide financing for buffer stocking of an agreed list of 18 commodities.

The General Assembly had been discussing all these issues ad nauseam and were tired. By the time the final report of the Eminent Persons Group was produced, there was no eagerness to get back to these issues. Some perfunctory gestures of support were made for the ideas in it, but the final report had little impact. So that was the end of the Group of Eminent Persons.

However, as a sequel, I heard later on that some people said that the Commonwealth Group was trying to disrupt the Third World and was promoting division by providing support for some aspects of the northern position. As a result, the Group of 77 developing nations refused to receive our Interim Commonwealth Report.

I consulted Sonny Ramphal and, after discussion, I suggested that we should arrange for copies of the report to be placed in the letter box of every delegation at the UN. After many of the delegates read the report, they realized that it was basically a somewhat modified, softer position on all the principal issues and that it might have the elements of a compromise. The Scandinavians, Dutch and French were supporting it because they saw it as a serious document that they should not reject and it might provide a way forward. Of course the British and Canadians were obliged to support it since they were part of the Group of Eminent Persons. There was therefore valuable support for the report among the developed countries, who faced the dilemma of choosing the Commonwealth proposals against the proposals of an alternative economic order that Dr Kissinger had placed on the table.

His proposals had some positive elements. In fact, if they had been agreed, the developing countries would possibly have been much better off than they are today. The US did not accept the 1 per cent aid target because it was difficult to get change on development assistance owing to the complexities of congressional politics.

The OECD (Group B) countries could not come out and declare their acceptance of the Commonwealth proposal, but they began passing the message that they would not oppose it if it was proposed as a solution by the developing countries.

However, it was never formally presented to the General Assembly because no one wanted to sponsor it, although there was considerable support in the corridors from both sides. The American proposal was not accepted and the Commonwealth proposal, *Towards a New International Economic Order*, was never put forward.

As to whether anything out of the report has been implemented, certainly the commodities aspect was put into action, albeit in a very truncated form that was not the fault of the Commonwealth. That is the reality of the international community.

The Non-Aligned Group

The concept of the New International Economic Order owed its origins basically to Algeria and Yugoslavia and, to a lesser extent, India. CARICOM prime ministers, particularly Prime Ministers Burnham and Manley, were major supporters. There was a critical meeting of the leadership of the Group of 77 in 1974 and Algeria was able to influence all the OPEC countries – who were not interested in the reform of the Economic Order but wanted links with the developing countries in order to secure their support for their pricing policies on oil. In addition, they wanted to extend their collective influence, not just as a result of developing countries protesting the high price of oil. That would have been inconvenient but would not affect the strategic interest of support for the Arab/Muslim cause in the General Assembly and similar forums. In some circles it was argued at that time that the support of the Group of 77 for OPEC was not so much economic as political. It was then alleged by critics that this was why OPEC paid attention to the Non-Aligned Group, because they were separate groups.

The Non-Aligned Group was political and that remained their principal focus, although they now deal with economic issues. It was started by President Nkrumah in Ghana, Prime Minister Bandaranaike in Sri Lanka and others. But it preceded the Group of 77, which started in 1964. UNCTAD I was meeting and the Group of 77 coalesced around the time of UNCTAD I. The Non-Aligned Group was in existence when I was an undergraduate in the 1950s, and therefore most of the OPEC countries tended to be non-aligned in the sense in which the term was understood at the time: as countries not allied to any of the major world powers. The Non-Aligned Group was political, but the Group of 77 was essentially economic.

I was very sceptical about a number of things in the Group of 77 and the NIEO. I was intellectually in favour of reform of the international system and thought originally the idea of buffer stocks warranted serious examination. There were buffer stocks in existence then, cocoa and tin, and I know a number of other people were discussing rubber, which eventually was the first agreement I serviced in Geneva. So I was in favour of stabilizing commodity prices, which is not anything out of the ordinary.

I would never go against an increase in development assistance if that could be arranged. There were some elements of it which instinctively commanded my support, but there were other proposals that had not been well thought out and required further work.

Of course, while I was still engaged in work on a New International Economic Order, I had at the same time, as Secretary-General of CARICOM, to keep my finger on matters under consideration there, where the Food Plan was supposed to emerge. However, as explained earlier, it was not emerging and finally collapsed because of the Williams/Manley/Burnham disagreement.

Interim Project Director, action programme for economic co-operation

While I was Secretary-General of CARICOM, I was persuaded by President Burnham and the Foreign Minister at the time, Sonny Ramphal, to assist them in implementing their responsibilities as members of the Non-Aligned Group. Guyana was asked to assume responsibility for a project on economic co-operation among the member countries that the UNDP had agreed to finance. The President and Foreign Minister appealed to me to take the project into my charge on an interim basis until they could find the right persons to assume full responsibility for it. I was very reluctant to do so as I was fully engaged with running the CARICOM secretariat and did not wish to add to my responsibilities at that stage. However, I understood the significance of the project for CARICOM and the unfortunate consequences that would arise should Guyana find itself unable to exercise its responsibilities for project delivery. Accordingly, I agreed that, notwithstanding my full desk at CARICOM, I would take on the project on a strictly interim basis while efforts were made to put a permanent head in place. The UNDP was aware of the staffing deficiencies in Georgetown, but could only find a young research assistant to work with me. Unfortunately, the arrangements for the establishment of a secretariat for the Non-Aligned project were never completed. The project was eventually returned to UNDP headquarters but no further information is available on it.

10

Working at the United Nations

International service

From the very beginning of thinking about career opportunities, I was attracted to the possibilities of developing my work on the Caribbean within a global environment. Indeed, this had influenced my choice of International Economics as the special subject in my undergraduate degree at the London School of Economics.

I had always started out with the proposition that, given the very small size of the Caribbean, one should approach the issue of its development within a global context. This was not a concession to notions of dependency but rather an interest in seeing how very small countries like the Caribbean could navigate within the world to take advantage of external opportunities for their development. From that perspective, the United Nations appeared as a vital link in the pursuit of development opportunities. Accordingly, once I began my post-university career I took a strong personal interest in the work of the United Nations from the point of view of developing countries seeking to use its framework and modalities to expand their development prospects.

To further clarify my outlook, I had always conceived that the best prospects for sustained development in the Caribbean might lie in a judicious combination of domestic, regional, bilateral, plurilateral and multilateral opportunities for enlarging their development prospects. On the surface, this might appear as a daunting prospect, but experience of successful small countries shows that these combinations are possible and underlie their success in the world economy.

Accordingly, the long and sometimes arid debates about import substitution versus export development rather overstated the reality. While others gave great emphasis to import substitution on both economic and social grounds, there was a tendency to understate the vital importance of the external aspects of development. I felt it imperative, therefore, to attempt to redress the balance and to give particular attention to the opportunities that lay ahead in the fields of international trade and capital flows.

It seemed to me then, and to be fortified by my own experience, that the Caribbean had to develop a greater capacity for dealing with the rest of the world in pursuit of its own development. Among other things, this required much greater familiarity with other countries with which co-operation in several areas could be contemplated, with regard to both private and public sector opportunities.

Accordingly, I was very anxious to build up knowledge concerning the global economy and the principal countries and groupings with which co-operation could be pursued. Although my primary concern was to give service in the region, I conceived that at some point a period of service internationally could usefully complement the knowledge and skills that I had tried to acquire in other ways.

As we shall see, this entailed hard choices when decisions had to be taken concerning my entry into and participation in international service.

Joining the UNCTAD secretariat, 1977

When I joined UNCTAD, I had been Chairman of the Commonwealth Group of Eminent Persons, assembled to examine proposals for the New International Economic Order (NIEO). As already explained, the group was established by the Commonwealth

Heads of Government to try and identify a consensus between developed countries and developing countries in the Commonwealth on areas of controversy, the main one being the establishment of an international producer/consumer Common Fund for Commodities.

The purpose of the Common Fund was to mobilize financial resources from both producer and consumer countries for the establishment of international buffer stocks of commodities. This was envisaged as being the principal instrument for securing greater stability in international commodity prices, important to the growth and development of the developing countries concerned. The simple idea was that the Common Fund would finance the purchase of commodities when prices were falling below agreed levels, and the commodity organizations concerned that had received financing from the fund would sell stocks when prices rose above prescribed levels.

This idea was not new. Prior to the discussions of a Common Fund, producer buffer stocks had been in existence for a few commodities such as cocoa and tin. The experience with those stocks had encouraged the idea that stocking could be undertaken for a much larger number of the commodities important to the developing world. A new feature of the arrangement would not only be the larger number of commodities involved (in the case of the proposed Common Fund, 18 commodities), but that in every case they would be financed both by producers *and* consumers. Until then, existing stocks such as cocoa and tin had been exclusively financed by producers.

Up to that time, producer/consumer co-operation in commodities had not been widely institutionalized, except in the case of rubber, sugar and coffee, where an institutional framework for producer/consumer co-operation had already been in existence or proposed. Accordingly, the Common Fund could build on these precedents in creating a financial framework for much more determined efforts to advance the commodity development of the developing countries concerned.

The question of buffer stocking had long been a feature of discussions of economic development. For example, significant commodity price instability was a feature of the interwar years and, to a certain extent, the Great Depression. They gave rise to an emerging school of thought that stabilization of commodity prices through buffer stocks could be a significant contributor to global economic recovery. Keynes himself came out in support of that idea. Against the background of greater intellectual consensus, and given the persistence of instability in several commodity prices, the developing countries thought that the question of achieving commodity price stability could be used as an opening salvo in promoting international action for greater stability and development in the world economy that would impact positively on the economic development of developing countries. This was one of the major elements prompting the formulation of a much wider programme of action to achieve a New International Economic Order.

As a result of discussions that had already taken place, the developing countries urged that the Common Fund be regarded as the centre of proposals for the NIEO. This led to the suggestion that UNCTAD should play a lead role in mobilizing support for this initiative.

Accordingly, great importance was attached to finding a suitable person to head the UNCTAD Commodities Division, which had been assigned responsibility for the UN secretariat's work on the fund. Indeed, when I joined the Division, the Common Fund was regarded as the most important individual project being pursued by the secretariat at that time.

As a result of my work with the Commonwealth Group of Eminent Persons on the NIEO, I fully recognized the importance of international trade in commodities to that discussion. In particular, we had very important exchanges of views in the group on the central role that the proposed Common Fund for Commodities could play in strengthening the economies of developing countries.

I was therefore very interested when the then Secretary-General of UNCTAD, Dr Gamani Corea, telephoned me to ask whether I would be interested in joining UNCTAD in any one of three capacities: Director of the Commodities Division, Director of the Division for Economic Co-operation among Developing

Countries, or Director of the Manufactures Division. After discussing the matter at some length with him, I opted for joining the Commodities Division because of the centrality of that issue to the entire development debate.

My appointment was settled with the UN Secretary-General in an exchange of letters between himself and the CARICOM Heads. In that exchange, it was agreed that because I was required to take up the UNCTAD post almost immediately, at very short notice, because the negotiations on the Common Fund had to start, it was agreed by the UN Secretary-General that I would be made available to CARICOM whenever they wished to have a major contribution from me.

Preparing for negotiating the Common Fund

On joining the Commodities Division, my first task was to settle its organization, since the United Nations had provided a large additional staff to take care of the negotiations. I had to settle the responsibilities and job descriptions of about 15 senior professionals the majority of which had to be recruited. This proved very challenging because I did not know in sufficient depth what work would be required on the Common Fund and the associated agreements for individual commodities. However, in that initial task I was greatly helped by Havelock Brewster, whom I had known before at the UWI, and Lucky Hulugalle, who knew the individuals involved and their work record and interests. As much of this as possible, if not all of it, had to be done before the Common Fund negotiations began in October/November 1977, in other words approximately two months after I assumed office.

As a result of these recruitments and some of the members of staff who were already involved in certain aspects of work on the Common Fund, I was able to appoint a special staff group on the fund which met virtually every day to discuss the different technical issues involved and to organize how the division would give support to the negotiators. I called this the 'Nine O'Clock Group', because we met at that time every day whenever I was in the office. I very much enjoyed this aspect of the work, which allowed me to acquaint myself fully with the technical issues and evaluate the responsibilities that I could assign to the individual staff members. The group remained in place for the entire negotiations and was very valuable to me in responding to the technical support requested by delegations.

My second task on joining the secretariat was to review the documentation on the fund, and it struck me that the required empirical content was not yet in place. In particular, very little investigative work had been done on the specific commodity interests of each developing country, with an appraisal of what their position was likely to be for the Common Fund negotiations and what specific commodities they would wish to see included in the fund.

What I found absent from the UNCTAD work programme were country studies assessing the importance of particular commodities to the economic development of individual countries. The proposed Integrated Programme for Commodities had become the dominant subject of international discussions and the Common Fund was to play the central role in the stabilization of commodity prices by providing financing for individual buffer stocks held by particular producer/consumer groups.

I asked the staff to let me see the dossiers that would inform me about the impact of these commodities on the economies of the particular countries concerned. I wanted this information to make an assessment of the possible impact of price stabilization on those economies. Ultimately, this would be vital information in assessing what the attitudes of those countries would be to the proposed Common Fund. However, I found that the available information on the importance of the commodity sector to individual developing countries was insufficient to allow the secretariat to make tentative assessments of the possible interest of individual producing countries in the Common Fund and related commodity agreements.

Accordingly, I took an immediate decision to reshuffle the budget in order to initiate a series of 30 Country Studies to ascertain the possible interest of these countries in price stabilization and the economic impact of such arrangements. For example, from the data available on the commodity economy of Malaysia, we could deduce what would be the likely impact of price stabilization of international rubber prices on that economy. Going further, we could attempt some informed judgements about what positions that country would take in the discussions/negotiations of an international buffer stock for rubber. From that analysis, informed guesses could also be made about negotiating positions on prices – what they might be prepared to accept as a bottom line – and other similar questions. Unless we could make informed judgements about the country impact of particular prices, it would be tantamount to taking shots in the dark about the acceptability of price ranges on the part of individual producing countries.

This was quite important material that allowed us to define which countries would be the principal beneficiaries if greater stabilization was achieved in the prices of specific commodities. Having so far identified the principal beneficiary countries, we were then able to define the countries that had a major interest in a possible Common Fund. We were also able to isolate those countries that were not very interested in the stabilization of prices as such, but had weak commodity sectors that needed to be strengthened.

This information gave some substance to the idea that had arisen among the developing countries for a two account structure for the Common Fund – one focusing on the provision of finance for commodity stocking and the other dealing with development measures, particularly for commodities where a price stabilization mechanism was not feasible. In other words, as a result of these Country Studies we were able to advise the developing countries about possible features of a second financing window for the Common Fund. The developed countries did not resist this approach, but they argued that they had only been asked to provide for price stabilization. If contributions were now needed for development measures, they should be financed by voluntary contributions. The negotiation conference agreed to this approach.

Negotiating the Common Fund

So the formal negotiations began in November 1977. Not having sufficient knowledge of how negotiations were organized in UNCTAD, I decided to feel my way by assigning individual staff members to particular political groups for the purpose of providing secretariat support. This had certainly not been done before in UNCTAD, where the prevailing notion was that countries would work through their groups in advancing their interests in negotiations. The secretariat would be available to support the conduct of meetings, not to provide substantive advice to individual countries or groups. I was therefore not sufficiently familiar with the UNCTAD methodology of negotiations and made a few mistakes along the way. It was an important learning experience for me, both in terms of the substantive issues involved and the methodologies being used for the conduct of negotiations.

Because of the short time available for preparation of the negotiations, I had virtually the entire Commodities Division working at full stretch in preparing for the meetings on the Common Fund as well as those on individual commodities. It was a very heavy staff load and some members began to complain about the long hours of work that I was requesting from them, but as they became involved in greater depth with the substantive issues and the commodities concerned, they began to respond with greater vigour and intensity. For my part, I realized that there was a great need to become involved with some of the central features of the negotiations.

Financing for the Common Fund

One of these central features was the proposals for financing the Common Fund. I also found when I took up office that the Work Programme lacked analyses regarding different constitutions for the fund. From the very beginning, the central issue was how the fund should be constituted. The developing countries considered that it should be open to all member states of the United Nations and should be organized as a source of financing for commodities, with every member state making a direct contribution to its resources. In other words, the fund should be a direct source of financing for buffer stocks of commodities.

The alternative view put forward by the developed market economy countries was that the fund should be constituted as a pool of funds contributed by commodity agreements. This issue proved to be very contentious. I did not myself find in our office any detailed analyses of these competing concepts and their financial implications. Indeed, there were practically no studies of the financial requirements for the fund based, in part, on the actual experiences of the individual commodity organizations. It was essential that this gap was filled without delay so that the negotiations could proceed on a strongly empirical basis. Indeed, it would not be unfair to say that the earlier discussions on the fund, to the extent that they included figures, were largely shots in the dark.

Having regard to these considerations, I recognized that immediate steps had to be taken to fill the knowledge gaps on the fund in the secretariat. I was equally concerned that no attempts had been made to solicit the opinions of the major commercial banks in North America and Europe involved in commodity financing: firstly, their perceptions of the need for such an institution as the Common Fund and secondly, their advice on the financial requirements for starting such a fund.

Once the negotiations commenced, I was able to indicate to delegations that it was our intention to consult the banking community. I felt that this could be an important step forward if we could present their views to the delegations as we sought to find an outcome for the negotiations. It took some time, but we were able to organize a meeting in Geneva of senior executives from major banks, and to discuss the matter thoroughly with them. In turn, they agreed during the discussion to embody their views in a report that went to all delegations. That report settled the issue of financing by proposing that an initial capital contribution should be made by all members to a total of US$600 million, while the remaining financial contributions would come from the buffer stocks seeking financing from the Common Fund. In other words, the fund would be a mixture of a source and a pool. Indeed, this recommendation was identical with the final agreement that was reached.

In 1976, when UNCTAD IV convened in Nairobi, they could only secure the agreement of the developed countries to establishing a Common Fund, but did not settle on the size and sources for financing buffer stocks. These issues were remitted to the negotiating conference.

At Nairobi the developing countries had argued for a fund with its own capital structure providing direct financing for buffer stocks of individual commodities. At that point, the developed countries considered that there was no need for an independent source of funds as such. The financial requirements for buffer stocking would be met by individual commodity agreements contributing the funds and financial assets available for financing their own buffer stocks. Accordingly, the differences between the two sides were summarized by stating that the developing countries wanted a fund constituted by contributions from members states of the United Nations according to their capacities to pay, whereas the other side proposed a pool of funds provided by individual commodity organizations with the financial resources made available to them by their members.

In preparation for the negotiating conference, the secretariat was encouraged to hold consultations with certain delegations, notably the OPEC countries, to ascertain how far they would be willing to contribute to the Common Fund's resources in addition to their contribution for individual agreements. These consultations proved rather tentative.

We were preparing proposals for the joint financing of the Common Fund. In consultation with certain influential delegates, it was suggested that the secretariat should probe the possibility of getting direct financing from developed countries and from the OPEC countries. In fact, in informal discussions with relevant sources, we had received the impression that OPEC was willing to provide a very substantial direct contribution. At the time, we were thinking of a fund with direct resources of $7.5 billion and it was being suggested that OPEC might be willing to provide up to $1 billion. That impression was certainly lingering among delegations from individual developing countries, but it was not confirmed by subsequent contacts with those donor countries.

Indeed, I wondered to myself whether those projections of donor interest had really probed the whole psychology of negotiations. A good negotiator must never be too impressed with his or her own views. They should never forget that their job is not to impose views, but to get the relevant parties to agree on the desired outcome.

One of my responsibilities was to see whether, on a very informal and non-attributable basis, a firm commitment could be secured from at least one major OPEC country, so that a very sizeable contribution could be levered from the developed countries. In fact, when I took the issue to the Secretary-General of the OPEC Fund and to delegations in the capitals, I found that apart from their direct contributions as members of the fund, OPEC was only contemplating a modest voluntary contribution, perhaps of the order of $50 million. This turned out to be quite a shock to the developing countries.

The actual amount fell far short of what the protagonists had originally proposed at UNCTAD IV. Following further negotiations and discussions it was finally agreed that the Common Fund would consist of two accounts. The first would contribute towards the financing of buffer stocking – but not necessarily all of the requirements – and there could also be contributions by individual states. The second account would consist wholly of voluntary contributions made principally by developed countries, while the OPEC countries would contribute $50 million to it. These outcomes fell far short of what had been originally envisaged, but reflected the depth of resistance to interference with the market which underlay the concerns of the developed countries. As for the OPEC countries, they too lost ground within the Group of 77 because of the disappointment experienced by some of the latter with the smaller than expected size of the voluntary contribution from OPEC.

It was felt by some developing countries that OPEC's participation had been mismanaged. Had there been greater success in securing much larger contributions from them, this could have levered much greater contributions from the developed countries themselves. In fact, having decided that a relatively large contribution would be required from OPEC countries, sufficient promotional work was not done by the other member states of the Group of 77 to sell the idea at the level of OPEC capitals so that they could be encouraged to make a sufficiently substantial contribution that would also serve as a lever on the developed countries to increase their own contributions.

On the secretariat's part there was, too, disappointment that the results fell far short of our initial projections and estimates. Overall, it was felt in some quarters that as a result of the outcome of the Common Fund negotiations and of UNCTAD VI, the stature of the UNCTAD secretariat as an honest broker in negotiations had been enhanced, but this was not necessarily a majority view among the developing countries.

Assessment of the outcome of the negotiations

It was UNCTAD's first experience in servicing a major global negotiation in which all member countries participated. Although critics regarded the outcome as disappointing, subsequent experience with commodities financing has more or less substantiated the importance of the mixed approach advocated by the commercial banks.

It should be acknowledged that insufficient technical work was done to demonstrate to developing country capitals the concrete benefits that would arise for them if the Common Fund was established. As a general rule, it was found that both the delegations and the capitals in developing countries were insufficiently briefed on the proposals as a whole.

In my own case, I felt a certain satisfaction in bringing a major international negotiation to a conclusion, qualified by disappointment about how far it fell short of what had been proposed in initial discussions of the New International Economic Order.

Scenario for an alternative negotiating focus

In considering the assessment made by some developing countries that the outcome of the Common Fund negotiations fell far short of the initial expectations, I have sometimes wondered whether the developing countries should not have pursued a different strategy in the negotiations. Although the immediate concern was the low level and price instability of the commodities coming up for consideration, the situation at the time seemed to warrant greater priority being given to price stability than to development.

Accordingly, the focus was placed on negotiation of the Common Fund itself, with consideration of the development needs for individual commodities being given subsidiary attention. Since the Common Fund and associated agreements have been established, the question has arisen as to whether a more satisfactory outcome could have been achieved if the focus had been placed initially on development agreements, with the issue of price stabilization through a Common Fund being given consideration at a later stage. The argument for that would be that development was not a controversial issue among the parties and it could be perceived that after proceeding successfully with the negotiation of individual development agreements the ground would have been more securely laid for proceeding with a proposal for a fund for stabilization that would rest upon those successfully negotiated development agreements. In the process, the financing of a fund for price stabilization could have been less controversial. Hopefully a habit of producer/consumer co-operation would have been in place, providing a stronger foundation for achieving consensus on the more difficult issues of price stabilization. All of this might represent attempts to be wise after the event, but it could also be viewed more positively as an attempt to build on the limited success so far achieved with commodity development in an atmosphere more understanding and supportive of the problems being confronted in the commodity sectors of developing countries. One might argue that the Common Fund, as now established, represents a very modest attempt at this approach.

As for UNCTAD itself, the Common Fund negotiations were its first step towards becoming not only a deliberative organization, but also one for trade and economic negotiations. However, it is not known what further steps have since been taken to build up the negotiating capabilities of the organization. It continues principally as a deliberative forum.

Returning to my duties at UNCTAD, I would say that, apart from the Common Fund, we gave a good deal of attention to agreements for individual commodities, advanced the work on some of them and brought others close to a consensus.

One of the development agreements we concluded was for jute, which was well received in the international community because of the state of poverty and under-development in the principal producing countries. But in a large number of other cases we had made substantial progress in reaching consensus, so that there were good prospects for an eventual positive outcome.

I was also very gratified at the progress then being made towards greater economic co-operation among developing countries and in technical areas such as shipping, and the least developed, landlocked and island countries. The work that was ongoing on technology transfer also represented a new area that UNCTAD had brought more forcefully to the attention of the international community. These were all areas in which UNCTAD played a pioneering role.

Appointment as Deputy Secretary-General

As to my personal situation, I was promoted to the post of Deputy Secretary-General in 1980, after an initial acting appointment of one year during the leave of absence of Bernard Chidzero, who was appointed Finance Minister in the first government after political independence was negotiated for Zimbabwe.

UNCTAD VI, 1983

The UNCTAD Conference convened every four years on the principle that it should rotate among the different regions of the developing world. In 1983 it was the turn of Asia to host the conference and that regional group agreed that it should be held in Belgrade. It was convening at the time when the negotiations on the Common Fund had reached a terminal stage, since substantial agreement on the text had been obtained. Nonetheless, given the then fragile state of the economies of most developing countries, it was thought that UNCTAD VI could seek to make progress on other development issues.

Figure 9 Addressing an UNCTAD meeting. To the left UNCTAD staff, to the right government delegates.

Among the country missions in Geneva, there was a certain feeling of weariness, having just resolved the outstanding issues with the Common Fund. The role of the secretariat in that situation was to build on the spirit of consensus emerging from the fund negotiations by proposing areas for discussion and negotiation that were more easily negotiable, so that the spirit of consensus could prevail and be deepened wherever possible. Accordingly, it was proposed that the central theme of the conference should be dialogue and consensus.

As for the secretariat itself, it too showed similar signs of weariness, but in my view it could not afford to miss any opportunities for further building on that atmosphere of agreement.

I discussed with the Secretary-General the possibility of getting the conference to focus on such an outcome by approving a resolution that identified the possible areas for consensus and included a commitment to work further on them in the post-conference period. The Secretary-General encouraged me to pursue the idea with the delegations. Accordingly, the conference ended up with such an outcome, which in essence meant agreeing to a future work programme in the four years between UNCTAD VI and UNCTAD VII. Some commentators, including members of the secretariat, considered that this was an unambitious result. In my view, the existing international atmosphere held no promise of anything more than that. I myself considered the post-UNCTAD VI period as an opportunity to build the credibility of the organization as a forum in which all parties in the international community could feel comfortable in advancing their development interests.

At the very personal level, I recall UNCTAD VI as a period of personal difficulty. First of all, the responsibility assigned to me for management of both the political and logistical aspects of the conference took a toll on my health. Fortunately, this was recognized by my personal staff, who arranged a weekend of rest and relaxation for me during the course of the conference. I remember the restorative effects of spending a weekend at a monastery from which I emerged feeling refreshed and ready to continue. I remember also that the conference took place at a time when I experienced a major personal loss with the death of a close school friend, Keith St Bernard, but in both of those situations I was significantly supported by my personal assistant, Mary Jane Bennaton, and my special assistant, Vivianne Ventura Dias.

Officer-in-Charge, 1984–85

At the end of 1984, Dr Corea's appointment as Secretary-General of UNCTAD came to an end. It was accepted that in rotating the office in accordance with the understanding that existed, an African national had to be appointed to the vacant post. The consultation between the UN Secretary-General and delegations in the General Assembly turned out to be somewhat protracted, and towards the end of that session the Secretary-General had been unable to complete his consultations on the nomination to succeed Dr Corea. As a result of the delay, there was some uncertainty as to the intentions of the UN Secretary-General. Some sources considered that Dr Corea should have been asked to remain until a successor

Figure 10 In conversation with Jean Ripert, Director-General for Development and International Economic Cooperation, my senior colleague at the UN Headquarters in New York.

had been appointed. I myself shared that view. Others held a different view. In order to avoid continuing disagreement on the matter, the UN Secretary-General appealed to me to serve as Officer-in-Charge and I did so until the end of 1985, when Kenneth Dadzie from Ghana was appointed Secretary-General of UNCTAD.

My service as Officer-in-Charge was characterized by post-Belgrade activities to advance the work on development co-operation in commodities and on economic co-operation among developing countries. This was focused on preliminary efforts to establish a Generalized System of Trade Preferences – the so-called GSTP – among developing countries. Work also continued on the special treatment of the least developed, landlocked and island developing countries. Altogether it amounted to a substantial programme of work.

Transfer to United Nations headquarters

Review of UN Economic and Social secretariats

There was a time when I had the unusual arrangement of doing two jobs – one in New York and one in Geneva. The UN Secretary-General had asked me to do a review of all of the economic and social secretariats in the UN, which meant that I had to travel very widely. Everywhere that the UN had a major presence, I had to visit to see how efficiency could be improved and whether it was possible to effect financial savings. I travelled to New York every Wednesday, worked Thursday/Friday/Saturday, left New York at six o'clock Saturday evening, went to my office in Geneva on Sunday, dealt with whatever was there to be done, and after Tuesday returned to New York. But it meant that I did not have an inch of private time. There was no space to do anything else.

Because of my interest in this inter-agency review that I was doing, I thought that since I had accepted the post of Vice-Chancellor at the UWI, I should seek an interim appointment in the UN for a period of one year during which I could complete the work I was doing and prepare carefully for our return to Jamaica. Those events are further dealt with in Chapter 15, devoted to my work at the UWI as Vice-Chancellor.

Taking into account, therefore, my obligations to the UN alongside those to my family, I proposed to the Director-General in New York that once a secretary-general for UNCTAD had been appointed, I would separate from UNCTAD and transfer to New York to complete the remainder of my assignments. He readily agreed.

Administrative Coordination Committee (ACC)

In August 1987 I transferred to New York as Assistant Secretary-General for International Economic Cooperation in the office of the Director-General.

In that capacity, I was also asked to serve as secretary of the Administrative Coordination Committee, which is a deliberating and decision-making organ with respect to the administration of the UN system. It consists of all the executive heads of agencies in the United Nations system, including the World Bank, IMF, ILO, UNESCO, FAO, and the executive heads of United Nations departments also attended. Because I was secretary of the committee, I became acquainted with all of the executive heads. Seeing their different interests and approaches made this a very interesting period for me.

One of the very important matters that came before the ACC was to reach agreement on a statement that the Secretary-General would present to the Special Session of the General Assembly on the occasion of the 40th Anniversary of the United Nations. Despite great effort on my part to assist the Secretary General to secure agreement on a text among the executive heads, those efforts were unsuccessful. Accordingly, at the ACC meeting convened just before the Special Session of the Assembly, it proved impossible to secure consensus. There was embarrassment at the absence of such an agreed text and also at the absence from the Special Session of some of the principal heads of government that were Permanent Members of the Security Council. This generated anxieties among some heads of agencies about what this situation might mean for the future of the organization.

Advisory Panel

In the light of the interest being expressed at different levels about the need for reform, particularly of the Economic and Social sectors in the United Nations, the Secretary-General decided that as an extension of the work of the review of the Economic and Social offices that I had done, he would invite a private group drawn from the highest-level members represented in the ACC to formulate recommendations for his consideration, about improving the management of the different parts of the system for which the Secretary-General was himself responsible. The group met in New York on weekends. I was appointed as a member/rapporteur and enjoyed the high level of discourse, and the recommendations accompanying it, that emanated from the meetings. In the light of the high quality of the discussions, it was a comparatively easy matter to extract the recommendations being made for reform. On completion of our work, we agreed that our report should be treated as a highly personal and confidential document, intended for the Secretary-General's eyes alone. As rapporteur, I submitted the report to the Personal Office of the Secretary-General in a form and by a route that I expected would ensure its confidentiality. It was no reflection on the office that shortly after my submission of the report the substance was apparently leaked to the New York media on the following day, to my utter astonishment. It was subsequently established that the leak did not occur through the Secretary-General's office. However, irrespective of the source, it virtually guaranteed that no action would be taken on the recommendations. I was deeply disappointed and frustrated because all the valuable work that this committee had undertaken had come to naught.

Since that period some innovations have taken place, the most important of which was the establishment of the Group of Twenty (G-20), which took place outside the United Nations. The group consists of the traditional major developed countries, some new members including China, India and Brazil, and attendance by the heads of traditional international financial institutions. It is silent on the issue of representation from the United Nations, although it is understood that from time to time the Secretary-General or his nominee has been invited to attend particular sessions.

This group has assumed responsibility for surveillance of the world economy and taking action on any major related problems. This represents an advance on the previous machinery, but it is not constituted on sufficiently representative criteria. In particular, it seems to assign a special status to the European Union, making specific provision for its representation at meetings of the group. There continues to be strong criticism of the composition of the G-20 and its modus operandi. This was reflected in the somewhat unorthodox – and some would say unfortunate – occurrences that took place during its Toronto Summit in 2010.

Guyana/Venezuela border dispute, 1990

I started the Guyana/Venezuela negotiations after I had assumed duties as Vice-Chancellor at the UWI in 1988. As a background, the Presidents of both Guyana and Venezuela approached the United Nations Secretary-General to request assistance in resolving the border dispute that arose because Venezuela thought that the British had encroached on their territory when they colonized the area. Both countries had agreed that I was acceptable to perform the role of 'Good Officer' in promoting a peaceful settlement.

Discussions had already been held with me in New York about doing these negotiations. I had, however, requested time to settle into the job at the UWI. Then Hurricane Gilbert struck within ten days of my arrival on the campus and I suggested to the UN that they find someone else. It was not until about 18 months later that I was able to take up any work on the border dispute.

At that time we were negotiating in different places, wherever we felt it was safe to do so without a substantial Guyanese or Venezuelan local community there that could complicate the situation. I argued that we just could not traverse the world looking for places where there were no Guyanese or Venezuelans. I suggested that although the presence of a diaspora could create difficulties, there were situations where this might not necessarily be the case. For example, meetings in large cities could possibly be organized even if there were local groups in residence there.

Accordingly, we agreed to meet in New York, in a large hotel where our presence might not be obvious to the public. Arrangements were made to hold a breakfast meeting in the suite that I had for that purpose. I was just about to retire on the night before the meeting when I received a telephone call from the Guyanese Ambassador to the UN. He informed me that he had just received a telephone call from President Cheddi Jagan of Guyana to advise him that he had dismissed the Guyanese negotiator who was expected to be their representative at the meeting. I protested that decision because the official concerned was extremely well briefed on the issues and his presence would ensure that we did not lose momentum in our work.

I insisted to the ambassador that a replacement should be appointed immediately so that the meeting could proceed as planned. Later on that evening he informed me that because the President understood the importance of the meeting and my concerns, he had asked his wife, Mrs Janet Jagan, who was a cabinet minister and currently visiting Boston on other business, to be Guyana's representative at the meeting.

I did not know Mrs Jagan and was somewhat apprehensive since I wanted to make the discussion substantive and keep it on a non-rhetorical level. However, Mrs Jagan attended the meeting and at the end of it the Venezuelan delegates expressed their satisfaction with our discussions and their outcome.

Over the years, despite the efforts at mediation made on both sides, virtually no progress has been made. Meanwhile, their respective nationals took initiatives to establish themselves. For example, when I asked the government of Guyana how many of their nationals were living across the border, they gave me a figure lower than the one I had secured from other sources. Eventually, both the government and I agreed that there were about 8,000 Guyanese working and living just across the border in Venezuela. I found it interesting to note that the Venezuelan government did not have an accurate figure on this matter. During an informal conversation with the President of Venezuela, he was surprised at the size of the figure I indicated to him, which, when he checked, proved to be approximately accurate.

Communication between the President and myself was very easy. He spoke fluent English, having attended school in Trinidad where he had absorbed both the language and the popular culture of the country.

I worked with three Venezuelan presidents while I was involved in the negotiations. Each had a unique personality, but I considered that I was able to communicate with all of them despite the differences in their styles. The first one, Carlos Andres Perez, was very friendly with Caribbean leaders, especially Michael Manley, and was actually a person of some foresight. The second one, Rafael Caldera Rodriguez, who was said to be a more private person than his predecessor, was in office for only a very short period, so it was not possible to advance the discussions significantly during that time.

I realized from my first meeting with his successor, President Chavez, that the momentum for the negotiations had shifted and doubted whether I myself would be particularly helpful to their progress. Accordingly, I telephoned the Secretary-General to acquaint him with this assessment. He accepted it and asked whether I could help him to find a successor.

I suggested a Barbadian colleague, Oliver Jackman, who knew Venezuela very well. He had served there, spoke Spanish fluently, and was a very sensitive individual who agreed to do it because he was just retiring from the Foreign Service in Barbados. Unfortunately, he died shortly after taking up the position. Thereafter, I believe in 2011, Norman Girvan was recruited for the position. Regrettably, President Chavez became ill and died and then Norman had a tragic climbing accident and died of his injuries in 2014. So I do not know what the situation is now, although there are press reports that it is being discussed once again.

11

Other international activities

For the record, and without getting into detail, I set out below a number of assignments that I undertook in varying fields during the course of my career. It illustrates the variety of experience that I was able to accumulate, virtually every assignment adding something new to my professional experience.

East African Community: assignment in Tanzania, 1977

I discovered, quite by chance, that one of the sub-committees of the UN General Assembly in New York is called the Advisory Committee on Administrative and Budgetary Questions, ACABQ; it was said to be the most powerful body in the UN.

I made this discovery in conversation at Amir Jamal's house in Tanzania. He was one of only two Asians who occupied positions of prominence in President Nyerere's government. He and I had worked together on the Commonwealth Group on the NIEO. Apparently, for some reason he was so impressed with me that on his return to Tanzania he urged the President to arrange to ask this person who was Secretary-General of CARICOM to work with them on the East African Community, particularly because at the time there were major differences between Kenya and other members of the community.

Amir called to inform me that President Nyerere wondered if I could come to Arusha for a few days to talk about the future of the East African Community. I advised him that, in practical working terms, it would be more appropriate to ask William Demas rather than me. He responded that he would then invite both Willie and myself. So we went and sat with the staff of the secretariat and discussed and drew up a plan designed to improve the administrative efficiency of the community. We then went to Nairobi and had meetings with the officials in the Ministry of Finance. I managed to persuade them to pay their contributions to the secretariat, which had been overdue. I took the cheque back to the secretariat in Arusha and they were amazed at the outcome.

I also had the privilege of meeting President Nyerere at his house. We had a very interesting conversation and I was very impressed with the simplicity of his life and lifestyle, which was unusual for a head of state.

While I was at Amir's place in Dar, he had a visitor who, Amir told me, was Chairman of the ACABQ. I really had no idea what that was and said so. Amir said that the ACABQ was vital. It was the UN Advisory Committee on Administrative and Budgetary Questions. The visitor introduced himself and we had a very pleasant evening together.

Later, in 1977 when I was at UNCTAD, my new boss Gamani Corea asked me if I knew anyone at the ACABQ, because we were in trouble with our budget. I told him that maybe I did know someone. He knew I was going to New York and asked me to see what could be done. In New York I called the individual and asked him why he was giving my workplace a hard time. Did he wish to send me back to the Caribbean? He laughed.

At the level of the UN secretariat, if the ACABQ is on your side, if they give the green light, the recommendation goes to the Fifth Committee which is formally responsible for these decisions. The ACABQ is the Advisory Committee, but the Fifth Committee usually accepted their advice without question. In between meetings of the Fifth Committee, the Chairman of the ACABQ has the authority to take decisions for the committee. So he is a very important person. Everybody in New York wanted to have this Tanzanian to lunch and dinner! He was a very competent person, no question about it. He was at Makerere and that is how we got talking about the people from the Caribbean who were on the staff at Makerere – Marshall Hall, Al Francis and others. We had a good time and he assured me that I should tell my boss that the budget would be all right; he would get it through the Fifth Committee the following day. He also said I would have to appear before the committee and warned me that the leader of the US delegation was very impressed with his own sense of humour. If he told a joke and people did not laugh, he never forgot it. When I eventually met him, he informed me that he had been to Jamaica and he tried to speak a little Jamaican and I laughed and complimented him that it was great that he had learned the language. So after that, he was my pal!

The UNCTAD budget was approved and I called Dr Corea that night in Geneva to tell him. When he heard, he thought I was Mandrake the Magician!

Zimbabwe's independence celebrations, 1980

UNCTAD not only brought me into contact with someone from my past, but allowed me to become involved in a developing country of great interest.

I became associated with a black Zimbabwean, Bernard Chidzero, because when I was at Oxford he joined me at Nuffield College. He and his wife were unable to find accommodation. At the time, I had been selected as Student of the Year and in that capacity had the privilege of occupying a three-bedroomed house. So I offered to have them stay with us until they found a place. They remained for about six months or so.

I lost touch with them because Bernard got a job with the United Nations Economic Commission for Africa (UNECA) in Addis Ababa. After a period in Addis, he was offered a job at UNCTAD as Director of the very Commodities Division I was subsequently invited to head. I was not aware of this when I visited Geneva to discuss my own employment.

When I arrived in Geneva to take up the post, I was told that he had just been appointed Deputy Secretary-General. We resumed our connection and had many conversations about African development, including the peculiar situation of Zimbabwe.

On the occasion of the independence of Zimbabwe, Bernard Chidzero was offered the post of Minister of Finance, on the basis of a leave of absence, initially for one year, from the UNCTAD. This required the approval of the Secretary-General of the UN, who consulted the five Permanent Members of the Security Council. It appears that there was initial reluctance on the part of some members, because they did not like the idea of someone with a political post still retaining a permanent job at the United Nations. However, the UN Secretary-General persuaded them to withdraw their reservations because of the high importance of getting the independence process in Zimbabwe off to as smooth a start as possible.

Accordingly, the post of Deputy Secretary-General became vacant at UNCTAD, which the Secretary-General of UNCTAD asked me to fill. I was very enamoured of this situation as it not only gave me an opportunity to get acquainted with the entire UNCTAD secretariat, but also to be a contact point between African delegations and the secretariat.

For my own part, I was very keen to contribute to Zimbabwe's development. While he was in Geneva, Bernard had invited me to associate with a group of young Zimbabweans studying or working in Europe who had expressed the desire to prepare a development plan for the country to which the leadership, after independence, could turn for ideas. So I went and in truth provided an input of economic knowledge that they did not really have. I attended a few of those meetings. It was a group of eight or nine people who met and they drafted a document which they gave to President Mugabe who was then still, I believe, in prison. He had it as a guiding document for when he was released and came into government.

Because of my involvement with the draft development document, I was included in the first UN delegation that attended Zimbabwe's independence celebrations. Subsequent to that, it was agreed that, because of my familiarity with the local situation, I should lead a UN Inter-Agency mission to Harare to assess the technical assistance needs with the new government.

On that occasion, we had detailed meetings with each of the government ministries. For the most part, the permanent secretaries were European and we were struck by how limited their views were on the needs of the country. For example, I was taken to see an internationally funded project for low-income housing. I was appalled to find that the project had no provision for bathrooms and showers. When I asked the permanent secretary then in office about this, he told me that the Zimbabweans did not want such facilities as they were quite prepared to carry out those functions in public. I was quite distressed by that view and went to see Bernard to report the matter. He, for his part, was quick to suggest that I should report the matter directly to President Mugabe and receive instructions from him. This I did later in the day when we met him for a quick drink and conversation.

President Mugabe told me that I should ignore the attitude of those officials, since their stay in the ministry would be short-lived and I should find other means of identifying the needs in housing and other areas of social impact. Fortunately, with the assistance of colleagues from the World Bank, we were able to put together a preliminary assessment of both housing and other social needs.

My own assessment of the situation was that President Mugabe's personality, which showed him to be a withdrawn and somewhat unfriendly person, could be attributed to his long period in solitary confinement in prison. At the same time, there was no question about his solid support from the people. Frankly, I attributed a large part of President Mugabe's attitude to the fact that there had been no settlement of the land question, as had been promised by the donor countries when the political settlement was made.

Altogether, while I wished the first Zimbabwean government every success in tackling the horrendous economic and social problems that had to be addressed, and was prepared to spare no effort in making whatever contribution I could, I was not very optimistic about the future of the country unless there were radical changes in attitudes and institutions.

The South Commission, 1987

I had transferred from UNCTAD in order to take up the position of UN Assistant Secretary-General for International Economic and Development Cooperation in New York, when President Julius Nyerere of Tanzania telephoned me to ask whether he could interest me in becoming head of the South–South secretariat being set up to support the work of the South Commission, which he headed. I reminded him that, notwithstanding my strong interest in the work of that commission, I had already committed myself to a position in New York that had family implications. Since I could not myself take up his offer, I promised him that I would identify a suitable candidate for the post. I had in mind Manmohan Singh, who was then with the government in New Delhi. He had been at Nuffield College with me, and we had liked each other from our first contact. Subsequently, I worked with him informally on some development issues and was very impressed with his high intellectual quality and his wise advice. I called him and told him about the establishment of the South Commission in Geneva and that they were looking for a head for the secretariat and that I had suggested him to President Nyerere, who had been asked to take initiatives to get the secretariat established.

Manmohan indicated a positive interest in the position. He told me that he was getting a bit restless at the Planning Commission. I followed up by saying that it would be a good move for him to change jobs. I reminded him also of the excellent medical facilities in Geneva for diabetics and promised to put him in touch with my own doctor, Dr Jean Philippe Asal.

Subsequently, I got a call from the Tanzanian Ambassador in Geneva, Amir Jamal, whom, as I said before, I knew very well and who was a very close confidant of President Nyerere. He told me that the President wished him to pass a message to me and that he wanted to see me on a private basis. I agreed readily to that and on that occasion he told me the President was insistent that I should become the head of the new secretariat of the South Commission that was being set up. I told Jamal that this was totally out of the question since I had accepted the position of Vice-Chancellor of the UWI and had promised the Secretary-General that I would spend a year finishing a review that he had asked me to do of all of the economic and social secretariats in the UN. I could not possibly turn back now, but I could recommend an excellent person for the position.

In any event, I was not sure whether that would be a job I would enjoy. Furthermore, I was also unsure that the international community was ready for a South Commission or that they would respond to it. But still, I think that at the end of the day, had I not had previous commitments and if they had really pushed me, I would have felt that I had to do it even if I had doubts about the outcome.

So Jamal told Nyerere and the latter sent a message to me to say he was devastated but could I suggest someone who could be considered. I told him that I considered Manmohan Singh to be my choice. He said he did not know him but would speak with Prime Minister Gandhi. She told him that I was being my usual self, coming up with something that she could not refuse, but which involved a substantial sacrifice. Then Manmohan, who at the time was Deputy Chairman of the Planning Commission, called me and remonstrated with me in a friendly fashion, indicating at the same time that he would accept the assignment and would make a preliminary visit to Geneva for that purpose.

He came and the substance of it all was that he agreed to take the job in 1987. Since I was leaving the secretariat, I was able to persuade Mary Jane Bennaton, my outstanding secretary for the period that I was at UNCTAD, to accept an offer from him in an equivalent capacity. She knew the files and was able to be of assistance with in-depth knowledge of the UN system and conditions in Geneva. Mary Jane stayed with Manmohan until he left the commission.

This South secretariat was financed by the Third World countries, I think OPEC contributed substantially, and India, although not an oil exporter, also made a significant contribution.

The South Commission Report was published in 1990 and several proposals in it were very deserving of acceptance and implementation. Had President Carter been in the White House then, my assessment was that he would have gone along with many of the recommendations, but he was no longer president, and the recommendations were too much at variance with Republican thinking. So the report eventually never came to anything.

We were all hoping for the World Development Fund, and at the time I told some members of the South Commission, as well as Manmohan, that they should press for the World Bank to take a lead in supporting the idea. Sir James Wolfensohn, who was then Managing Director of the World Bank, was a very open personality. After several discussions with him, I felt that there was a chance of bringing him along in support of the idea. We had good exchanges and he demonstrated promising flexibility on a number of matters. I was not certain that he would accept the specific proposals but I considered that it was worth a try. However, there were some people in the South Commission who did not share my optimism. They persisted with the proposition that the South should not expect any support on this matter from the Bretton Woods institutions. Accordingly, they insisted that they should go ahead and set up their own institution, the South Bank. I figured from my experience with the Common Fund that they would not be able to mobilize a critical mass of developing countries who had the resources to make this possible, and I did not believe that the OPEC would do so either. The same reasons why they did not produce the required resources to set up the Common Fund for Commodities would also apply to the South Bank. But Manmohan worked very hard and wrote an elegant, very sensible, very balanced report. He managed to get them to moderate several avant-garde ideas held by many of the Third World countries. Accordingly, the South Commission Report of 1990 could have attracted the support of a number of countries, both developing and developed, who were supportive of its moderate recommendations. They might have associated themselves with its recommendations. But there was no disposition on the part of the developed countries to start another round of development negotiations.

However, both the Common Fund for Commodities and the South Commission eventually had an impact on thinking. A number of countries took a softer view of development issues and as a result of UNCTAD thinking there was better receptivity for ideas on development, but the report of the Brandt Commission and the work of the South Commission did not translate into action.

For instance, Willy Brandt's reputation of being a listener to the Third World, even if he did not implement actual change, spread through the German government and through the European Union, where the Germans had great influence. As a matter of fact, on a number of issues in our negotiation of the Lomé Convention, which became the Economic Partnership Agreement (EPA), the Germans helped us considerably. Had it not been for them, there are some things we would not have secured in Lomé IV, such as a more generous commitment of development assistance; and they were willing to listen on the vulnerable commodities, although I would not say that they would have gone the whole way in accepting the proposals being made by developing countries. The French also were traditionally supportive on commodity issues, though not so much on monetary and financial matters.They tended to be more flexible on commodities because of their long historic links with Africa.

The British were not as helpful as the ACP countries might have wished, although they were supportive in advancing decisions through their back channel connections with the ACP. These private discussions, in which Ramphal was the principal participant, were helpful in concluding the work on Lomé IV.

Chair, Review Committee, Commonwealth Scholarship and Fellowship Programme, 1993

I was appointed Chairman of the Review Committee with a request that we review the Scholarship and Fellowship Programme in order to make it more in tune with the needs of Commonwealth developing countries, and that we set out any improvements that were desired in the rules and procedures.

This was not a very contentious issue and we were able to conclude our work quite easily, securing consensus on the changes then being proposed.

Advisory Board for the Centre of Caribbean Studies, University of Warwick, UK, 1993

Warwick wanted to set up a Centre for Caribbean Studies. They were under some pressure to do so because Sonny Ramphal was Chancellor at Warwick and he was strongly in favour of it. A faculty member who was from Guyana was also pressing for its establishment.

The Vice-Chancellor asked me to be a member of an outside group that he wished to convene to consider the proposal and make recommendations. We recommended the establishment of the centre and an initial budget for its operation. The university accepted our report and established the centre.

I am not myself familiar with the work that the Centre for Caribbean Studies has since done, but my information is that it has been a moderate success. In general, Caribbean Studies at Warwick has advanced rather well, but they tend to specialize more in the areas of literature and history than in contemporary development studies.

Moderator, review of International Commodities Situation, the Common Fund for Commodities, Brussels, 1993

I was asked to return, as the 'Father of the Common Fund', to act as moderator of a review that was taking place at the headquarters of the fund in the Netherlands. The idea behind the review was to generate pressure for an enlargement of the fund's resources. I am not certain how far the recommendations were implemented, but the information which has reached me suggests that the fund still remains a very small version of what had been initially envisaged during the UNCTAD negotiations.

Although the review meeting was not very productive, I was pleased to be present because I met several of my former colleagues who worked with me at UNCTAD as well as some delegates who were accredited to the UN in Geneva during those years.

External Advisory Group, the World Bank, 1994

The Vice-President of the World Bank, responsible for Latin America and the Caribbean, felt strongly that the bank was too reliant on its own advice and should have an input from the countries they served. A very noble ambition! I knew from the outset it would not get very far, because I was not confident that a meeting of minds could occur on the topics brought up for discussion. I regret to say that my forecasts proved correct.

We had one meeting where there were good discussions, but after that the idea petered out because the established interests were too powerful to be modified by outside ideas.

Chair, IDB/OAS Independent Group of Experts on Smaller Economies and Western Hemisphere Integration, 1996–97

In those days the World Bank had a great enthusiasm and a general perception – which it no longer has, and in fact enthusiasm for integration also went out of the window – that economic integration in Latin America and the Caribbean was proceeding somewhat more satisfactorily among the larger economies than the smaller, in particular Central America, which had started off rather well.

The first time I had to review it, I was rather enthusiastic and quite irritated when someone in the ECLAC office in Mexico, from which I was working, said: 'Don't bother being so enthusiastic about Central America.'

I said: 'How can you say that? Against the background of what you're trying to achieve in the Caribbean and the very poor Central American countries.'

He said: 'OK.'

But of course, what really upset the pace and in fact sustainability of Central American progress was the El Salvador crisis, which took up all of their energy and attention. El Salvador had been the manufacturing centre in Central America and therefore was leading in the industrial development of the sub-region. Their civil war from 1980–92 lasted such a long time that it is doubtful how far they have recovered from it even today. It did a lot of damage to the economy and the society. It cost a lot in terms of their leadership and resulted in a heavy migration of people.

I never had a satisfactory explanation for the degeneration that occurred there. I was very close to a Salvadorian who worked with Pérez de Cuéllar, and he was very upset about the situation. In fact, he tried to get me involved in some reconciliation process, but at the time I had other prior matters that took up my attention.

As for the Central American integration process itself, we were asked as an Expert Group to assess the situation with a view to identifying alternative sources of stimuli for the integration process. We were not very successful in that endeavour. I have the impression that we had one meeting in Washington and we also had one in Costa Rica, which pleased me no end because I got to know a little bit more about Costa Rica.

A number of Jamaicans had migrated there and owned businesses and so on in the capital. On one occasion I was walking in San José when all of a sudden I heard a Jamaican accent, but by the time I turned around to enquire the person had crossed the street. On another occasion, I was sleeping one night and heard two Jamaicans arguing vigorously. I thought I must be dreaming but I put on my dressing gown, walked to the door and there were these two security guards. So I said, 'Are you guys from Jamaica?'

'Yes, mon.'

'What you doing here?'

'We bawn here.'

'So how can you say you're from Jamaica?'

They were from the Jamaican community in Limon and began telling me about where they came from, where their parents came from in Jamaica. They provided me with considerable information. Then they said: 'We must take you on a visit to Limon.'

I was planning to go there before leaving Costa Rica, but it did not happen because our meeting ran beyond the schedule.

As for the report on integration which Gerry Helleiner and I wrote, I tried, unsuccessfully, to locate it at the IDB, including in the Library in Washington. However, I hope that it was useful to the World Bank.

Member, Board of Governors, and Chairman, Human Resources Committee, International Development Research Council (IDRC), 1999–2005

I served on the Board of Governors of the IDRC for two terms of three years, which was the usual period of service. While I was there I was chairman of the Human Resources committee. I thought that the work was very interesting and useful. The board members displayed considerable collegiality and it was altogether a very rewarding experience for me.

The projects that came under my purview while I was there that I felt could make a difference in the developing world included Distance Education in several African countries. One of the great things about it was that it was a programme to teach computing to children. It was making children from the ages of 10 to 15 computer literate. I was keen on that.

I enjoyed excellent working relations with my colleagues on the board and with the president and her staff. However, I did have a problem with international travel commitments and I found myself unable to participate in some of the field visits to different regions of the world. Accordingly, I did not offer myself for re-appointment.

Executive Committee of International Lawyers and Economists Against Poverty (ILEAP), Toronto, 2002–6

I was invited by Professor Gerry Helleiner to participate in a small group of economic advisors, funded by CIDA, UNDP and some other agencies – often depending upon the project being undertaken. The terms of reference for individual advisory groups varied according to the problems being addressed, which were usually international development problems requested by individual developing countries or by agencies with which they were working.

We had a very bright young French Cameroonian as the Executive Director, with a very small staff – altogether a group of three. He was extremely capable and there was a young lady, a Canadian who had just got her master's degree, serving as research assistant, and a secretary. That was the establishment.

The Dean of the Faculty of Law at Toronto was a good friend who allocated two rooms in the Faculty to give us an office. We would meet three or four times a year as the situation required. And we had some very interesting discussions. We really argued a lot about the various issues that were referred to us. We shared certain common perceptions but with wide variations in our approach, but in the course of the discussion we would arrive at a consensus.

Gerry Helleiner, who was Professor of Economics at the University of Toronto, agreed to serve unofficially as our chairman.

I remember some of the particular problems on which we advised. For instance, a minister of finance from an African country would ask us how to approach a particular debt problem that they were having. The Director would canvass the African group to ascertain their views on the problem. He would hold discussions with them and someone would suggest that our group be brought in to offer the required advice. He would dutifully record what they had to say and would then circulate it to us for comments. We would comment, have a discussion and then formally make a submission to the Minister of Finance. In those days we would send a fax. So even though we had not met as a group, we might still be working together on a problem. The chairman would send things to us. We focused on Africa to start with, because they were the neediest in terms of technical advice.

My colleagues decided that we needed consulting advice and decided to recruit some Third World consultants in order to build a capacity over and above our small group. That was how ILEAP brought in expertise and assisted countries.

I stopped participating in ILEAP several years ago, when I was medically advised to reduce my workload. However, I enjoyed the experience thoroughly!

Group of 77 South Summit in Havana, 2000

The Group of 77 Summit was expected to be a landmark event promoting substantive co-operation among developing countries and setting up institutional machinery to support it.

Cuba hosted the Group of 77 South Summit in Havana on 10–14 April, 2000, a meeting to which I was invited as an advisor. As is customary at these international events, the CARICOM secretariat helped in finalizing the draft speeches of the Heads of Government attending. Since there were many heads attending, the CARICOM secretariat was in particular need of assistance in dealing with the large number of speeches. I offered to assist and while doing so received a call from Sonny Ramphal who had been asked to do the same thing. He said: 'How far advanced are you on a speech?'

I said: 'Pretty well advanced.'

'Well listen, before everyone starts saying the same thing, let us spend a little time together to make sure that we do not duplicate the substance of the texts.'

I went over to his residence and was there reading what he had done and contributing my suggestions so that overlapping would be eliminated, when the telephone rang. I heard him saying: 'We'll be here until about two o'clock, you know. We have to finish these speeches for this afternoon. But can our host wait until two? We'll try and finish quickly enough and come over.'

I said: 'Sonny, what are you up to? What have you committed us to?'

'President Castro wants us to come and have lunch with him.'

We left the texts with the secretaries to be typed and went on to see the President. The Protocol Officer met us, took us inside and I saw this vast library to my left, going down all along the wall. I was very impressed with the collection.

The Protocol Officer brought us in and that's when we realized it was only the two of us having lunch with the President. Then the latter arrived. We sat down to a very simple and tasty lunch, which suited me fine, as it suited Ramphal.

We began talking about the substantive issues before the conference and then moved on to the institutional machinery, principally the proposal for a secretariat. President Castro had an interpreter there but I quickly surmised that he understood everything that we were saying in English. My memory fails me on the details of what followed. But on leaving the meeting Ramphal mentioned to me that in one of his asides the President informed him that his name had come up as a possible candidate for the Secretary-General and he was in support of that. I recall Ramphal saying that this was somewhat premature, and he would advise caution in taking that discussion forward.

Actually the South Summit was the second time I had met President Castro. I was in Havana for the Group of 77 Ministerial Meeting on one of the UNCTADs and he hosted a reception. When I went in, the person who introduced me said: 'McIntyre is the official handling the Common Fund for Commodities.'

The President said: 'Oh! Very important for us in the South, very important. Congratulations. You keep up the work.'

On this second occasion, he remembered me. When I went in I said: 'My name is McIntyre.'

He said: 'I know.'

I said: 'Do you, Mr President, remember the Group of 77?'

'I do.'

I was very impressed with his mastery of current developments.

In the early days the South–South Summit was ad hoc: some countries proposed the organization of a meeting and took the lead in making arrangements for it. There was no organization behind it. Now the whole idea was to establish a secretariat for the organization, which would make possible greater continuity in its activities. The first meeting was held in 1974 at Bandung. Periodically a country offered to host and they would look after the meeting, preparing and drafting the agenda, that sort of thing. The secretariat work would be done by the host country.

As to Havana in 2000, you would not have thought that the agenda came from such a highly ideological source. It was very empirical. No major judgemental issues at all. Just simply the nature of the problem and the options, without necessarily coming down on one side or the other. A lot of people commented on it. In fact several people thought that we, the English-speaking Caribbean, had had a hand in it, but we did not.

I remember that on a previous occasion at a meeting of the Non-Aligned Foreign Ministers in Georgetown, Willie Demas and I were attending the meeting as advisors. The meeting was going on and on and on, and Willie and I were sitting next to each other. It was three o'clock in the morning when the Algerians thought we were asleep. So they got up and proposed that the conference should condemn preferential trading arrangements with developed countries that were divisive of the South. The participants seemed to be very well disposed towards this idea until Willie got up and said that we would not go along with that proposal at all. The English-speaking Caribbean was very pleased with their quotas for exports of sugar and bananas. So we would not subscribe to that. We did not think that these preferential trade agreements were compromising us to such an extent that we should abandon them and thereby endanger the situation.

The Algerians were surprised. They thought we were asleep. They simply said: 'OK, Mr Chairman, we won't push this at this moment.' They and some other delegations were always watching us at these meetings, where we were sitting and to whom we were talking.

Altogether, my participation in the South–South Conference was a very useful experience, although the idea of the establishment of a secretariat never took root.

SECTION 4

ADVISORY WORK FOR NATIONAL GOVERNMENTS

12

Assignments in Trinidad and Tobago

Citrus negotiations

The government of Trinidad and Tobago was having problems with the British government over citrus, which was then quite a major export of Trinidad and Tobago. The industry was developed during World War II at the prompting of the British government. The latter was committed to providing orange juice for children in Britain during the war and continued it after the war as part of their National Health Scheme. They had a long-term contract with Trinidad and Tobago to supply orange juice and the country went into citrus in a big way, only to discover that when that period had passed, the Labour government was out of office and the National Health Scheme had changed. The British government was no longer interested in buying citrus. Trinidad and Tobago now had to sell it on the open market.

Prime Minister Eric Williams was very upset about this. He had an elderly Englishman, a large planter in Trinidad and Tobago called Sir Harold Robinson, who lived in London and occasionally came home to attend to things. He was easily the most knowledgeable person in the Caribbean on citrus. The Prime Minister wanted to initiate some negotiations with the British government for the purpose of reaching a new agreement for citrus, even though it had become a market transaction. He felt the

British government had to provide certain supports to citrus farmers in Trinidad in view of the fact that they had encouraged them to make substantial investments in increased production. He spoke to Willie Demas, who advised that I should be asked to participate in discussions with them in London, since I knew a lot about international trade in commodities such as citrus. The Prime Minister asked him to raise with me my willingness to be part of their delegation to discuss the matter with senior officials in London.

While expressing a willingness to be part of the delegation, I mentioned to him that since I was not a Trinidadian, I could not ask the government of Grenada to provide me with the necessary diplomatic status to participate in those discussions. They found a way of solving it.

When I first entered Trinidad in December 1964 to work at the university, the immigration officer pointed out to me that since I did not then have a work permit to remain in the island, they would give me two weeks to clear up my status. I went to the Registrar's Office at the university and was advised that I had to go to the Immigration Office myself to secure the necessary approval, which I decided to do. On my first visit I was advised that I could not see anyone because meetings were arranged through an appointment. Accordingly, I made an appointment and went back a second time and was told that the official was busy and would call me when he was free to see me. He never did call.

When Willie raised with me the proposal of going to London, I said that I would not be in a position to go as the emissary of the government because I was being harassed at the airport over whether I had a work permit or resident status.

The solution was to provide me with a highly embossed document which I could present in London should enquiries be made as to my status. The document designated me as the Special Emissary of the government. So when I returned to Trinidad and presented the document to the immigration officer, there was great consternation. He called his colleagues because they had never seen such a document. And that was the last time I was ever asked anything about my status in Trinidad.

I arrived in London, got to the Hilton Hotel where I had a reservation, which impressed me enormously at the time, and called Sir Harold Robinson, who expressed satisfaction at my arrival and indicated that we had considerable preparatory work to do. He asked me to see him at three o'clock on the following morning, and I did as he requested.

I did not know at the time that he was suffering from insomnia. He used to roam all over the house at nights, engaging in a variety of activities, but he had an encyclopaedic knowledge of the citrus industry. I went as he had instructed me and he really taught me, went through everything. We prepared a document for presentation at the Ministry of Trade. I worked with him for about ten days. It was a very good learning experience for me. First of all, how to draft these documents. I did not know too much about that but he showed me how to do it. Secondly, the substantive knowledge of the subject, which I did not have, but I felt when I left that I really understood international trade in citrus, its problems and its possibilities. The British government was very impressed with Sir Harold. They obviously knew him and we had very amicable discussions and came to agreement. They presented the agreement to their minister. We sent the agreement – in those days, it had to be sent by telegram, or telex, whatever it was – to Port-of-Spain, and it was subsequently received and confirmed and agreement reached on marketing agreements for citrus that lasted, I suppose, for another ten years or so – until the Lomé Convention came into being.

This work really laid the foundation for the work that I did later on Lomé in the sense that, first of all, I did not know anything about negotiation until Sir Harold Robinson taught me some techniques. After I returned to Trinidad and Tobago, he would every now and then send me papers and say: 'You should be interested in this.' He was a nice person. Very irascible on occasion, but very knowledgeable.

So I completed this assignment within the first six months of arriving in Trinidad. On campus I also had my responsibilities for managing the economics programme. Having done this assignment on citrus, Dr Williams was impressed and appointed me straight away to the board of the Industrial Development Corporation (IDC) and to a number of other boards, so I was very busy in Trinidad.

Political disturbances

Although I left Trinidad and Tobago in 1967 to take up the post of Director of the Institute of Social and Economic Research (ISER) at the UWI Mona campus, I still remained in close touch with Willie Demas.

In 1969 Willie telephoned to tell me that the government was having to rethink its entire social policy. Trinidad and Tobago got representative government in 1956 and eventually independence, like Jamaica, in 1962. The early years of independence were characterized by unprecedented prosperity because of the discovery of natural gas. At the time, Trinidad and Tobago was the only country in the world exporting natural gas. The oil companies took full advantage of that. The government and the country experienced a significant inflow of financial resources. As in all situations like that one, such as the experiences in the OPEC period, considerable public money was being spent and, in some cases, wasted. Although there were some concrete illustrations of the prosperity of those days, they were inadequate to impress the young and growing population. Far from generating social peace and greater stability, it generated considerable instability, especially among the young who saw around them concrete evidence of a prosperity that had not reached them. This was especially the case among the young Afro-Trinidadians living in the low-income areas like Laventille, the largest and most significant one.

The response was essentially that of the African-Trinidadian population because the Indian-Trinidadians were basically rural and less militant about social problems. They generated most of the production of domestic agricultural crops. With rising incomes, they were reasonably prosperous. There was a whole string of small, family farms in an area just outside of Port-of-Spain, which was so successful that several of these farmers were able to send their children to university. But a generation gap developed even among those groups, where parents had different expectations from their children.

The Indian sections of the population did well because the public prosperity meant greater prosperity for them as far as the demand for food was concerned. In any case, they had their own agenda with the African population in the sense that they co-existed peacefully but there was not a lot of contact between them. Actually, one of the most interesting things was that the University of the West Indies managed to bring some of the young people together, so that in the demonstrations I am about to describe there were some Indian students who had caught up with the rhetoric of the time.

Dr Williams had become increasingly concerned by the fact that, far from the prosperity generating greater social harmony, it was generating quite the reverse. There were a lot of splinter groups developing and the population was very restive. In conversation with Willie, he observed that something was wrong with the development strategy that the government was following because, evidenced by the restiveness among the young population, they were not getting commensurate results.

The government of Trinidad and Tobago had embarked on a very vigorous programme of education through the establishment of Junior Secondary Schools all over the island, but it still did not close the gap between those and the very prestigious schools where the middle-class and upper-middle class went, because they did not have the same quality of teachers. So the Junior Secondary School Programme was not achieving the results that had been foreseen.

Then the government started the Better Village Programme to encourage villages to compete among themselves to see what amenities they could establish on their own initiative with secondary support from the government. This had been yielding somewhat better results, but was still insufficient to meet the needs of the time. Dr Williams was really very perturbed about the fact that the conventional way of development planning did not seem to be working in Trinidad and Tobago, because of its multi-ethnic and multi-cultural population, and the high percentage of young people in the total population, who were becoming restive. He suggested to Willie that he should seek the involvement of his

177

close friends in discussions of the situation and what could be done to ameliorate the restiveness being displayed.

I was in Jamaica, very much engaged with whatever I was doing. But Willie and I used to have these long telephone conversations at night. After nine o'clock in the evening Willie would ring me or I would ring him and we would speak for two or three hours. In fact the telephone company in Trinidad said to Willie: 'Mr Demas, we're going to stop charging you because what we'd charge you, you could never pay these bills.' Actually, as recalled elsewhere, when Willie retired, the telephone company presented him with a free telephone for the rest of his life. It was very amusing and the big crowd at the retirement function roared with laughter.

We spoke nearly every day. I had spoken to him frequently before, but when this situation began developing, which was in 1969 or thereabouts, we spoke on several occasions during the day because the situation was changing all the time. And then, of course, there were the Black Power riots in 1970.

Demas and I struggled to identify possible remedial action. We hit upon the idea of the government taking a multi-sector approach to the development of small businesses, be they small farms, or small firms doing a variety of manufacturing and distribution. To support them the government would set up a comprehensive package of development incentives and support. We came up with this idea of a People's Sector. At first the Prime Minister was not attracted to the idea of 'people's' because he said it sounded very much like a Socialist/Marxist solution, which really it was not. Nonetheless, I said in reply to Willie, 'Tell him that that should be part of the attraction, because the popular young leaders are using socialist rhetoric, so if one says the People's Sector, one is using the language of the day.' We drafted a document which Willie presented to Dr Williams, who, as was his habit, very patiently sat down and crafted this into a major policy statement on the economy. But it was too late. It fell flat. Of course, it required dissemination and explanations, but the pace of the movement quickened so much that it just fell flat. Nobody paid the slightest attention to it. Dr Williams was very depressed by that, and it occurred to him that he might not be relevant any longer.

I was confirmed in that assessment late in 1970 when I went to Trinidad for a university meeting, which he was chairing as Pro-Chancellor. I got into the hotel and went flat down with a terrible attack of the flu. The doctor came and advised that I should cancel my appointments for the next 72 hours. I was very surprised when a member of the hotel staff arrived to tell me that Dr Williams was there to see me. His arrival in the hotel attracted a great deal of curiosity. He came and expressed regret that I was ill and could not participate in the meeting. I enquired how the meeting went and he was not too happy with it.

On the subject of the document to which I had contributed, he indicated that all the work that Demas and myself had done had come to naught because the population was not interested in the ideas that had been put forward. I tried to reassure him by pointing out that such presentations took some time to be understood and absorbed by the groups for which they were intended. However, from his subsequent response, it became apparent that he was not going to pursue the matter. He sat down and indicated that he had already devoted numerous sleepless nights to thinking about the problem and at this point felt that he had done all that he could to achieve a better understanding between himself and the young population. The conversation ended with him reiterating his feeling that he might no longer be relevant to the young people and he doubted whether he had sufficient time left to rethink a new strategy for the young population.

I remember that conversation so well. And that's the last time I had any direct contact with him. I came away from it with a sense that it would not be long before he gave up. But in fact he did not leave office at that time.

13

Principal assignments in Jamaica

Literacy Campaign Evaluation Committee, 1970

While I was Director of ISER at Mona, in 1970 Prime Minister Hugh Shearer asked me to head an evaluation of the literacy programme. I spent the better part of two years with a group looking at the problem, proposing and developing a programme of remedial work in literacy. It was one of the best groups with which I have ever worked.

The Jamaica Movement for the Advancement of Literacy (JAMAL), which was introduced by the PNP, came after the change of government in 1972.

Having evaluated the state of literacy and found that the illiteracy rates were alarmingly high, we proceeded, while continuing our investigations, to propose a significantly expanded programme of remedial action.

The Evaluation Committee was very reliant on the considerable experience of Marjorie Kirlew, supported by Rita Girvan and Elaine Melbourne. The committee decided to do some pre-testing of the programme that we were recommending to the government.

In view of the limited resources then available, we proposed that the programme should be built up on the basis that volunteers would undertake the bulk of the teaching and other support activities. From our initial contacts with university graduates, we were optimistic that a well-constructed appeal for literacy teachers and other forms of support for the programme would be successful.

We developed a long list of volunteers, largely but not exclusively drawn from university graduates. We then proposed a programme of action principally based on utilizing the services of volunteers.

The proposal was submitted to the Prime Minister, for the purpose of securing government endorsement and support. He thanked me very warmly because initially I had been somewhat reluctant to take on the assignment so soon after I had assumed duties as Director of ISER.

There was a change of government when elections were held in 1972. Douglas Manley, whom I knew rather well because he was at Mona with me, indicated that he had been appointed Minister of Youth and Community Development and that included the literacy programme. I arranged for him to be briefed by Marjorie Kirlew on the substance of our work and recommendations. He found our proposals to be rather modest and inadequate in the light of their own assessment of the scale of the problem.

Marjorie subsequently reported that she had had discussions with the minister and that he desired a much more ambitious project than the one that we had formulated. He was of the opinion that Jamaica should aim at a programme along the lines of that introduced in Cuba, which would set out to eliminate the problem in a very short period of time, say six months. I responded by saying that Cuba had not solved the problem in six months, since I was familiar with the results of that programme. I had been in fairly continuous contact with UNESCO, which had been monitoring the progress of the Cuban programme.

Several weeks elapsed and we then heard that an appointment had been made of someone not known to have expertise in the field. I was distressed, because I was convinced that, based on the information at my disposal, the appointment could have negative outcomes. A more suitable appointment would have been Marjorie Kirlew herself, who was regarded locally and internationally as Jamaica's leading literacy expert.

After many false starts, eventually Dr Joyce Robinson was appointed when JAMAL was started – by which time, if I remember correctly, the government was almost out of office. Dr Robinson tried to get the programme back on track and to some extent she did succeed. However, the programme was delayed because well-prepared and efficient management had not initially been put in place to address this serious problem.

Jamaica bauxite levy negotiations, 1973–74

In April 1972 I was on my way home one afternoon when I heard the news on the car radio that I had been appointed as one of the members of a bauxite advisory group that had been established. I was unable to ascertain from the announcement what were the responsibilities envisaged for the group. If it was intended that the group should undertake action research on opportunities for increasing the contribution of bauxite to the local economy, I was certainly not the obvious choice in that situation. Had I been consulted beforehand, my own advice would have been to invite Dr Norman Girvan to be a member of the group because of the substantial research that he had done on the local industry. I had then concluded that I should indicate my unwillingness to join the group and instead propose that an invitation be extended to Girvan.

By the time I got to my office on the campus next morning, I was told that some people were saying that I went to Jamaica House and asked Mr Manley to put me on this advisory group! This was the worst kind of gossip-mongering since I was not in the habit of seeking positions or assignments. Accordingly, I made it plain to the government that I was not in a position to accept the appointment.

It must have been a year or so after this particular incident that I received a telephone call from the Prime Minister asking me whether I would see Pat Rousseau, who was undertaking a job for him on bauxite. I agreed to do so.

Pat came to see me at home and said that they were examining this question of how to increase the contribution of the bauxite industry to the local economy. They wanted to find a way of getting a substantially larger return for the country. He asked me to look at a document which he, Richard Fletcher and Mayer Matalon had prepared. They had come up with the idea of a levy on bauxite and wished to discuss it with me.

I had a long discussion with him and then he asked whether I would join the group preparing the study. I agreed and he also told me that he wished to associate Trevor Byer, energy advisor to the government of Jamaica, and Erwin Angus, who was then Permanent Secretary in Mining and Natural Resources, to serve as advisors. Byer's reputation had preceded him to Jamaica, as an extremely bright thinker with a prodigious capacity for work. Erwin Angus was also very competent. What I liked about him was how very careful he was on detail. He understood the issues. Carlton Davis, Senior Principal Scientific Officer, Scientific Research Council 1973–75, became an indispensable advisor to the group and later developed as Jamaica's leading expert on bauxite. Linton Minott was a long-serving public servant who became secretary of the commission. All of them formed part of the team advising the group. So this is how I became part of the Bauxite Negotiating Team. I spent nearly all my time out of office on it.

Our preparatory work for the meeting with the bauxite companies began. The first thing I asked members of the secretariat was whether they had requested the SEC 10K reports. Every year the United States Securities and Exchange Commission requires detailed reports from all the public companies in the United States, setting out the results of their business. The bauxite companies were producing these reports. I had never seen them but I knew of their existence. Only some members of the team answered in the affirmative. They then contacted the Jamaican Ambassador in Washington and asked him to have copies of these reports sent down. We got them, studied them and this is how we got all the information on the returns that the bauxite companies were securing on their investments in Jamaica. The reports were studied in very great detail.

We then had a meeting with Prime Minister Manley to consider whether the government should ask for negotiations with the bauxite companies. At this meeting were most of the people who would eventually serve on the negotiation committee.

The Prime Minister invited contributions from those present about whether there was prima facie a strong case for asking the bauxite companies to increase substantially their tax contributions to the government. After an expression of views, the Prime Minister concluded the discussion by giving his considered judgement that a strong case existed for requiring a substantial increase in revenues from the local industry. Accordingly, he instructed that preparatory work should continue and arrangements made for holding negotiations with the companies.

Pat Rousseau, who had been leading the preparatory discussions, continued as chairman of the negotiating group and, accordingly, had a very wide mandate. Associated with him was Mayer Matalon, one of the most impressive people that I have ever had the privilege of working with on technical and policy matters. Since Rousseau and Matalon, together with Richard Fletcher, were attending to most of the substantive issues, I concentrated my attention on economic issues and principally on assessing the data available on the financial performance of the companies involved.

In our preparatory discussions we were extremely well served by the contributions of our advisors, especially Carlton Davis, who had mastered a good deal of the technical and financial material, and Trevor Byer, who concentrated on the scientific side. Taken together, with inputs coming from other government officials, the committee eventually felt itself sufficiently prepared to proceed to negotiations with the companies, and so advised the government.

We invited the bauxite companies' team for conversations. We were making the presentation, but what the other side did not know was how well-prepared we were.

They had recruited a professor from Yale University as a consultant to do a study on the industry for them which they would present as their starting point for negotiations. The representatives of the companies came to the first meeting and offered the study for consideration. At the same time they indicated that because of their very busy schedule they would be unable to spend more than one day discussing it. We replied affirmatively and said we would study the report and be ready for discussion on the following day.

I was responsible for that response, while my colleagues were somewhat anxious that in view of the size of the study we might not be ready as proposed. I promised my colleagues that I would give the study my best effort.

I took the report, went home, retired to my study and stayed there for most of the night in order to identify the points that had to be discussed with the companies. The most important of these was their price assumptions, namely, the price they were using for accounting purposes and on which taxable capacity could be calculated. A considerable amount of their transactions were intra-company transactions, for example Alcoa Jamaica to Alcoa US (Aluminum Company of America Inc.). It was not a market transaction. This was not a market price. It was simply the price that they fixed for their intra-company transactions.

From their earlier discussion, I had felt that the company representatives had not studied the matter very carefully but had accepted unquestioningly the work of their advisors. In fact, what I discovered very quickly by going through the report was that the consultant had operated with the same price assumptions as we had, but the companies were not aware of it. So when the meeting resumed the following day, they started the discussion with the lack of realism in our proposals which, if they were to accept them, would ruin the industry.

At that point, I asked them what were their price assumptions on which their estimates of profitability were being made. The manner in which they handled the study that they had asked us to consider suggested to me that they were not too familiar with it. I decided therefore on the tactic of asking them questions about the content of the study. My hunch paid off. When I quizzed them on the price assumptions, they equivocated and proposed that we ask Professor Peck, their economic advisor from Yale, to deal with it. Professor Peck started by enquiring as to my great interest in the price assumptions. I replied that I would like to know because our group had been less familiar with the details on the industry and clearly we had to ensure that we were in agreement on the bases on which estimates of profitability were being made.

The company representatives began fiddling with the study, and then I referred them to different pages in it where it appeared that the price assumptions being used for the profitability calculations were identical to the ones that we had used in our paper, about which the companies were apparently unaware.

I said: 'So we are ad idem. We have nothing against one another, we are ad idem on a price we should use for the purpose of this negotiation.' Well, the representatives of the bauxite companies were astonished to find that their study used the same price that we had been asking them to accept, which they were resisting when in fact their own study and proposals were based on it!

The companies had been charging, or paying before that, 35 cents, and we were both discussing 42 cents plus. So there was now a 7.5 cent increase, which was a major difference from the levels that were then in existence. They were shocked because here were they talking to us about a 35 cent price per lb and their document was proposing a 42.50 cent per lb price. They proposed an adjournment of the meeting on the basis that I had treated the Yale economist very badly in the exchanges that we had on his study. To them, this was unacceptable. In my own case, no offence had been intended. Later, in conversation, the advisor assured me that he was not at all upset, since the vigour of our exchanges represented what took place at his own university in discussions of faculty studies.

The bauxite companies had felt that they should bring down a highly regarded authority from a major university to impress our delegation, which they thought consisted of a group of inexperienced people. Professor Peck, for his part, later explained to me that he had not himself worked on the report, but had secured a graduate student to prepare a draft which he had not himself had sufficient time to review. He went on to say that he was told that there was a local economist on the negotiating team, but he did not imagine that I would have such impressive academic credentials. Had he known, he and his assistant would have taken a totally different approach. Indeed, once the companies understood that our team was using unassailable data, they realized that we had scored a psychological victory.

The only company that had been close to our approach was Alcan, since in settling their liabilities in Canada they were accustomed to detailed scrutiny of their financial situation. Accordingly, we found very close correspondence between Alcan's payments to the Jamaican government and what our estimates would have been of their tax liability.

The American companies did not change their negotiating team because the representative from Alcoa, Charles Winckler was, in fact, warning them that the bauxite companies would have to pay more, much more, and that the local negotiating team was not just a group of uninformed people. He was absolutely convinced that they had to pay something much closer to the real taxable income than they had been paying. Charlie Winckler was a true professional and he had always been very uncomfortable with the situation as far as taxes were concerned. From the outset we could see from his replies and his input into the conversation that he was just doing his job. From the beginning he was sending signals that he was not happy with the situation. I remember telling my colleagues to pay careful attention to Winckler's responses. The team was subsequently advised by Mayer Matalon, who had gone to see Winckler and confirmed our impressions about him. Mayer also had a conversation with Leslie Ashenheim, who was initially against the levy, and who began by saying that we were going too far in proposing it. Mayer asked him to go and see Charlie Winckler. After that meeting, Ashenheim advised us to negotiate for as much as we could get because after his conversation with Charlie Winckler he was convinced that the companies were not levelling with us. Once Leslie Ashenheim said that, the JLP decided to support the levy. The levy was passed without a dissenting voice in parliament. This was an unprecedented occurrence in bauxite matters.

Chairman, Task Force on Financing Education, Government of Jamaica, 1989–90

This was the first government assignment that I took up when I returned to Jamaica as Vice-Chancellor of the UWI. There was then a current debate in the public domain about how additional resources could be found for financing the development of education.

The government set up a Task Force, which they asked me to chair, to examine the situation and come up with suggestions for improving the flow of resources into education and for the efficient management of them. It was a very well constructed group, consisting of experienced people drawn from the private sector, the teaching profession and other sources.

In order to accommodate the different time constraints of individual members, it was decided that the group should meet before the beginning of the working day, which meant at 6:00 am.

We worked very hard, in particular on the concept that in future education would be financed by an independent foundation with contributions coming from the government and other sources in the community. It was considered that such an arrangement could help to reduce the politicization of education expenditure, which was identified as a principal problem affecting the sector.

We thought that the government would set the policy in terms of educational needs, while the foundation would concern itself with the mobilization of resources from government and other sources, both local and external. The foundation would also monitor the expenditure of those resources, reporting to parliament and the country at appropriate intervals. The membership of the foundation would be broadly based to include representatives both of the education sector and the community as a whole. Apart from its disbursement of funds made available from government, private and external sources, it would have a broad mandate to undertake investigations into problem areas and make appropriate recommendations.

We submitted the report and received virtually no response for some time, after which the whole report sank like a stone, but it served the purpose of reacquainting me, after a period of absence, with the realities of Caribbean public life.

Not surprisingly, the issue of adequate financing of education has remained current over the years as governments wrestle with the problem of finding sufficient resources to meet the burgeoning needs for greater expenditure on education.

Committee to review the structure of the Jamaican government, 1991–92

This committee was commissioned by the Prime Minister. The chairman was Professor Rex Nettleford. When he was allocating tasks to individual members, Marshall Hall, Arthur Brown and myself agreed with him to assume responsibilities for the commodity bodies: the Banana Board, the Coffee Industry Board, and so on. We looked at all of them, interviewed people in great detail and looked at the process of modernization of the commodities sector.

Notwithstanding our efforts, the recommendations of the report were not accepted and followed up by the government.

Chair, task force to assess the impact of tourism on the Jamaican economy, 1995

Carlyle Dunkley, then a minister in the government, called me on behalf of the Prime Minister to ask whether I could be persuaded to chair a group being set up to examine the impact of tourism on the Jamaican economy. I was extremely hesitant to do so because of multiple commitments, both in my office and with other governments. However, after gentle persuasion, I agreed to accept the assignment provided I was given freedom to select the other members of the group.

As I recall, the members were O.K. Melhado, who had been chairing a committee on tourism; Oliver Clarke, Managing Director of *The Gleaner* newspaper and very conversant with the operations of the private sector; Anthony Abrahams, who had been Director of Tourism; and Marjorie Henriques, who for some time had been a senior official at the Planning Institute of Jamaica (PIOJ) and was very knowledgeable about the workings of the local economy. All of these were people with whom I enjoyed a cordial relationship and most of them had worked with me before on an assignment requiring exceptional hours of work.

Given our other commitments, the members of the committee, like myself, had great difficulty in finding an acceptable time for meetings. We finally decided we should meet at 6:00 am so that our work could be done before the normal office period began. We worked energetically and in short order had assembled most of the data on the tourist sector that was required to examine its impact on the economy.

In the course of this process, I had started thinking about what is known as a 'satellite account' for tourism in the national accounts: that is, a separate account for tourism that would show the flows of expenditure into the sector and the outflows of expenditure that would constitute the incomes going to different parties in the form of wages and salaries and non-wage payments, such as interest. This would constitute a much more acceptable method of identifying income flows going to different parts of the economy.

The whole idea of a satellite account had been developed in France. The person who had developed the French accounts was teaching at the University of Montreal. I called him and he was very excited that someone was going to use his methodology and offered to come to Jamaica to train the people assigned to the study at no cost other than air fare and accommodation. However, I could not get approval, at the working level, for his visit.

In the absence of a satellite account, I constructed a rudimentary version based on statistical data that Marjorie Henriques was able to assemble from available sources. Notwithstanding its very preliminary nature, the data were able to show that tourism was a much larger contributor to the local economy than had been conventionally assumed. There was also very valuable work done on identifying the problems of Ocho Rios and what needed to be done to correct them. This part of the Task Force report was largely developed on information unearthed by Anthony Abrahams, with support from Maurice Facey.

We finished our work on schedule. Although I say so myself, the report was of good quality and, notwithstanding data limitations, it provided valuable insights on how the local impact of the tourism industry could be increased. The typical calculation missed income and expenditure flows that made a significant difference to the result. The development of satellite accounts would correct that problem.

The task ahead for the government was to set up the necessary machinery including the training of the requisite staff so that the information flows needed to calculate the impact of the tourism sector would become regularly available.

I was therefore somewhat perplexed by the fact that after much energy had been spent on trying to get me to organize this work, no acknowledgement or responses were received about our report. I gathered that some members of the government were unhappy with the conclusions reached on the impact and wanted further investigations to take place before any action would be approved on the report's recommendations. The matter has since rested there.

I was deeply disappointed, and embarrassed that I had persuaded the other members of the group to take part in the proceedings when they had a number of urgent matters requiring their attention. I was also disturbed that the report had not been sent to the representatives of the tourist industry for their information and comment.

In the meantime I have, on more than one occasion, been approached by ministers of tourism who appear to be very interested in the idea of developing satellite accounts and were apparently awaiting approval from cabinet to proceed with the work required. However, I am not certain whether any action has taken place.

14

Assignments in other Caribbean countries

Grenada

From the time that I concluded my stay at university in England, I considered that, as the land of my birth, I had a special responsibility to Grenada. This did not in any way conflict with my basic commitment to the West Indies as a whole. However, in my initial period back in the Caribbean, I had a personal difficulty with the governments that were then in office in Grenada under the leadership of Prime Minister Gairy.

I was particularly troubled by several reports I had received about the financial irregularities of those governments, not to speak of my strong objections to incidents concerning personal attacks on individuals for whom I had high esteem, especially members of my family. In their case, this occasioned so much personal insecurity that it led to their emigration. In those circumstances I did not feel it appropriate for me to provide any assistance to those administrations, although they included personal friends from schooldays.

That situation changed with the coming into office of the Bishop/Coard administration. Then, I subordinated my personal views to the wider recognition that this regime was very popular in Grenada.

Head of interim government after the political and constitutional crisis

As a result of the political crisis in Grenada which led to the death of Prime Minister Maurice Bishop and other high-level government officials, there was a virtual breakdown in the machinery of government. It appeared that after a series of consultations, both at home and abroad, the Governor-General was advised to appoint an interim government to deal with the affairs of the island until a new government could take office following elections.

I was then approached by the Governor-General to head an interim government that would remain in office until the elections had been held. This was an extremely delicate matter since the Governor-General was acting on his authority without consulting any of the local political interests. I was myself somewhat hesitant about assuming these responsibilities, but after consultation with the Secretary-General of the United Nations and of UNCTAD, I was encouraged to make myself available for a period of one year. I indicated to the Governor-General that I would pay a short visit to Grenada to discuss the details of my assignment. On my arrival there, I managed to put together a preliminary list of members of an interim cabinet and, by so doing, constituted ministers to head existing government departments. Having laid the groundwork for the assumption of office by the interim government, I returned to Geneva to make the requisite arrangements for my assumption of office in Grenada. On my way back to Geneva, I stopped in New York to acquaint the Secretary-General with the substance of my discussion. He was very supportive and indicated to me that, on a strictly informal basis, the representatives of the five Permanent Members of the Security Council had indicated to him that their governments would not raise any objections to my being granted a special leave of absence to head the interim administration. As I have already indicated, a difficulty had arisen in a comparable situation in Zimbabwe.

When I returned to Geneva, I was advised to visit my doctor to acquaint him with the situation and get his advice about how to handle my treatment while I was in Grenada. He suggested that I see the Professor of Ophthalmology in Geneva. She undertook her own examination of my eyes and gave me the most unwelcome assessment that they were in a bad state because I had lesions on the retina of one of them. If I did not follow the proposed treatment, there was a strong possibility that I would become blind. She indicated that she wished to consult with her parent group in Boston, and the conclusion reached was that the treatment involved my remaining in a dark room continuously over an initial period of six weeks, when the matter would be further reviewed. The immediate implication of this was that I could not take up the assignment in Grenada. I advised the Governor-General and suggested that he should proceed to appoint the interim administration and to ask one of them, Nicholas Brathwaite, to head it. He agreed readily and also accepted all of my other recommendations for the membership of the government. Although I was deeply disappointed to be deprived of the opportunity to help my country in this exceptional period of difficulty, I was somewhat reassured that the interim administration would have people of quality to undertake the task.

A major difficulty arose in the misrepresentation of the reasons why I had not gone to Grenada. The Geneva correspondent of a major newspaper published a front page article saying that I had decided not to go to Grenada because of a 'diplomatic illness'. According to his accounts I was reluctant to abandon my high lifestyle in Geneva. Fortunately, my family and my office decided not to inform me of the article, which I could not read myself because I was confined to a dark room on my doctor's instructions. Very much later, my doctor was introduced to the correspondent at a social function and informed him of the injustice that had been done to me. My wife and I were later to meet him by accident and he was extremely apologetic for the error that he had made. Nonetheless, for some time afterwards I occasionally met members of the public who referred to the newspaper report, believing it to be true. I quickly put those impressions to rest.

Development programme following Hurricane Ivan

A further opportunity to help Grenada was provided in the aftermath of Hurricane Ivan in 2004. The damage done by the hurricane was extensive, both to housing and other infrastructure, particularly schools, major roads and health facilities. The Prime Minister of Grenada contacted me to ask whether I could help them to put together an economic recovery programme, suitable for submission to external donors. I agreed to work with the administration in Grenada for an initial period of six months. Accordingly, I took up residence within two weeks of coming to an agreement with the Prime Minister on my assignment.

Upon arrival, I secured an office in the Ministry of Finance and selected an initial team of three young UWI graduates, with occasional support from others. Our initial task was to prepare proposals for external funding and to arrange a donors' meeting to discuss it. In a very short period of time we drew up a draft proposal involving an initial contribution of US$260 million. This was intended for contribution by individual donor countries and agencies. Additional sums were targeted towards institutions such as the World Bank and the European Community. I was very encouraged by the full acceptance of our proposals by the countries concerned. I was also very satisfied with the herculean efforts of the group working with me who laboured for very long hours to produce, in a comparatively short period, a document that was accepted by the donors' meeting without any amendments. I should also mention the very commendable efforts by the Financial Secretary, Mr Antoine. All this had the effect of giving the post-hurricane reconstruction a very good start.

After I had completed the donors' document and met with them, I experienced a bout of illness that eventually required my return to Jamaica, but nonetheless I was gratified that the programme had got off to a good start with the initial funding commitments.

Guyana

National economic strategies: nationalization of bauxite

With all the work I had to do, I also found myself helping with bauxite negotiations. I was surprised when President Forbes Burnham of Guyana wrote me a letter at ISER sometime in the early 1970s, prior to the bauxite negotiations in Jamaica, requesting me to become a member of a group that he was appointing to undertake a review of economic policy, centred around issues of the ownership of resources.

I called Willie Demas, who was already in Georgetown as Secretary-General of CARICOM, to get his understanding of the purpose and scope of the mission.

In reply, he encouraged me to come to Georgetown because he thought that I could be a leavening influence on the radical advice that the government was receiving from other sources. He indicated to me that the government was interested in hearing from other sources about the approach it should take in trying to take control of the principal natural resource industries, which were sugar and bauxite.

The meeting turned out to be a general review of natural resource development and ownership; in fact, in my contribution to the discussions, I focused almost exclusively on the issue of taxing these resource industries. When we adjourned, we were each given a particular assignment. Demas and I were asked to look at the fiscal system and what improvements could be made in securing more government revenue from the natural resources sector. Other people were given assignments more directly related to the question of public ownership.

On the issue of public ownership, it was apparent during the initial exchanges that decisions had already been taken to proceed with nationalization. The issue then largely became a management one – how to proceed with legislation to provide for public ownership, what would be the arrangements for compensating the companies concerned, and how would the top management and senior staffing be organized.

At that time, local participants in the group were somewhat dismissive of the importance of management problems such as recruitment of senior executives to run the companies, training of executives and other personnel in financial management and in the technical work required to run the plants efficiently. Demas and I warned our colleagues about the management problems that had to be solved but there was a tendency to minimize the importance of these issues.

Accordingly, there was a clear intention to proceed without the degree of preparation we were proposing. Demas and I politely withdrew from the proceedings. The other participants – George Beckford, Kari Levitt, Norman Girvan, all from the UWI and whom we knew very well – were more positive and did not give as much priority to the issues of management. However, they were not the people pushing for nationalization. It was really the Guyanese technocrats, among them Haslyn Parris. He was a very bright person who had done mathematics at Mona and was a very impressive individual. President Burnham had, understandably, a very high opinion of him, and decided to appoint him to head the nationalized bauxite company. However, his performance was impaired by his lack of operational experience.

The government of Guyana had been fortunate with the nationalization of sugar. Its desire to nationalize coincided with the desire of Bookers Sugar Estates Ltd to reduce its ownership in Guyana. Bookers took the nationalization of sugar very much in its stride. The person who represented Bookers at the time was Anthony Haynes, originally from Barbados. He co-operated with the government and after Bookers was taken over continued selling the sugar for the local company.

President Burnham was impressed with how Bookers dealt with the problem of nationalization and kept making comparisons between them and Alcan, who were more reluctant to cede ownership. However, in the end they did not persist with their opposition to it, partly because of company policy and the Canadian government's sympathetic attitude in favour of local ownership and management of a country's resources.

It is useful to recall that Prime Minister Trudeau and President Burnham knew each other as students in London and were therefore sensitive to each other's positions. Accordingly, they both worked for a settlement of the issue through negotiations.

Commonwealth Group of Experts on Development and Adjustment in Guyana, 1989

The members of this group were Michael Faber, Institute of Development Studies, University of Sussex, and Gerry Helleiner,

Professor of Economics, University of Toronto, in association with Vishnu Persad, Director of Economics at Marlborough House, and myself as chairman.

The group undertook a careful review of the existing policies relating to economic recovery and development and formulated a revised strategy. The report, entitled *Guyana: Economic Recovery Programme and Beyond*, was published by the Commonwealth secretariat and was carefully reviewed by the government of Guyana, which adopted several of its proposals.

This permitted Guyana to overcome the hesitations of the international community about some of the ongoing approaches and strategies then being followed by the government. It facilitated the government in returning from a situation of relative isolation to one of ongoing support from external institutions and agencies.

Herdmanston Accord, 1998

It turned out to be fortuitous that I had had that initial meeting with Mrs Janet Jagan in 1989–90 during the negotiations on the Guyana/Venezuela border dispute.

There was a big problem in Guyana because of the long-standing difficulties between the citizens of Indian and African descent. It was reported that they were marching, firing guns and actually fighting each other in the streets.

I received an official message from the government of Guyana asking me to be part of a reconciliation panel of three. Sonny Ramphal, Henry Ford, a very well known lawyer from Barbados, and myself were invited to arbitrate the dispute to resolve outstanding issues, which were largely political and constitutional. I do know Guyana quite well, and am very interested in its future.

There was quite a lot of publicity that we were coming to 'solve the problem', as if we could solve the racial problems in Guyana. We were reluctant to stay at a hotel for obvious reasons, so we were accommodated at a place called Herdmanston House, which had hitherto belonged to one of the large companies. There were a lot of rumours and everyone was anxious to give us information about the situation and the latest happenings. The most encouraging aspect was that the head of the army was Indian and the head of the police was African and they were very good friends. We had a meeting with them and were pleased to see the good understanding between them. They promised to ensure that there were no demonstrations in the streets while we were trying to negotiate.

Our next step was to meet with Mrs Jagan, who was the President after her husband's death in 1997, and with Desmond Hoyte, who was the leader of the opposition party. Both Sonny Ramphal and Henry Ford, for personal reasons, thought that it would not be appropriate for them to meet with Mrs Jagan. Sonny assumed that he would be thought to be on the side of the opposition because of his service during President Burnham's government, while Henry assumed that because years ago he had won a very expensive case against Mrs Jagan and her husband which had cost them a great deal of money, she would not have forgiven him.

Since I had no such stories to tell, I was elected as the negotiator.

I telephoned Mrs Jagan to ask for an appointment. She was very accommodating and said that three o'clock would be convenient for her. After checking my diary, I confirmed with her that after my luncheon appointment tomorrow, I could come at three o'clock. She then indicated that she meant three o'clock in the morning, not in the afternoon. When I told the other members of the team, they were very amused.

I asked for a wake-up call at 2:30 am with some coffee and when I arrived at the President's house it was obvious that she had been working for some time in her study. She offered me tea.

To open the conversation, I started with the difficulty of political leadership and asked her how she liked the business of being head of government and head of party, especially as her husband had been in that role for so many years. She replied by asking me if I thought that people in Guyana liked her. She said they did not like her, they respected her because she was Cheddi's wife. She then asked me if I thought she was not liked because she was white. I said I was not sure, but I would not rule it out. She then said that, from time to time, she thought that was the case. But I do not really think that was so. I believe she was a strong woman and the Guyanese were not accustomed to a strong woman being in charge and, in addition, she was not Guyanese. I assured her that she was in charge and I was convinced that she would carry out her functions very well.

I suggested that we discuss the various points for the negotiation and started with the most difficult, contentious issues. To my great surprise, she agreed to every single proposal that the team was about to make. The most difficult was to ask her to forgo the remainder of their parliamentary term and have the election in six months. She was in the second year of a five-year term and we were asking her to give it up, so that elections could be held and a fresh start made. She agreed. We then went through the entire list of proposals, discussed it, talked through the implications of them all and she agreed to everything. I was elated. And then she said we now have to go and tell the cabinet. This was about 5:30 in the morning.

I suggested that perhaps the meeting with the cabinet should be postponed to allow her to catch up on her sleep. She assured me that she would never sleep after getting up in the morning. She usually had a cup of tea and that was when her day began.

We went down to the cabinet room where the entire cabinet was assembled; some of them were half asleep. The President then introduced me and began her presentation by saying that we had just spent almost three hours discussing the matter and had come to the following agreement. Some members of the cabinet tried to interrupt her and she responded by asking them to allow her to complete the presentation, since she was the President and someone had to take responsibility for the agreement. At the conclusion, she asked if anyone had any objections. There were none. She then told them that she expected them to respect and honour every single line of the document. Finally, she then thanked them and wished them a good morning.

When I returned to Herdmanston House, the other team members were at breakfast. They were astonished to learn that Mrs Jagan had accepted every one of the proposals and had signed the document. I told them that they should now meet with Mr Hoyte and have him sign as well. We could meet for lunch, write the report and arrange a press conference. Well, it turned out that they could not get Mr Hoyte to agree. He questioned everything in the document. It took them the entire day before he finally agreed and signed. This agreement was the Herdmanston Accord.

The Guyana elections were brought forward and Mrs Jagan's party won in December 1998. The opposition could not claim that they were not given a chance. Mrs Jagan won as a democratically elected president and continued in power until August 1999, when she resigned due to ill health with a heart condition, though she lived for another ten years.

Belize

Advisor on economic co-operation, 1970–74

While I was Director of ISER at the UWI, Mona, I was privileged to serve in a variety of government negotiations. One of them was being advisor to the Belizean delegation negotiating their boundary with Guatemala. The reason I became involved was that when I was at the LSE, Raphael Fonseca, a senior civil servant from Belize, came to the UK on a one-year course for senior civil servants that the British government used to organize. I became friendly with him and we would discuss a large number of issues having to do with Belize's development.

On one occasion when they were having difficulties at the border with Guatemala, there were a series of disputes in which the British had to send troops to police the border. They agreed to have discussions on the question of settling the disputes. Fonseca suggested to Prime Minister George Price that they should invite me to be an advisor to them for these negotiations; having discussed the situation with me when we were in London, I knew something about the subject and had some ideas on it.

It appeared that the British government was surprised when they were told that I was going to be an advisor for the negotiations. The High Commissioner in Jamaica told me that I would be part of their delegation since Belize was not an independent country. He further said that the negotiations were secret and I should not discuss them with anyone. For the purpose of maintaining secrecy, they had decided to give me a code name – it was Bentley. Thereafter, I was only to be referred to by that name.

The first meeting took place at the Tower Isle hotel in St Mary, Jamaica. I went there to join the Belizean delegation. At the hotel check-in desk I was asked for my name, but could not remember the code name that had been assigned to me!

So I thought, this just suits me. Why have I got myself into this awful mess? I was just about to give up, walk out of the hotel and take a taxi back to Kingston when Raphael Fonseca showed up. He said: 'Ah, Mr Bentley, how are you?' So the problem was cleared up.

When we arrived at the conference room, the Guatemalans were sitting on one side of the table and the British and ourselves on the other. When I looked around, I realized that one of the people on the Guatemalan delegation was a good friend of mine, Gert Rosenthal. But I decided not to show any knowledge of anybody at all. Nor did he. We had a very fractious discussion, but at the end it was agreed that because there were a number of technical points that had to be resolved, we needed to meet again.

It was always a problem finding somewhere we could meet because we did not want to meet where there was a Belizean/West Indian community, or for that matter, a Guatemalan community. People would know we were meeting and things were very tense at the time, or so it was said.

Anyway, for the negotiations in March 1971 the governments had to choose very carefully and they chose San Francisco for our meeting. On arrival in the US, my procedures had been completed in advance so that I was allowed to dispense with the usual immigration and customs requirements. When we got to the hotel, my suitcase was there in a room that had been reserved for me. I thought this fascinating. I made contact with the Belizean members of the team. It was agreed that we would meet close to midnight to liaise with the British members of the team. When we got to the conference room, we were told that the British were unable to make any contact with the Guatemalans, but that enquiries were underway. We were subsequently informed that the Guatemalan representatives at the talks had been unfortunately detained in Guatemala and would not therefore be in a position to join the meeting.

Since we had received confirmation that they were no longer able to attend the meeting, it was decided to arrange for a one-on-one at a location to be agreed between the two sides. Belize appointed me. The Guatemalans appointed Gert Rosenthal. We agreed to meet in Mexico.

About a month later, we arrived in Mexico, checked into the hotel, and met in the lounge. We agreed to have a discussion and both indicated our willingness to find agreement and draft a suitable proposal. After some discussion, we agreed that what Guatemala wanted was an outlet to the Atlantic Ocean. This was understandable given their geographic situation. If they get to the Atlantic they can trade with Europe. We agreed that Belize also needed a good port on the Atlantic.

We came up with this idea that the two sides, before they could get agreement on the other very prickly points, would agree to build a multilane highway as a joint venture, stretching from the border to the sea, which would give Guatemala free access down to the sea. Belize would also use it and both sides would benefit. In fact, they could charge a fee to people using the highway and share the revenue and the facilities. We prepared the proposal on the basis that the project would be financed by the British government at a rough estimated cost of approximately £5 million. This was going to be the beginning of a better relationship. We considered that this could be a significant start with joint management and confidence building, which would be indispensable conditions for reaching an agreement on a total package.

We went back to our respective countries and reported the conclusions that we had reached. But the British Treasury turned it down on the grounds that the £5 million that we had suggested as a rough approximation of the cost was not acceptable to the British authorities.

I told the British that if they did not accept the proposals they would spend more, in the years to come, on troops and Harrier jets going to Belize to protect the border. And of course, this has turned out to be the case. At present, 30 years later, the two sides have agreed to work jointly on a project to build the highway along the lines that we had proposed. It would be interesting to know the eventual cost of the project.

The irony of it is that, on a visit to Belize while the negotiations were taking place, I mentioned to Prime Minister Price that I was negotiating about a place that I had never seen. He was amused and immediately arranged for me to visit the border on the following day.

On arriving, I took the opportunity to walk around the area and observed that there was nothing interesting there. There were a few women washing clothes in the stream, some men were playing cards, and everyone seemed cordial towards one another. I was left wondering whether the dispute was only between governments and not between those resident in and around the border. This might well have been the case, although border disputes are not just between peoples but also have wider implications at the national level. Nonetheless, I sensed that, setting aside the national implications, some goodwill gestures such as the proposed highway might go a long way towards solving the problem.

Organization of Eastern Caribbean States (OECS)

Chairman, Technical Advisory Committee, Constitutional Reform in the Leeward and Windward Islands, 1974–75

In 1973–74, Dr Eric Williams exhibited a high degree of interest in CARIFTA and, later, CARICOM. When I first went to the CARICOM secretariat in 1974, he was extremely helpful. In fact, he telephoned me before I assumed the post to ask me whether I could assemble a team and do a report on the constitutional future of the Windward and Leeward Islands. In governmental circles in the region there was uncertainty as to whether it would be feasible to make a viable arrangement for the independence of all of them, since some of them were not independent. Certainly, their membership of CARICOM required the achievement of that status because, as colonial territories, they had to seek the prior approval of the British government before associating themselves with any decision that had external implications. The entire situation was rather untidy.

After our conversation, Dr Williams placed at the disposal of ISER US$150,000 to prepare a report. I managed to interest two colleagues, Vaughan Lewis and Pat Emmanuel, to undertake the work. They did the report and actually finished it in 1975 after I had assumed the post of Secretary-General in Georgetown. There was $40,000 remaining from the advance that had been provided. I sent the report to Dr Williams and the other Heads of Government in the Windward and Leeward Islands. Dr Williams sent a message back thanking me for the report and asking me to send it out to the Heads of Government involved to ascertain their reaction to it.

I telephoned the Hon. Robert Bradshaw, then Prime Minister of St Kitts and Nevis and at the time regarded as the elder statesman in the OECS, to arrange the meeting. He suggested that we aimed to have it over the Easter weekend in Barbados, which would give adequate time for its consideration in the various capitals so that his colleagues would be equipped to participate in decisions about it.

I contacted the other Heads, and each of them agreed on the timing and location of the meeting. However, on Good Friday morning, I received a telephone call from Patrick John, then Prime Minister of Dominica, who indicated that he was not available to attend because of prior commitments. Accordingly, he wanted to know whether he could send a representative. Then I received a similar call from Antigua saying that the Prime Minister was unable to attend, but wanted to know if he could send a representative. My response was that this was a matter to be discussed by the Heads of Government concerned. It was important that they give their personal endorsement, or otherwise, to the report. The final result was that only two Heads of Government were able to attend: Robert Bradshaw, St Kitts and Nevis, and John Compton in St Lucia. I called to tell them the outcome of my enquiries. Compton responded by asking what was the point of just two Heads of Government meeting. He could more conveniently discuss the recommendations of the report with Robert Bradshaw on the telephone and endeavour to have a meeting of minds on the subject.

Prime Minister Bradshaw was very upset and indicated that he would not be attending any further meetings on the subject, since he felt that his colleagues could have made a greater effort to free themselves for the weekend.

On Easter Tuesday, Dr Williams had someone telephone me to find out the outcome of the meeting. Could I give him my report? I had to tell him that the meeting did not take place. He was extremely disappointed and took an immediate decision not to involve himself any further in the matter. I then tried to persuade him otherwise by writing him a personal letter to encourage him to remain committed to the consideration of the study. He declined my suggestion and showed no interest in the balance remaining from the advance, indicating that I should do whatever I wished with it. Accordingly, I arranged with the university bursar to place the remaining amount at the disposal of the ISER and told Vaughan Lewis to use it to advance their work on the political development of the OECS.

As far as the OECS countries were concerned, they never met to consider the report.

Dr Williams' profound disappointment with CARICOM was not only because of the Guyana/Jamaica imbroglio on the matter of associate status with the Council for Mutual Economic Assistance (COMECON). It was also based on his profound disappointment with the OECS.

Chair, Commission on OECS Tax Reform and Administration, appointed by the OECS Monetary Council, 2002

In an effort to modernize the tax systems of the member states of the Organization of Eastern Caribbean States, the monetary council of their central bank agreed to the establishment of a technical group to undertake a survey of the taxation systems, with a view to increasing the revenue being collected.

The Governor of the Central Bank, who was very well known to me, asked me to chair the group. It included the most experienced economists and financial analysts drawn from the member states and the Central Bank, who provided the secretariat. It was extremely well-organized and discussions were of a high order. In my own case, it brought me up to date on the fiscal situation and prospects of these states.

We travelled through the individual countries in order to get the commission better known to the local sectors of opinion, especially the business community. The discussions were very lively and informative. Our methodology was that we would work during the day, and in the evenings we would make ourselves available for discussions on television and radio. We participated in a panel so that the public could telephone in questions about our work. We visited all of the member countries of the OECS and met all the important interests: the cabinet and senior civil servants and the private sector, including the trade unions.

We broke into sub-groups to deal with particular matters. I kept broad oversight of the entire exercise, but I was particularly interested in the issue of value added taxation.

As far as the subject of our discussions was concerned, in several states the issue of value added taxation turned out to be among the most contentious, but on the whole we sensed weary acquiescence among most representatives of the private sector.

As a result of all the material we had assembled from our investigations and discussions, we were able to submit our report through the Governor of the Central Bank for cabinet discussion in each state.

Without getting into the detail, it was apparent that our report was broadly acceptable to individual countries and most of them agreed to introduce the value added tax. Those who were hesitant at the outset eventually agreed to do so.

Apart from the local reception of the report, it was well received in the international community as a genuine effort to improve fiscal performance in the interests of further and more sustainable economic growth. Undoubtedly this has had a positive effect on the standing of the individual states among international donor agencies.

The member states expressed satisfaction with the outcome of our work and indicated interest in continuing to retain our services for further investigative work on taxation and other matters.

However, a heavy schedule of commitments did not permit me to accept the proposal, although I retained a very strong interest in the fiscal and economic performance of the states concerned.

Antigua and Barbuda

Chair, Royal Commission of Enquiry into the Medical Benefits Scheme, Antigua and Barbuda, July 2002–3

The question of the operation of the Medical Benefits Scheme in Antigua had been an issue of public concern, largely centring around questions about how the financial affairs of the scheme were being administered because it was based on taxpayer contributions. There were also concerns about the people who had received benefits from the scheme.

I spent 18 months on the enquiry, of which at least 12 months were spent resident in Antigua. I started virtually from scratch, set up offices in some rooms in the local hotel where I was staying, and finalized the arrangements for the commission with the government.

There were three of us, the other two being a local accountant and a Queen's Council from Sierra Leone, resident in the United Kingdom. We worked with a legal advisor from Barbados.

Our first task was to set up an investigative team to look into the technical operations. Because of the complex nature of the subject, we decided to request the services of a team from the Royal Canadian Mounted Police (RCMP), which had a high international reputation for dealing with white collar crimes. The government of Antigua requested the team through official channels. A positive response was quick in coming and the team started to work very shortly after our arrival in Antigua. They did a fantastic job and substantially assisted us in discharging our mandate.

One of the most important issues for consideration was the decision taken by the government to build a new hospital for Antigua and Barbuda that would essentially have been funded under the scheme. The project was generally welcomed by the population, but concerns were raised because it appeared that the construction of the hospital had run into financial difficulties, substantially exceeding the original estimates.

This was the principal reason why the government took the decision to establish the enquiry. It would be inappropriate to go into further details of our work since having reported to the Government, it would be for it to decide on further disclosures of information.

SECTION 5

DEVELOPMENT OF THE UNIVERSITY OF THE WEST INDIES (UWI)

15

Vice-Chancellor, 1988–98

Early interest

When I joined the staff at Mona in 1960, I became almost immediately involved in the ongoing discussions among other staff members in the Faculty of Social Sciences about the future of the university and what should be its strategic aims. This experience was enriched by the scholastic exchanges that I was able to have with the contacts that opened up as a result of my secondment to Princeton and Columbia universities and my participation in high-level exchanges, of which the Rio Conference on Inflation and Growth stands out as a very seminal occasion.

As a result of these experiences I developed particular views on the development of the UWI and how it should try to locate itself in the academic world at large. While I was Secretary-General of CARICOM, Vice-Chancellor Preston gave Gerald Lalor the assignment of discussing with the CARICOM committee set up for this purpose what particular projects they would submit for financing from the European Development Fund. The Heads of Government had already agreed that the university should get some of the money. Lalor came to Georgetown with a 'wish list' of projects. When he came, I listened to what he was going to propose and then said to him that I did not find the list sufficiently impressive. He replied that this was what Vice-Chancellor Preston wanted. So I called the Vice-Chancellor and told him that in the light of my experience with the European Community, I doubted whether this would be an attractive package to them. The Vice-Chancellor then gave me carte blanche to change the project list and so I informed Lalor when we met the next day.

When the meeting convened, Lalor presented my version of the list, and I followed by saying that, in the light of my experience with Brussels, they would be impressed by a list that indicated that we were thinking as a region and giving emphasis to human development, an area to which they attached considerable importance. The meeting agreed and in the end the university got a very substantial sum from the first and second Lomés.

From then on, the future of the university and its development needs attracted my attention and I developed concrete ideas that I would later seek to implement while I was Vice-Chancellor.

I had met Vice-Chancellor Aston Preston just by chance on a flight to Bogota in 1986. I do not remember what either of us was doing there. We started chatting and he said he would like to have a conversation with me about the future of the university. Among other things, Preston indicated that he wanted to establish a Business School at Mona. The United States Agency for International Development (USAID) had expressed interest in providing support for such a school. They hoped that the university would break new ground and identify suitable leadership. Subsequently, Preston telephoned me in Geneva to say that he had a proposition to put to me about the leadership of the new business programme.

I replied that I did not think I would be available, because I was in the midst of the Common Fund negotiations. I would therefore have to decline his invitation, but I fully supported what he was trying to do and hoped he could find someone else to lead it.

He went on to ask whether I would be willing to meet with him at a convenient time during the coming months to discuss the project, and I agreed. In thinking about a possible date for a meeting, I indicated to him that because of a standing arrangement that the CARICOM Heads had made with the UN Secretary-General for me to attend meetings of CARICOM Heads as requested, I would be going to the next meeting of the Heads being held in Georgetown. Preston said that he would also be there, and we could possibly meet during that time to have the conversation. Indeed, if that was not possible, I could arrange to come to Kingston immediately after the meeting for a few days, before returning to Geneva.

Very shortly after that conversation, I received a message that Vice-Chancellor Preston had died. I was in a state of shock because I had so recently been speaking with him.

CARICOM Heads initiative

I went to the Heads of Government meeting as I had originally planned, with no thought about being involved with university matters. As a matter of fact, John Compton, Prime Minister of St Lucia, saw me in the lobby as I arrived at the conference hotel and asked me to assist him in preparing a draft proposal in the field of tourism that he wished to put to the Heads. Accordingly, I asked him to mention to the chairman that I would be somewhat delayed because I was helping him with finalizing a proposal.

I was just settling in to that assignment when Sonny Ramphal came to tell me that the Heads wished me to come to the plenary session because they wanted to discuss the vice-chancellorship of the university with me.

It seemed that following Vice-Chancellor Preston's death, the CARICOM Heads of Government had initiated an informal process in parallel with the university's own process to identify a successor. The actual authority for the appointment resided in the University Council. I was somewhat hesitant to participate in a process that could be thought of as conflicting with the university's statutes. So I told Ramphal that the Heads were not in a position to make such a proposal to me, since the appointment of a new vice-chancellor was the prerogative of the University Council.

He countered my statement by saying I should not be concerned with the constitutional aspects of the discussion; they were, after all, Heads of Government of the states participating in the university and it was in order for them to have a discussion with me on the matter.

215

So I went down to the plenary meeting of the Heads and reiterated what I had told Ramphal, adding that there was also the question of my family's reaction to the proposal. It was represented to me that the Heads were anxious to speed up the process of identifying a replacement. As one prime minister explained to me: 'You are not looking for work, the work is looking for you!'

On my return to Geneva, I did in fact discuss it with my family and there were pros and cons.

Some time after that, I was invited to Kingston for an interview with the committee set up by the University Council to select the Vice-Chancellor. I was one of three candidates. I was subsequently informed that I had been selected by the committee.

Arthur Brown, who usually visited Geneva in the summer for meetings of the UNDP and ECOSOC, came to my home as he usually did and urged me to make a decision about accepting the post. Arthur, in his capacity as chairman of the Mona campus council, was ex officio a member of the University Council. They had asked Arthur to encourage me to accept the position, because the other candidates were not appointable. I enquired from Arthur whether he knew what the terms of the appointment were, because I was not uncomfortable in Geneva.

He promised to find out and then returned to tell me that he did not want to mention the difference in salary to me because it was so substantial. I indicated to him that I would have to give the matter considerable thought since my family, particularly the children, were well-adjusted to Geneva.

After further consideration, I decided to accept the job offer at the UWI with effect from September 1988. The advantage of this was that it gave me sufficient time to arrange my family affairs, including the children adjusting to an entirely new and somewhat unfamiliar schooling system.

Eric Williams Memorial Lecture

In May 1988 I was invited by the Governor of the Central Bank of Trinidad and Tobago to deliver the Eric Williams Memorial Lecture. I thought that the establishment of the lecture was a timely and appropriate initiative and I accepted his invitation. In thinking about what I would talk about, I recalled that, prior to the establishment of the university at Mona in October 1948, Prime Minister Williams had himself done a lecture on the idea of a West Indian university. In searching for a copy of the lecture, I was advised to visit the Public Library at 42nd Street in New York. I was very impressed with the comprehensive collection of Caribbean papers that the library had at that time. And indeed, I was able to locate a copy of the lecture without any difficulty.

I read it and there were several ideas in it that were still relevant. Accordingly, I decided to construct my idea of a West Indian university as the topic for my lecture. I did this and entitled it: 'The West Indian university revisited: aspects of the intellectual task ahead'. Dr Williams' ideas were never fully taken into consideration when the UWI was originally established. Subsequently, some of his ideas were taken up, but perhaps not quite in the way he had envisaged at the time.

As part of the agreement on Chaguaramas in 1962, the United States Government gave a substantial grant to Trinidad and Tobago. Some people thought of this as representing payment of rent for the Chaguaramas Base during World War II. One part of the payment financed the construction of the John F. Kennedy College of Arts and Sciences, a concept that Williams and the Americans had developed which I thought made a lot of sense.

Dr Williams had the idea that within the university there could be two systems of instruction. The John F. Kennedy College, named after US President John F. Kennedy, would teach on American lines, of which the principal features were: a credit system, four years undergraduate study, a broad education, not highly specialized. It was designed to meet the personnel needs in sectors such as teachers for primary education, civil servants, and other sectors where a non-specialized education was the appropriate starting point. The university would have been unique. It would have had two systems of instruction, side by side. There need not have been any conflict between them. It was just a different concept.

The John F. Kennedy College approach could have generated a supply of teachers, because an American undergraduate degree is actually far better than the British type for primary and the early stages of secondary education teaching, because you get a much broader base. For teachers, especially at the pre-secondary level, this is much more important than simply studying two or three subjects over the course of their degree.

The US government also gave money for an Institute of Caribbean Studies and for an Institute of Legal Studies, which would have preceded the establishment of the Faculty of Law because it was felt that some Caribbean legal scholarship should be available for the faculty so that they could rely on West Indian/ Caribbean legal scholarship for part of their teaching. Looking back over that period, these were then innovative ideas.

It would be interesting to see the actual Chaguaramas Agreement, because for Dr Williams, who had been at variance with the Americans over many matters, it was a good settlement. However, the university was not given full responsibility for the implementation of it and was only brought in to take responsibility for individual items in the agreement.

Development objectives for the UWI

I am still pleased with my Memorial Lecture. I was deeply impressed by Dr Williams' lecture, as well as other material that I was able to consult, and was strongly of the view that the university should, as a matter of priority, set out clear development objectives for itself against the background of those for the region as a whole.

From the literature that I consulted and the personalities with whom I was able to discuss the matter, I came to the UWI with very strong development objectives. The first was that the university should adopt and implement its principal development objectives as quickly as possible; the ultimate aim of these would be to expand its presence and impact within the region, with the direct objective of stepping up the latter's economic growth and social impact.

The Eric Williams Lecture convinced me that no time should be lost in attempting to fulfil that endeavour, both through an expansion in campus enrolment and in off-campus academic programmes, including distance learning. Perhaps of equivalent, or some would argue greater, priority would be efforts to enlarge its research programmes, both in terms of numbers of personnel involved and the disciplinary spread of research areas.

It was already apparent that the region was lagging behind in terms of the volume and spread of research activity. In particular, it appeared that priority attention should be given to work in the fields of science and technology, where the data showed that the region was lagging behind high performing developing countries, especially in Asia. Among other things, this suggested that the university should consider becoming a 'window on the outside world' for the region.

However, I did not anticipate that some members of the university who were in the audience would take exception to some of the ideas expressed in my lecture. I opened up areas of controversy before I assumed office, which on reflection was probably an unwise thing to do.

I suppose it is not unusual for new heads of established institutions to experience differences in views about how the institution should be run. But I underestimated the degree of difficulty I would encounter on assuming the post of Vice-Chancellor.

The impact of Hurricane Gilbert on the UWI

I arrived as Vice-Chancellor of the UWI on 1 September 1988, and on 12 September, Hurricane Gilbert, a category five hurricane with winds over 170 miles an hour, devastated Jamaica. When the first estimates of the damage to the UWI from the hurricane arrived on my desk, I did not know where to find the next cent. To ascertain the insurance situation, I decided to call the local companies that held the university's insurance, so that I could be fully briefed on the matter.

At that meeting, two representatives started talking to me about the 'average clause'. I disagreed very strongly and told them that under no circumstances would I be prepared to agree that they could compensate the university on that basis. I reminded them that since the university was set up in 1947, about 40 years ago, there had been no insurance claims. They now had a chance to satisfy the first and only claim for damages. I would not accept any resistance to our claims. If they continued doing so, I would make a public statement. Therefore my advice was that we should adjourn now to give them an opportunity to consider the matter and come back with a more acceptable response.

All of the companies except one agreed to settle without the average clause. So every time I saw the head of the dissenting company, I would nudge him about the outstanding settlement. Eventually, about one year after, it was settled without the average clause. So that gave us at least a start with the financing of the necessary repairs and rebuilding.

Hurricane relief and rebuilding efforts

Dr Enrique Iglesias, then President of the Inter-American Development Bank (IDB) came to see me and said he would recommend that the UWI be granted a loan from the bank of up to

Figure 11 First day as Vice-Chancellor, surveying Hurricane Gilbert's damage.

US$80 or $90 million. Eventually I think we got about US$60 million, not because they were not willing to give us more but because I would have had to get government guarantees for a larger sum, which was problematic.

Then the Hon. Dennis Lalor came to see me, in his capacity as an insurer, and suggested that I should try to raise some money locally. I told him that I had just arrived and did not know the local community sufficiently to make an approach. He then offered to host a breakfast for me to meet some of the leading personalities in the business community.

On that occasion, I suggested to the gathering that they establish a local endowment fund to emphasize that the financing being sought was not just for covering the hurricane damage, but ultimately was aimed at the development of the Mona campus. They set up the Development and Endowment Fund with contributions of $1 million per member. The fund eventually raised over US$100 million. I assisted Dennis Lalor only marginally; he took the project forward on his own initiative. I very much appreciated his assistance and continue to regard his actions as laudable.

The Jewish community was also very supportive in our rehabilitation efforts. Maurice Stoppi, who was a friend of mine from the 1960s whom I had not seen recently, came with Ainsley Henriques to see me on the campus, had a look around and asked what they could do to help. They indicated that they had seen the damage done to the halls of residence and were very concerned about the situation of the students, who had to continue living in the rooms because they had nowhere else to go. I suggested to them that a very valuable interim measure would be to construct a study room at each of the halls that the students could use outside of their classes. They readily agreed with that and decided to recommend a project to their local community of building one temporary study room for each of the four halls.

Maurice and Ainsley took this idea forward with commendable speed. In short order, work commenced on the study rooms. When the university officially re-opened, the students came back and showed immediate appreciation for the quick response of the Jewish community. I associated myself with that response by writing to the contributing governments to advise them of the initiative.

We got undertakings of a similar nature from other companies in the private sector. Among them were the local bauxite companies, Alcoa and Alcan. On the whole, I would say that the private sector made a valuable contribution to resolving the difficulties arising from the hurricane.

The UWI's 40th Anniversary

Despite the damage done by the hurricane and the necessary attention that my senior colleagues and I had to devote to that situation, we recognized the timeliness of continuing with the preparations for celebrating the 40th Anniversary.

As we saw it, this was an appropriate occasion to bring back the alumni and together with the current student body to recognize the need for institutional strengthening and start a programme of fundraising for it.

After internal consultations, it was agreed that we should organize a special programme of events that would serve to bring

Figure 12 Dr Enrique Iglesias, President of the Inter-American Development Bank, on a working visit to the UWI.

together all of the stakeholders in the university, together with participation by the public, so that the image of the institution could be lifted and pledges of support secured for major developments.

In the course of those consultations, I obtained support for the idea that we should hold a major 40th Anniversary concert to start the process of fundraising. I thought that we should seek permission to hold the concert at King's House, the official residence of the Governor General, the head of state, and make it a black tie event at which we would feature the Neal and Massy Trinidad All Stars Steel Orchestra, based in Trinidad and Tobago, which enjoyed a high and rising reputation throughout the region for the outstanding quality of its performances. Sydney Knox, Chairman of Neal and Massy, drawing on the co-operative work that he had done with me when I was at the St Augustine campus, was exceptionally helpful in making the orchestra available at no cost to the university.

Mr Dhiru Tanna, Managing Director of Neal and Massy, Jamaica, supported the project by a vigorous sale of concert tickets to members of the private sector in Jamaica, which led to a complete sell-out of the tickets for the event.

On the Mona campus itself there were mixed views about the appropriateness of the initiative; some people indicating that this was not a suitable initiative for the Vice-Chancellor. I made it plain that I disagreed with those views and pointed out that the university would be US$25,000 better off as a result of the event.

The Governor General of Jamaica was very co-operative in making the King's House lawns available for the concert, as were the Heads of Government of CARICOM, most of whom attended the event. The concert was a resounding success and was followed up by a tour by the orchestra in the United Kingdom to give performances in different parts of Britain where there were significant West Indian populations.

The West India Committee in London, especially its representative David Jessop, arranged for a firm of jewellers in Regent Street in London (I believe that it was Mappin & Webb but may be wrong) to convert their store into a dining room where we could have a high-priced dinner under the patronage of Her Royal Highness Princess Anne, who was then assisting the Hurricane Relief Fundraising Committee. Nearly 200 tickets sold out in a day. The demand for tickets vastly exceeded the available space.

The West Indian community, many of whom could not afford to attend this event, had the opportunity to attend the many All Stars functions when the band went on tour at other locations in West Indian communities around the country. This served to promote their involvement in the celebrations and the fundraising activities that were associated with it.

Implementing the initial vision

Development priorities

Given my views on the urgency of tackling the reconstruction after the hurricane, I sought to involve the senior management group in thinking through the possible university response and becoming alert to finding solutions and acting on them. I was also anxious to draw upon the thinking of the faculties as a whole and sought opportunities to hold discussions with them. One of my principal objectives was to develop and sustain effective communications with the faculties on all of the campuses as far as opportunity permitted.

It was not logistically easy to arrange because of their geographical dispersion. However, I tried to convey critical messages through the deans about what I saw to be major development priorities. I am not certain the extent to which these efforts made any impression. But the way in which the university was organized, it was expected that there would be a free flow of ideas communicated from the centre to the campuses and faculties there located. Equally, I looked forward to hearing campus views from the principals and campus deans. I am not certain that this arrangement worked as well as had been hoped by the framers of the constitution.

Accordingly, wherever opportunity permitted I tried to communicate directly with the faculties. This was largely possible at Mona where I was located, but even then, I do not recall great success in that endeavour.

My recollection is that the then Dean of the Faculty of Social Sciences, gave me an oral invitation to speak to the faculty. This was taken up and I was glad to be in exchanges with faculty members some of whom had been my early colleagues when I was myself a member of the faculty, I was most indebted to the Dean, Dr. Don Robotham, for that initiative, He himself, had a number of very productive conversations with me which led me to opening up areas for university action. Among the faculty itself, I received several insights that were later to translate into special initiatives.

I also recall a meeting with the Faculty of Arts and General Studies where useful discussions took place on some topics of concern to them.

At a more informal level, as I moved around all of the campuses, I had the opportunity of many conversations with faculty members that enlarged my thinking and helped me to avoid several misjudgements and errors.

In the light of all the capital investment that had to be made to repair the damage inflicted by Hurricane Gilbert, it seemed a good opportunity to also proceed with the formulation and implementation of a ten-year development plan, about which preliminary discussions had already taken place, at least on the Mona campus. This could also be used as an opportunity to upgrade the facilities across the university and to involve both external donors and the alumni in that effort.

I decided to set up an administrative structure for formulating and implementing the development plan. This took the form of upgrading the structure of my office to make it the co-ordinating body for the plan, while relieving me of duties as principal of the Mona campus, which was already being proposed on other grounds.

Accordingly, for those and other reasons, I secured acceptance of my proposals for an increase in the number of pro vice-chancellors to eight, to include one for planning in my office, and some modification in the office of the campus principals in order to accommodate the greater workload that would arise in implementing the plan at campus level.

The Development Plan was drawn up as a ten-year plan (1990–2000), with targets that included the following:

- Increase in enrolments by 50 per cent to 18,000 students; this was actually achieved five years ahead of target, i.e. by the 1995/96 academic year.
- Increase in outreach work and off-campus enrolments, including bringing non-campus countries closer to the mainstream of the UWI's work.
- Strengthening of post-graduate studies and research.
- More multi-disciplinary programmes of study and research in emerging areas, e.g. environment and women's studies.
- Increase in R & D in Science and Technology, in areas critical to the region's economic growth.
- New initiatives to upgrade studies in the humanities and the creative arts, for example in literature and language studies.
- Greater inter-campus linkages and complementarities in teaching and research.
- Mobilization of resources up to US$300 million to cover implementation of the plan through bilateral and multilateral development assistance, public appeals, private sector contributions and outlays provided by contributing governments.

In order to implement several of the academic goals in the Development Plan, it was agreed that the semester system should be introduced during the 1990/91 academic year. This proceeded with very few hitches and opened up possibilities for academic improvements above and beyond what was initially foreseen.

The establishment of the Association of Tertiary Level Institutions (ACTI) was an important institutional innovation that strengthened the links between the university and non-university tertiary institutions, as well as among themselves.

In particular, I recognized the high importance of extending the university beyond its physical locations on campuses to contribute to continuing education both in terms of preparation for access to the university and as a critical resource in responding to priority development needs.

There was also the parallel importance of building the research capacity of the institution as part of the effort to build the knowledge economy of countries in the region as they sought to take advantage of new possibilities for diversification and investment. Equally important was the outreach programme to communities as a whole, providing initial training and education that would allow them to take advantage of ongoing opportunities for development.

All of these concerns called for a fresh attempt to define development priorities and to identify modes and programmes of education and training, focused on the development issues that the region faced.

With regard to development work, I consulted the files on these subjects left behind by my predecessors. Among these was one by Sir Arthur Lewis that focused on setting up a very high level international support group that would assist in approaching major institutions in the field of development assistance. These would include the international development banks, foundations and bilateral donors, and others involved in providing major support to developing countries or their prime institutions. The overall purpose of the group was to give visibility to the university among the principal countries and institutions involved in international development.

The target list of individuals to be approached was an impressive one, including major personalities in the international donor community. Although not entirely ruling out the possibility of direct approaches to some of the individuals, I felt that my own attempts should be somewhat more modest, not myself having the global stature of Sir Arthur.

Drawing on the list, I constructed a more modest version that I felt myself capable of approaching. This included the major international foundations, mainly in New York and London, and international development agencies, principally in the UN system. I then drew upon contacts in the international development world and asked them to introduce me to the list of potential donors. At the same time I also made attempts to identify donors in the private sector and individuals who could represent the university in seeking out co-operation opportunities.

I then shared the list with my senior colleagues with a view to finding out if they had any ideas for improving it, and enquiring whether they would be able to help in the initial contacts with the people and institutions involved. This was an entirely new area for most of them, so I concluded that it was my signal responsibility to start the process of contacts with the donors and institutions concerned.

Fundraising efforts

After an initial visit to New York, I realized that our energies should be focused on that city, where most of the relevant institutions were located or were easily accessible. It was also apparent that efforts to contact alumni and other supporting groups might most advantageously be focused on contacts available in New York.

One of the early initiatives taken was to establish a private foundation as the repository of funds received from different donors in the United States. This involved cancellation of an earlier arrangement for administering scholarships for students attending the UWI from Barbados and Guyana. Approval was then secured from the US Treasury for a wider scheme to re-establish a foundation for the purpose of providing opportunities for US citizens to receive tax-deductable status for any contributions made to it for funding scholarships and development projects at the UWI.

Figure 13 Addressing students at the Faculty of Medical Sciences.

It was apparent that if we were to follow the approach of focusing on New York we should set up a very small but effective business office there. I received the prompt support of the government of Jamaica, which provided the university with a small office in its consulate. I also gave attention to setting up a small back office group in my office at Mona to help me in taking the necessary initiatives both in the Caribbean and outside and to supplement the efforts that were supposed to emanate from campuses and from the central offices of the university.

The office was staffed by Ms Kelly Magnus and Elizabeth Buchanan (now Mrs Buchanan-Hind). I relied very heavily on them for sourcing information on the universities in the United States with which we could work, including efforts to arrange joint activities with African-American colleges and universities.

Perhaps the most important innovation was the holding of fundraising events in cities where UWI graduates were significant. These took the form of annual dinners in New York and Toronto, the latter being an outstanding contribution by Elizabeth Buchanan-Hind that continues to the present. The staff were also very involved in arranging fundraising concerts in Kingston and elsewhere in the region. Mrs Buchanan-Hind took a further interest in organizing sports events, especially cricket matches with visiting teams from abroad. The Vice-Chancellor's Cricket Match was an innovation in this area that has continued. These activities have now blossomed into annual events, as have other sporting initiatives involving activities on the road.

The approaches which we made to foundations bore early fruit both in New York and London, yielding significant grants from three foundations in the United States and two in the United Kingdom. Altogether, as a rough estimate, I would say that over my period in office contributions from foundations exceeded US$1 billion.

Much of that was due to my own personal effort. The important thing about fundraising in New York is to get on the contributions budgets of companies. One needs, therefore, to build a relationship because you are most unlikely to get a contribution after just an initial visit.

As an example, I can never forget Johnson & Johnson. I went to see the man responsible for contributions there. After I had put my case, he promised that he would put the UWI on their contributions budget two years from now for an initial amount of US$250,000. He indicated that they always started small and saw where it would go over time. I was pleased and thanked him and sent him a note confirming our understanding. However, UWI's staff in our New York office failed to follow it up.

Many years later, I was sitting in the Miami airport reading a newspaper when I was hailed by someone calling my name. It was the man from Johnson & Johnson, who enquired what had happened and why the university had not followed up on the arrangement. I was astounded to learn of this but told him that I was no longer at the university.

It was demoralizing, the extent to which the follow-up on my initial fundraising efforts was allowed to lapse.

In making my rounds to different companies, it occurred to me that one way of building their commitment to the UWI was to ask them, as a starter, to provide summer internships for UWI students. Given their standing, they would have no difficulty in getting visas for the students. I started with very high level engineering companies and got positive responses immediately. One company provided openings for six students from the Faculty of Engineering at the St Augustine campus. The students performed so impressively that they received offers to return in the following summer. Some of them did, but on completion there was no follow-up by the university to see if appropriate jobs could be found for them in the Caribbean. Accordingly, all but one remained in the United States.

Later on, other prospects for support came onto the horizon. The group in my office was expanded to include a Pro Vice-Chancellor for Development and additional project personnel. This group was able to take immediate responsibility, working with the principals and the relevant campus personnel for the management of large grants from the Canadian International Development Agency (CIDA) and the European Union.

The work to secure greater involvement of the alumni would necessarily take more time because of the promotional and organizational requirements. Nonetheless, this was also pursued in collaboration with the campuses and by the establishment of a more substantial and effective office on alumni affairs at the central administration. In the case of the medical alumni, support facilities were provided since the faculty already had designated staff who were able to take forward development initiatives.

Returning to the basic issue of developing an effective organizational structure for sustained fundraising efforts, it was evident that what had been established, in particular the office in New York, was inadequate in terms of continuing contacts with the donor community. This required a capacity for ongoing promotion of the university's possibilities and needs. It became apparent that the university lacked that capacity either at headquarters or out in the field. Accordingly, many initiatives that we considered could not be taken forward.

One of these involved working together with the African-American universities and colleges in appeals conducted through the media in the United States. Our efforts in that regard held promise, but were short-lived because we did not have enough resources on the ground to build up the necessary promotional capacity. However, this remains a field worthy of further exploration in the future.

Opening 'windows to the world'

A person who was extremely helpful was Gunter Freidrich. He was German but a global citizen. We became friends when I was in Europe. Gunter had enormous contacts; there was hardly anybody in the world he did not know, or knew how to get to them. He came to see me very early after I returned to the university. I took him to the Mona campus and he said: 'Look, this is a very interesting institution. I don't know many developing countries which have an institution like this. You've got to put it on the map! Get important people in the world to know of its existence and the work it is doing. Bring your politicians in. You be the broker. Bring in the leadership from outside, so when people think of the Caribbean, they think of the University of the West Indies.'

Figure 14 Rosalie O'Meally and me in conversation with University of Toronto officials during a visit to the institution.

He made the suggestion that the UWI should organize a review of regional co-operation in the world so that the lessons from those experiences could be discussed and conclusions drawn about what initiatives seemed particularly promising for CARICOM to implement.

When he gave me this idea, I sprang into action. He provided me with a target list of the major personalities that could be invited. We had the meeting in Port Antonio and it was highly successful. Delegates spoke frankly about their situations and, speaking off the record about Europe, we heard things that we would never have heard in the context of the Lomé discussions. It was foreseen that the meeting would also facilitate a general exchange of views among prime ministers and some of the top representatives of groupings.

I positioned Jamaicans to speak at different times during the conference, following on my idea that since the governments seemed hesitant to deal with the big issues of the time, the university should take an active role.

The meeting went well and that encouraged me to hold a second meeting on finance. It was held in Montego Bay, at the Half Moon Hotel. We got the Deputy Managing Director of the IMF, the Senior Vice-President of the World Bank, and the President of the European Investment Bank. The latter was a very impressive person. He said that he brought greetings from his wife, who had served as my interpreter for a negotiation with the Prime Minister of Luxembourg during the Lomé negotiations. I remembered the occasion. She had interpreted very well and at the end of the negotiations I thanked her and sent a little token of thanks. Years after, she had remembered it. Her husband indicated that she had wanted to attend the meeting, because in between the meetings I had told her about Jamaica and the Caribbean, and now she had an opportunity of visiting Jamaica with her husband. Unfortunately, prior commitments stood in the way of that.

Through my UN connections, I was able to ensure good representation from both the public and private sector. We also secured good representation from the private sector in Jamaica and Trinidad, but not from other countries in the region.

What particularly disappointed me, however, was the lack of follow through from university delegates, whom I assumed would have been sufficiently stimulated to follow up the contacts made at the meeting. I had assumed that my colleagues would take initiatives to follow up and build ongoing relationships and contacts with the institutions that were represented. I saw this as one opportunity to build the institution's 'window to the outside world', but my ambition in that regard was premature.

When I could not get support from my colleagues for continuing with these high level meetings, Anthony Hill sold me the idea of approaching the organizers of Davos (the World Economic Forum) about holding a meeting in Jamaica. The Forum is an independent international organization committed to improving the state of the world by engaging business, political, academic and other leaders of society to shape global, regional and industry agendas. The meeting brings together some 2,500 top business leaders, international political leaders, selected intellectuals and journalists to discuss the most pressing issues facing the world, including health and the environment.

I checked into it and asked a member of its staff to arrange for me to meet the head of the WEF, who was then scheduled to visit Jamaica. The meeting took place and I proposed to him that he should organize a meeting in Jamaica. He said that he had not thought of it, so I suggested that he should do so and develop a proposal that could be studied by the government of Jamaica and relevant private sector interests.

We began discussing the possibilities. In our discussions, he said he always made preparations three years ahead of time, because of the amount of planning needed to organize a successful meeting. He then proposed a date four years ahead.

I was planning to proceed with the initiative as a university project, but, again, I did not get sufficient encouragement from my colleagues to pursue the matter. So after the Montego Bay meeting I decided to change tack and try other alternatives. There was no point in being a lone prophet, running around the place advocating similar events, if I could not convince my colleagues and contemporaries that this was something that we should do because it would have benefits for us in terms of exposure in the world.

Financial assistance for the UWI's development

The Ford Foundation

Bill Carmichael and I were assistant professors at Princeton together, and he not only set up the Cornell connection for me to introduce Management Studies at St Augustine in 1965, but also, later on, facilitated me quite a bit with the Ford Foundation, where he had become Vice-President. I had raised over US$1 million for ISER at the Mona campus before I left in 1974, and when I came back as Vice-Chancellor I resumed the relationship with Ford. Then they came to me and said they were reviewing their policy and indicated that the UWI had been the second largest international grantee from the Ford Foundation and it was time they retired us.

I responded that the foundation could not send the UWI into retirement without a gratuity. So we got an additional million dollars when I was Vice-Chancellor, which was extremely generous of them.

At the time, the university Bursary was overloaded because of its own need for restructuring. I concluded therefore that we required some assistance from outside in managing any new grants. In the case of the Ford Foundation I arranged for the endowment to be managed by people from the private sector who had the necessary expertise in investing in the US market, where they could secure a wide range of portfolio opportunities.

Accordingly, I asked Dennis Lalor, who was already managing the contributions made by the private sector to the Mona Development and Endowment Fund set up in response to Hurricane Gilbert, to arrange for the day-to-day management of these new funds.

They arranged to place the funds in the United States, as the Ford Foundation Endowment. I told them they could not mix it up with their endowment for two reasons, the principal one being that it was for use by the university as a regional institution and not for any particular campus, whereas the Jamaican Endowment Fund was for the Mona campus. They understood and invested it as agreed. The income from it was used for a variety of research and academic purposes. I do not know what the status of the endowment is today.

The Wolfson Foundation

When I became Vice-Chancellor I encouraged staff members to come to see me if they had any ideas about development projects. Errol Morrison was one of the few staff members to take up the invitation. He indicated to me that although he was in the Biochemistry Department, his real interest was in tackling diabetes. He told me that they had been trying to develop voluntary support groups all over the country, but needed a diabetes centre that could be the focal point for the outreach and research that they were doing. I reacted very positively to his ideas and asked him how much funding would be required to make a start. His response was that they could use as much as I could get.

I promised to keep their needs in mind while I was in London contacting potential donors. I went to see David Jessop and told

Figure 15 With Harry Belafonte, a strong supporter of the UWI's fundraising initiatives.

him that I wanted to find a foundation that might be interested in helping me on diabetes. He recommended that I go to see the Wolfson Foundation, founded by Sir Isaac Wolfson. I went to see the Executive Director of the Foundation, who indicated his great interest and asked me to send him a proposal.

So I returned to David Jessop's office and drafted a proposal that I sent to Errol, asking him to fix it up any way he thought appropriate. He faxed it back and I submitted it.

The Director of the Foundation approved it but queried whether other Caribbean countries could be considered. I agreed and included Barbados, since I was aware that there was a group in Trinidad and Tobago who were already working on this because of the high incidence of diabetes at that time among the different racial groups. They were interested in putting in some money and I knew that Dr Teeluksingh at the Faculty of Medicine at St Augustine was thinking of it but did not need resources at that time, though possibly at a later stage.

I revised the proposal and included £250,000 for Jamaica and £250,000 for Barbados and the Eastern Caribbean. The total sum was approved.

Errol told his group about the grant from London and discussed ways of taking the project forward. Mrs Jean Anderson, sister of former Prime Minister Seaga, quickly volunteered to make a start with securing counterpart funding for the diabetes centre. In a very short period of time her group raised the required amount and the centre was established.

They decided that they wanted to honour me and it was agreed to establish an annual Alister McIntyre Distinguished Lecture to be delivered by dignitaries from across the world who have made significant contributions to diabetes. On one occasion the invited speaker was Dr Jean Philippe Assal, who was my doctor when I was in Geneva and saw me through several health crises. He also helped friends of mine from the Caribbean. The Diabetes Association have kept the annual lecture going, over all these years. I usually show up for a photo opportunity with the invited lecturer.

Fulbright Fellowships

The Faculty of Arts more or less disagreed with the proposals I made to them, including some that were designed to develop a more comparative approach to the teaching of languages and literature.

First of all, I managed to secure more Fulbright Fellowships than previously. They usually received one Fulbright Award every two years. I managed to increase that to two per annum over a three-year period.

This was arranged when I met the US Secretary for Education and she invited me to Washington. I had written to the US Ambassador in Jamaica to say that I understood his government was instituting a North American Free Trade Agreement (NAFTA) group of research institutes or research universities and I would like to ask that they accept the UWI as one of the NAFTA universities. Ambassador Glen Holden said he had referred it to Washington with his endorsement. This led to an invitation for me to visit the department in Washington. On that visit, the Secretary of Education told me they could not admit the UWI because we were not in NAFTA. This was for institutions in the three member countries, namely the US, Canada and Mexico. However, she indicated that a more feasible arrangement for the UWI would be to increase the number of Fulbright Fellowships that we were receiving. Accordingly, it was agreed that the allocation to the UWI should increase from one every two years to three annually.

I thought we should use the opportunity to broaden the scope of our teaching. For example, we should have a course on North American literature, which was not available at the time because the teaching was organized around thematic, rather than geographic, lines. Professor Eddie Baugh, who was the expert in that field, was quite well disposed to the idea. Members of the Faculty of Arts and General Studies criticized the initiative at faculty level, while showing a personal interest in securing awards when applications were being advertised.

Networking opportunities

Rockefeller University

I had met another source of support through Peter McLeish, a Grenadian who had actually married into my family. This was Professor Torsten Weisel, a Swedish scientist under whom Peter had done his doctorate. Dr Weisel became President of Rockefeller University in New York, and during that time was a co-recipient of a Nobel Prize. Peter had done his medicine and science in North America and got a job at Rockefeller.

When I was at the UN in New York, prior to coming to the UWI, Peter invited me to supper on one occasion to meet Dr Weisel. We had a most fruitful conversation during which he promised that when I became Vice-Chancellor he would do his best to help me strengthen the Faculty of Natural Sciences.

I had heard from several sources before I came to Mona that people in the community/region were concerned that the UWI was falling behind in science, so I developed the idea of seeking the services of a group of West Indian scientists in senior academic positions in North America to undertake an evaluation of the

Faculty of Natural Sciences, as a basis for securing additional resources for its development.

I had myself come to the view that the advancement of the region's capability in science was a major element in achieving greater and more sustained economic development. Accordingly, I regarded the review as the first step in strengthening the scientific capability of the university. With the review of the faculty in hand, I felt that we were ready to start the process by mobilizing resources for it. I therefore felt that I should use whatever time was available to begin making academic contacts for support in implementing the review. I went to see Professor Torsten Weisel, who had earlier promised to assist me with the faculty's development, to secure his advice on how to proceed.

He responded very positively to the proposed review, and indicated that he would be ready to support its implementation. He said that he would just like to come to spend a few days on campus; he did not want any publicity or to do a lecture. For the first few days he asked to be allowed to just move around the campus by himself.

After the first week of his visit, I invited him to come and have breakfast and share his impressions with me. On that occasion he started by saying that he regretted to tell me that his first impressions were that our scientists were very lazy. On being asked why he thought so, he responded that on a Saturday night not a single light was on in the labs. If there were high-performing research people there, they would be in their labs on a Saturday. That is the difference between people who make it and those who do not. Based on that impression, he could hazard a guess that none of those scientists would make it.

He spent a further three or four days with us and as he visited the departments he gave me periodic reports on those people he met that seemed to have good prospects and those who did not impress him.

He then proposed that we should work on a development plan. He would offer me three places per year at Rockefeller for promising staff. The places there are competitive, candidates have to sit an exam to get admitted as a researcher, but exceptionally he would offer three research places every year for the next five years. The places could be assigned to each campus or on any other basis considered appropriate by the university. The places would be provided and accommodation close to the university would be available.

That arrangement was made, but it was never taken up by the Faculty of Natural Sciences. The only member who showed any interest in it was Errol Morrison, who was then in the Department of Biochemistry and visited Rockefeller for a week. He returned to Mona and expressed high appreciation for the excellent facilities and very high standards of its faculty.

Returning to my original point about the lack of receptivity on the part of some members of the Faculty of Natural Sciences, I would not say that this was true of the other faculties, although here and there I ran into criticism of the developments that I proposed for the university. This was by no means an exceptional situation since by their very nature university faculty members tend to be critical of change.

Networking with South Africa

I made a series of efforts to bring the needs of the UWI and the Caribbean to the attention of several eminent global personalities

Figure 16 With President Nelson Mandela and Sir Shridath Ramphal, Chancellor of the UWI.

involved in Third World events. I used the occasion of the high-level seminars being held throughout the world to develop contacts to communicate our development needs and seek their support in alleviating them.

In my personal conversations during those meetings, I explained to my audience that I wanted to give the students a better sense of the contemporary world. They were interested in the subject of decolonization, especially the situation in Africa. I thought that maybe a start could be made by making them better acquainted with apartheid as then existing in South Africa.

Through the contacts that I made, I was able to secure an immediate response. In short order I was contacted and told that a highly recommended speaker from the African National Congress (ANC) had been identified and could become available to visit the university. I responded enthusiastically.

I announced the impending visit of the representative of the ANC, his name and his work with the ANC. He was scheduled to give a lecture in the Assembly Hall at the UWI. The place was packed. Beyers Naudé arrived and the audience was stunned! When they saw me bringing up this white man to the platform, they were taken aback! They did not quite know what to do.

Figure 17 General Colin Powell in the university council room with the Chancellor, me and other senior university officials after receiving an honorary degree.

He started off by saying: 'I am quite sure like other audiences you are surprised to see a white man coming to talk about the African National Congress. But you see, I have been a member of the Congress from the outset.'

Then he explained. He'd lost a son in the whole struggle. He had been to jail several times. By the time he had finished he had the entire audience in his hands. In closing, he said: 'Let us now sing the anthem of the National Congress' and everybody stood and sang. It was a very moving occasion. It was shocking for the students, but I was glad to shock them, to see that race is not something owned exclusively by them. It is a problem with people of all different kinds in the world. I was so pleased. He was outstanding.

His visit was only outshone by that of Nelson and Winnie Mandela, who came to the university during an official visit to Jamaica. The three of us had a conversation in my office for about 45 minutes. They also met with Sonny Ramphal, who was the Chancellor of the university and whom they knew intimately because of the incredible role he had played in securing Nelson's release from prison and mobilizing support for the immediate achievement of independence. It was a memorable event to see the response of the crowd to both of them, but rather specially to Winnie. This was apparent in the high excitement of the crowd that congregated, particularly at the Undercroft, to view their visit to the university

During his address to the gathering of students and staff in the Assembly Hall, Nelson Mandela explained that he had to come here first, after his release from prison, because Jamaica was the first country to take action against the apartheid regime.

The catalystic initiative that Jamaica took in 1948 under the leadership of Norman Manley contributed to bringing the South African issue to international attention. Thereafter Sonny Ramphal, as Commonwealth Secretary-General, took up the cudgels and systematically mobilized Commonwealth support for the release of Mandela and the independence of South Africa. Getting action on the matter was not easy because of the strong resistance of the British government led by Mrs Margaret Thatcher, who as the prime minister at the time was extremely reluctant to respond to the urgings of the majority of the Commonwealth countries and the Secretary-General. In the course of discussions, Canada and subsequently New Zealand joined the ranks of the majority. It was literally a case of the United Kingdom standing alone, with only reluctant support from Australia. When the government of Australia changed its position under the leadership of Prime Minister Malcolm Fraser, a very reluctant British prime minister and government decided to withdraw their opposition to the release of Mandela and political independence for the country.

Medical networking with Guy's Hospital, London

From the outset, I attached the greatest importance to international networking as a means of broadening the outlook and contacts of UWI staff and students with other institutions around the world. Some of this was already in progress, but I wanted to widen the scope and extend the number and variety of institutions with which co-operation could be pursued. One of the initial areas where such opportunities occurred was in the field of medicine.

On a visit to London on university business, I encountered Professor Kenneth Stuart, who was then attached to the Commonwealth secretariat. Professor Stuart introduced me to the School of Medicine at Guy's Hospital, which had a long record of contact and co-operation with the UWI. On that occasion I mentioned to Dr Cyril Shankland, the Dean, that although we were very mindful of the important co-operation that the school had sustained with the UWI, I was somewhat concerned that in London itself, where the school was located in a part of the city in which large numbers of West Indians lived and worked, there was no particular treatment and advisory services geared towards that community. He promised me a response within a matter of days.

He then came up with a proposal that the UWI and Guy's should jointly set up a Centre for Caribbean Medicine in London that would be a facility to provide the West Indian community with advisory and treatment services targeted towards their major medical concerns. Both institutions would assign staff to the centre. UWI staff would go to London to work in the centre and would be replaced in the UWI by comparable staff from Guy's, being rotated on a basis to be agreed. I considered this to be a very timely initiative as it would open up opportunities for UWI doctors to go to the UK to do their work towards an advanced standing in one of the medical fields or in pursuance of a research interest, while according opportunities to the Guy's staff sent to the UWI to advance their research and clinical interests. For his part, Kenneth Stuart offered to accompany me to see representatives of the British government with a view to securing appropriate funding from them for the project in the Caribbean.

I was totally perplexed when the Faculty of Medical Sciences at Mona turned down the proposal on the grounds that they were being used to advance the interests of other institutions.

Participation in the International Network of Medical Schools

The rejection of this project for a Centre for Caribbean Medicine occurred at a time when Guy's were in the process of establishing an inter-university project for advancing medical education within a select group of medical schools around the world. These included schools in France, Poland, Germany, Japan and the United States. Guy's had offered to sponsor the UWI for membership in this select group and they had early indications of the willingness of the other institutions to accept the UWI.

I was also disappointed at the Faculty of Medical Sciences' lack of willingness to participate in this group. It struck me that membership of the group could have opened up enormous opportunities for UWI staff and students and placed us at the centre stage of medical education.

Proposed medical networking in Malaysia

Another missed opportunity arose in Malaysia. For some time, UWI faculty members had been going on a visiting arrangement to that country under the auspices of the Commonwealth Group for Cooperation in Medicine. They had developed a high reputation among staff and students at the medical faculty in Kuala Lumpur.

On the occasion of a visit I made to Malaysia, I was asked to see the Prime Minister of Malaysia, who told me that they had very ambitious plans to transform the Faculty of Medicine at their local university into a major medical facility for teaching and research. At that time they were sending students to St Augustine to do the pre-clinical part of the medical programme. So impressed were they with the quality of the medical teaching that they wished to expand the links with the UWI to cover the entire medical degree programme.

The Prime Minister asked me whether we would consider coming to Kuala Lumpur to set up an entire medical school and staff it for an initial period. For its part, the government of Malaysia would make generous provisions to meet all of the project's cost on a cash basis. My initial response to the Prime Minister's proposal was that it would enhance our stature and improve our impact on a basis that would, among other things, be academically and financially advantageous. I foresaw that we could draw into the effort not only current faculty but also our alumni. One could also envisage it as offering opportunities to enrich the education of our own students.

Unfortunately, my views were not shared by the faculty and I had to politely turn down the invitation from the Prime Minister of Malaysia. This was a major disappointment for me, if only because I considered the Faculty of Medical Sciences to be in the best position to initiate a comprehensive programme of networking with overseas institutions, thereby enlarging the presence and impact of the UWI in pertinent areas. The faculty was, after all, the first to be established at Mona.

Initiative to strengthen links between the UWI and universities in the Dominican Republic and Haiti

In furtherance of the agreement between CARICOM and the European Union under Lomé IV to place emphasis on regionalism, a project had been developed to promote inter-university co-operation and linkage between the UWI and institutions in the Dominican Republic and Haiti.

The project was co-ordinated by a unit established in my office. Several graduate programmes were initiated on the three UWI campuses and similar steps were envisaged in the other participating countries. As far as the UWI was concerned, students enrolled for courses, some of which were in entirely new fields as diverse as tourism, natural resources management, and coastal and marine management.

The necessary university agreements were made to service the programme. Unfortunately, while a very positive start was made with student enrolment and securing the services of visiting and established faculty, most of the programmes were very short-lived because there were inadequate resources to finance them after an initial period.

The financial viability of the UWI

The basic strategy was to raise as much of the development funding needs as we could, relying upon the regional governments to meet the recurrent costs. When I arrived at Mona in 1988 there was unfortunately a slippage in the regularity of government contributions. I set out very early in my office to have an active dialogue with them on the matter. I was gratified at the positive reactions coming from them, always with a promise to eliminate arrears and follow that up with actual payments. The most significant amount came from Trinidad and Tobago, which at one stage, owed the university about US$400 million. I raised the matter very forcefully with the Prime Minister at the time, and I am glad to say that he responded promptly and paid off the entire amount. Among other things, this allowed us to repay a long-standing debt to a local commercial bank.

Looking towards the future, I have to emphasize the central importance of financial viability, both in the current and capital operations of the central administration, as well as those of the individual campuses. To my own way of thinking, this is a major challenge that the institution has to confront as it seeks to make its way forward. I believe that there are approaches and opportunities

Figure 18 On the Cave Hill campus with Sir Allen Lewis (right), Chairman of the University Council and Sir Carlisle Burton, Chairman of the Campus Council.

that can be followed up to put the university in a safer place. However, this is a matter for the current administration, not the subject of retrospective reflections.

All of these problems can be expected to continue as the region attempts to surmount a number of weaknesses that exist currently in their public and private sectors. What seems to be needed are more determined efforts by all parties to sort out how they can, in co-operation with the university, find ways to meet its current and capital needs, and to access sources of funding both locally and abroad that can be marshalled in support of the situation. A new spirit of determination should pervade the discussion among the regional parties involved.

An assessment of my work at the UWI

Despite many disappointments, some of which are reflected in the preceding sections, I remain convinced that in a rapidly changing world strategizing to develop a global outlook among the faculty and students at the UWI is indispensable for their own survival and prosperity as well as that of the region.

It is common knowledge that the world map is changing in directions that had not been identified earlier, as development possibilities arise in new alliances at country and company level to take advantage of the possibilities for economic and financial co-operation. As a relatively small part of the world, the Caribbean has to make exceptional efforts to find its place in these global networks.

When I try to assess the totality of my impact at the UWI, I am more inclined to focus on my failures than on my successes. The ambitions which I held for the institution were not, for the most part, realized to the extent that I had hoped. Although the university did have standing in the outside world that preceded my assumption of office, I felt there were many further opportunities that could be grasped to consolidate and enhance that standing.

Certainly, I was, in general, impressed by the high quality of the staff and their commitment to the advancement of the institution.

Figure 19 Demitting office as Vice-Chancellor – Receiving the Chancellor's Medal for Excellence. On the left Professor Rex Nettleford, my successor. To the right Sir Shridath Ramphal, the Chancellor.

My criticisms were not meant to detract from that. I suppose also that one should give due weight to the views of people who, by education and training, were taught to be critical.

Because of these requirements, unique and countless tasks devolved on my personal office which played a critical role in ensuring that liaison between the Vice Chancellor, the Staff on the different campuses and the students were preserved and strengthened. In undertaking these roles, I think of the invaluable work done by Ms Rosalie O'Meally, my executive assistant who represented my ears and eyes in all of these areas. I think also of Mrs Joyce Byles, my Personal Assistant whose knowledge of the University and its staff at all levels represented a valuable resource. I think further of Mrs Jean Smith whose extraordinary knowledge of the Jamaican community, especially the government, continuously provided critical support in the discharge of my functions. I should also indicate appreciation for the other staff in my office who all showed commendable enthusiasm for whatever assignments were given to them.

There can also be little doubt that my colleagues were motivated by very genuine sentiments in favour of the development of the region; it should not be surprising that there was, at the same time, a strong orientation towards the campus and the country in which it was located. This was particularly noticeable among staff members who had received most, if not all, of their education within the UWI, and had little enthusiasm for the global vision that I was trying to promote.

At the same time, one should also acknowledge the outstanding staff members who were visionary in outlook, although they had not had any of their education abroad and in a few instances had not been to a university at all. One such individual was Sir Philip Sherlock, who had an amazing academic career and stands out among the great leaders of the UWI.

When I place my efforts in the wider context of the university, I can see that progress was made in a number of areas. As an example of this, an Appendix contains a somewhat imperfect list of activities which were undertaken during my tenure by myself and, in some instances, together with senior colleagues in my office.

I leave it to others to make the ultimate assessment. I can only say that I left the institution even more convinced than I was originally about the extraordinary role it can play in the advancement of the countries of the region. Altogether, I retain very strongly positive views about the institution, its current and potential impact.

I leave for last what should essentially be first. It is that the principal purpose of a university is to provide opportunities for development of young people through education, research and associated activities, essential to their development to enable them to take their place in the adult world. In the flurry of activity in which one tends to be engaged, it is important to be reminding oneself continually about this objective. Having to travel between three campuses as well as to keep one's finger on extra-mural activities, as well as community service, one could find oneself with little time left to contribute towards student development.

Having in mind this objective about the centrality of student welfare and development. I conceived of making an address that was broadcast simultaneously to the student body as a whole at the beginning of each academic year. It was a small gesture, but I thought that it created one opportunity for the students to hear directly from me on issues of central importance to them, occurring both within the institution and outside. That initiative was apparently not considered important at the level of campus administration. Accordingly, the arrangement fell flat at virtually all of the campuses.

This issue of the centrality of student development was linked also to another deep seated belief which I held regarding the regionality of the university. I felt very strongly that the university should be seen as a central institution in the development of regionalism. This objective had been set out in the very earliest documentation about the establishment of the institution. Accordingly, I was very keen to make it plain to the student body and for that matter, the faculties as well, that regionalism was an indispensable part of our mission. Again, I cannot say that I made much progress with that idea, although there was a degree of loyalty to it among the members of staff. I suppose I should summarize this particular point by saying that despite the campus loyalties that developed as the university spread itself through the region, there remained an awareness of remaining faithful to the regional mission that our founders had provided. The senior administration at the Cave Hill campus showed particular awareness of this objective and I should acknowledge the co-operation extended to me by members of the senior administration of that campus.

Despite the degree of scepticism that tends to surface in public discussion throughout the region about the contemporary value of regionalism, I myself in the light of all of my involvement with the region and with the outside world, continue to hold to the view that 'we do it better, when we do it together.'

Figure 20
My wife
Marjorie and
me, enjoying a
light moment.

Figure 21 My two sisters, Pansy and Joy, and me at a cricket match.

*Figure 22 My brother
Dunbar and his wife
Maureen relaxing at our
sister's hotel in Grenada.*

*Figure 23 My
daughter Helga's
wedding.*

Figure 24 My three sons, Arnold, Andrew and Nicholas, and me.

Figure 25 William Demas.

16

Very brief thoughts about the future

The tendency continues of not following up the recommendations made by specialist groups at the request of governments. This is where the participants gained their most satisfaction and equally experienced their greatest frustration. However, I should qualify these remarks by noting that I have received several honours for public service; these are listed elsewhere at the beginning of this book. Indeed, I very much hope that, notwithstanding the disappointments I experienced, young people will seek a different result by coming forward readily to render public service in their community.

I would say that my association with William Demas has been the most rewarding part of my professional life. No question about it. Sir Shridath Ramphal also played a significant part in my professional life. I much admired the lucidity of his brain, his prodigious capacity for work, and his unbounding energy and commitment to the Caribbean.

Willie died in 1998. He was a person who paid absolutely no attention to any medical advice. He had the most idiosyncratic habits as far as eating was concerned. He was not diabetic like myself but he had other medical issues and his heart eventually gave out. But I have never seen anybody so totally devoted to work. His commitment to the Caribbean was legendary. That is why Dr Eric Williams had such a high admiration for him and had hoped that he would return to the government of Trinidad and Tobago after completing his service with the CARICOM secretariat and the Caribbean Development Bank. He did so eventually, for a comparatively brief period serving as Governor of the Central Bank of Trinidad and Tobago.

The last time I saw Willie was in Jamaica in 1998. I invited him to Mona because the university had received a grant from a foundation to do some exploratory work on the future of the Caribbean. William was leaving government service and I asked him to come to Jamaica to do the opening essay. He accepted the invitation and started writing.

He remained about two months and wrote a draft with some very good ideas in it, but he wanted to return to Trinidad. There were some areas in the draft that needed further thought, so I suggested that he take it back to Trinidad to do any additional work that was needed. He went, and died within a month.

His wife Norma is a wonderful person. She assured me that she had done a very thorough search for the draft, but was unable to find it. She thought someone might have taken it.

I have had a chance to reflect on the passage of my generation who went into public service. They were all imbued with the strongest sentiments focused on securing the future of the region at a time of political independence, coloured by continuing support for forms of regionalism in a changing world environment.

Reggie Dumas, a friend of mine, has recently sent me an email to tell me that the government of Trinidad and Tobago has inaugurated a Distinguished Public Service Award and he was to be the first recipient. I was reflecting that I met him on a ship in 1954 when we were both going to university in England. I was going to the LSE, he was going to Cambridge. After graduation, he returned to Trinidad and Tobago and had a very impressive career in the government service.

So I was thinking of him and in a sense he is representative of that generation of young Trinidadians who were all highly nationalistic, highly committed to returning to public service. They all went, got qualified, largely in England, went back and constituted the hard core of expertise in the government of

Trinidad and Tobago. There was a similar experience here in Jamaica and elsewhere in the Caribbean.

What has happened, of course, is that over these 50 years, the stock has been depleted and has not been sufficiently replenished. A large number of people today have decided that their future is better secured outside the Caribbean than inside it. Individual reasons differ from person to person. Some do not feel they are getting sufficient financial reward, or in some cases moral satisfaction. Accordingly, a large number of Caribbean professionals are to be found in North America and other developed areas.

I was reflecting on that earlier generation and thought of all the various outstanding people who constituted part of it. I suppose it is my generation. But I am not boasting about myself. I also thought about people, from both the public and private sector, who did not consider that they were getting sufficient job satisfaction and appreciation for what they had been doing.

One thinks of the people who have contributed to educational development; those who have helped to develop schools around the country, or to start schools where there were none; those in education, social services, particularly in health, in central and local administration, in justice, whose contributions have not been sufficiently acknowledged. This is to be observed across the Caribbean.

Over the course of my career, I did not expect it to involve opportunities for meeting various world leaders. It was my good fortune, after leaving university, to fill positions that were very visible and involved meeting personalities at a very high level. This afforded me unique opportunities to exchange views with individuals having vast experience in leadership, problem solving and dispute resolution.

The first 50 years of independence have passed and we need now to reflect on the initial feelings of optimism and purpose that characterized thought and action among the principal personalities engaged at the technical level of policy making, which is not in any way to diminish the importance of the political leadership.

From the outset of my academic and public life, my thoughts have been about the Caribbean. I have always thought that small size represented a fundamental consideration, and not necessarily only a constraint. Historically and in the contemporary field, there were several examples of countries, or parts of countries, overcoming the limitations brought about by small size. This had largely to do with the choices of production that permitted escape from the limitations imposed by restricted domestic markets: taking advantage of opportunities for linking with other markets, and avoiding the other constraints imposed by such limitations. This led me to the conclusion that the problems that might otherwise be imposed by small size could be overcome through judicious investigation and persistent pursuit of opportunities.

As I reflected on the matter, I came to the conclusion that a major effort had to be made at the level of research and development to unearth the most promising opportunities for production and trade and the development of appropriate human resources for those endeavours. It was this perception that guided me in preparing for the leadership responsibilities that offered themselves at the University of the West Indies. In response to the mandate provided by its founders, that it should become *Oriens Ex Occidente Lux* – 'a light rising from the west', I had from the outset the notion that the UWI could lead the development effort by illuminating an array of possibilities unearthed through persistent research and development investigations.

Moving this perception forward, I concluded that the principal component of a development strategy for the countries in the region, taken individually and together, entailed persistent efforts to identify the most promising areas for production and trade and to pursue them relentlessly through building relationships with countries and business partners. I saw this idea being pursued throughout the principal sectors of the economy, whether in agriculture, manufacturing or the services sector. Within that conception, regional integration among the CARICOM countries could be viewed as a first step, as member states purposefully pursued those opportunities for production and export that could later lead to further accessing partnerships and business opportunities with states of similar size and scope for investment, production and trade. This perception led to the notion that at the multilateral level, the countries of CARICOM should pursue openings for joint development by co-operation with other similarly placed countries within the hemisphere and beyond.

I was particularly interested in investigating possibilities with some of the Caribbean and Latin American countries that were of similar size and endowments. Going outside of the Caribbean, I was attracted to possible relationships with countries such as Mauritius, Hong Kong and Singapore, as well as in certain parts of Africa. It also seemed to me that larger countries like Malaysia, India and China could be pursued for purposes of attracting entrepreneurship, knowledge, global markets and investment. In other words, I was myself persuaded that globalization should be pursued through the linkage of production and trade with countries possessing those particular geographical endowments that could complement those of the Caribbean countries.

I sought to advance these ideas through public speaking and through participation in a number of relevant exercises requested particularly by regional governments and regional and international agencies. In a majority of instances, these perceptions and suggestions did not fall on fertile ground. I remain strongly convinced that the failure of countries in the region to pursue strategies along these lines basically pinpoints the course that has to be pursued in the period ahead.

I reflect that in the first three decades of independence, representatives of the Caribbean serving at the international level were regularly pursued by those from other developing countries to ascertain our views on international development issues and the strategies that could be pursued. My impression is that our countries have lost ground in this regard. My continuing hope is that we can find our way back to that situation and in so doing chart a more productive course for the future. I remain an unapologetic regionalist with an underlying confidence in the capacity of the peoples of the region.

Appendix
Activities of a vice-chancellor

Recommendations of the Burton/Mills Report

The Burton/Mills Report, entitled *Separation of Central and Campus Administration*, was commissioned by the Finance and General Purposes Committee (F&GPC) of the University Council to review the administration of the university; it was prepared in May 1988 by Sir Carlisle Burton, an eminent Caribbean public servant, and Professor Gladstone Mills, Professor of Public Administration, Mona campus.

	Activities / Remarks	Status
1	Complete the administrative separation of the posts of Vice-Chancellor and Principal, Mona campus and formally delegate a Pro Vice-Chancellor as Principal, Mona	Completed
2	Choose a site for a new Vice-Chancellor's office building on the Mona campus	Completed
3	Prepare brief for architect	Completed
4	Schedule a series of regular visits to the three campuses and university centres across the region	On-going
5	Appointment of executive assistant	Post established; appointment made June 1989
6	Select and appoint Deputy Principals	Completed August 1990
7	Organize fundraising machinery and appoint office staff	Completed August 1990
8	Commission University Registrar to allocate registry personnel	Completed December 1990
9	Commission University Bursar to allocate bursary personnel	Completed
10	Commission PVC/Director, Planning, to allocate planning unit personnel	Completed August 1990

11	Canvass governments on support for a bond scheme	Not being pursued at this time
12	Obtain annotated register of ongoing research	Not begun
13	Issue guidelines and objectives for new research initiatives, including policy on advisory committees/boards	Not complete
14	Review university centre estimates	Completed
15	Commission study to rationalize salaries of senior staff across the three campuses	Study completed April 1991 and implemented
16	Commission study of financing system, including a university unit of account	Being pursued by OPAD in relation to the new tuition fee structure
17	Commission study of committee structures and use	Completed August 1989; implementation to be initiated by the University Registrar
18	Commission study of communications system	Not completed
19	Commission study of university publishing facilities	Completed February 1992; University Press established June 1992
20	Commission university-wide development plan, 1990–2000	Completed April 1991
21	Amend the University Statute to effect complete separation of posts of Vice-Chancellor and Principal, Mona campus	Completed

Some activities initiated by the Vice-Chancellor

	Activities	Status
	Improving physical infrastructure	
1	Rebuilding the Mona campus after Hurricane Gilbert struck the island on 12 September 1988	Completed May 1989
2	Redesign and rebuilding of the main entrance to the Mona campus	Funded by a grant from the government of the United Kingdom; completed September 1990
	Improving general administration	
3	Initiated weekly senior management meetings across the three campuses using UWIDITE (University Distance Teaching facility)	Commenced September 1988; ongoing
4	Initiated annual management retreats	Commenced May 1989; ongoing
5	Reorganized the office of Vice-Chancellor and established five sub-offices of Pro Vice-Chancellors	Completed August 1990
6	Commissioned university-wide management audits of the Registry, Bursary and Maintenance Departments	Completed June 1991
7	Secured financing from the Inter-American Development Bank (IDB) (university centre project) to implement the recommendations of the management audits	Completed October 1994

8	Designed and implemented the semester system	Completed; introduced October 1991
	Improving academic performance	
9	Review of the Faculty of Natural Science	Completed December 1989
10	Review of the Faculty of Education	Completed December 1992
11	Review of the Faculty of Law	Completed January 1993
12	Self-study by the Institute of Social and Economic Research (ISER)	Completed September 1992
13	Introduction of a summer semester programme	Began Summer 1995
14	Linkages with eminent academic institutions overseas	Ongoing
15	UWI/Mexico Technical Agreement	Commenced July 1991; ongoing
16	Chair in Management Studies funded by the Grace Kennedy Foundation	Professor appointed January 1991
17	Chair in Caribbean Sustainable Development funded by Alcan Jamaica Ltd	Professor appointed; assumed April 1994
18	Chair in Actuarial Science funded by Colonial Life Insurance Co., Trinidad and Tobago	Professor appointed
19	Chair in Latin American Studies funded by the government of Venezuela at the Cave Hill campus	Not completed
20	Joint bilingual graduate programmes with PUMM, Dominican Republic, under Lomé IV programme	Negotiations completed; programme began 1994
	Improving cultural and leisure lifestyles on the campuses	
21	2000 Lecture Series	Commenced February 1990; ongoing
22	Latin America Centre: a university-wide initiative that develops programmes to build bridges of understanding and co-operation between Latin America and Caribbean countries	Established at the Mona campus; ongoing
23	Grant from the Lord Moyne Trust for the creative arts at the three campuses	Established 1992
24	Donation of study/reading/leisure activity rooms by the Jewish community	Completed June 1990 at the four halls of residence at the Mona campus
	Public relations and communication	
25	Appointment of a PR consultant to the centre and re-vitalization of the public relations offices at Mona and Cave Hill as well as establishing a PRO at St Augustine	Established August 1991; ongoing
26	Monthly newsletter from the Vice-Chancellor's Office	Commenced February 1992; lapsed
27	Simultaneous university-wide broadcast address by the Vice-Chancellor to the academic staff and student body at the three campuses at the start of each new academic year	Commenced September 1990
28	Twice-yearly lunch with university Deans, hosted by the Vice-Chancellor in rotation at the three campuses, to facilitate exchange of ideas and plans for the university by consensus	Commenced May 1990

APPENDIX

	Regional development and research	
29	UWI/Canadian International Development Agency (CIDA) Institutional Strengthening Project: provision for strengthening the UWI's capacity to respond to critical development needs in human resource development in the Caribbean region. The goals of the project are to assist with the development of the strategic planning, financial management and regional co-ordination capacities of the University Centre; to contribute to a sustainable development programme and to assist with the upgrading of regional HRD planning capacities and teaching skills on an in-service basis	Commenced June 1990; ongoing
30	Inter-American Development Bank (IDB)/ Caribbean Development Bank (CDB) Loan Project for Science and Technology	Negotiations completed May 1992
31	Association of Caribbean Tertiary Institutions (ACTI)	Established November 1990; ongoing
32	UWI/The Andrew Mellon Foundation project for research in Caribbean economic and international relations	Commenced August 1992
33	Ford Foundation Endowment Project for research in the social sciences	Commenced academic year 1993/94 with a programme for US$120,000, utilizing endowment funds of US$60,000 and matching funds from Appeal Committees
34	UWI Centre for Environment & Development	Professor appointed 1992; Centre established 1993
	Improving financial situation	
35	Report on the tuition fee structure commissioned	Completed June 1991; implemented with amendments October 1993
36	Reduction/elimination of arrears by most of the CARICOM governments contributing to the university	Commitments obtained in writing from those in default as of August 1991; only two governments had not completed arrangements
37	Emphasis on a fundraising campaign	See below
	Fundraising and alumni relations	
38	National Appeal Committees established worldwide	Ongoing
39	Revitalized and established Guilds of Graduates branches worldwide	First gathering of graduates held in April 1993
40	International summer schools	Ongoing; to be expanded to the three campuses
41	Fundraising campaign targeted to individual and corporate donors in the USA	Commenced 1993
42	Negotiations of grant under the Lomé IV programme	Commenced 1993

Index

References to the author are indicated by the letters 'AM'. Page numbers to figures or photographs are in *italics*, followed by the letter 'f'.

INDEX